Anglo-Zulu War of 1879

THE DEATH OF LIEUTS. MELVILL AND COGHILL

Anglo-Zulu War of 1879

Illustrated with Maps of the Campaign

The History of the Zulu Campaign

Waller Ashe and E. V. Wyatt Edgell

With a Short Historical Record of the
17th Lancers or Duke of Cambridge's Own
During the Zulu War
by J. W. Fortescue

LEONAUR

Anglo-Zulu War of 1879
Illustrated with Maps of the Campaign
The History of the Zulu Campaign
by Waller Ashe and E. V. Wyatt Edgell
With a Short Historical Record of the 17th Lancers or Duke of Cambridge's Own
During the Zulu War
by J. W. Fortescue

FIRST EDITION

Leonaur is an imprint of Oakpast Ltd

Copyright in this form © 2016 Oakpast Ltd

ISBN: 978-1-78282-561-6 (hardcover)
ISBN: 978-1-78282-562-3 (softcover)

http://www.leonaur.com

Publisher's Notes

Contents

Preface

Some apology or explanation may be deemed requisite, for delaying the publication of this *History of the Zulu Campaign* for more than a year after its conclusion. The little book itself was written very shortly after the capture of the king, Cetywayo, and the tardiness of its appearance has been, to a certain extent, intentional on my part.

Although it may seem ungracious and, perhaps, ungrateful to cavil at the war criticisms and descriptions which, by every post and telegram, adorn the pages of contemporaneous journalism, I would submit that the practice of writing *ex cathedrâ* on war topics the day after an engagement, is too early to allow us to examine motives as well as facts, so that we may form conclusions to which we can only justly arrive, when "*Time, the corrector, where our judgments err*," has softened prejudice and exposed partisan feeling. The worst and most valueless criticisms on Waterloo were given to the world immediately after the fight of Mont St. Jean.

The most unreliable, and indeed erroneous, opinions in regard to the splendid errors of Inkerman and Balaklava, appeared before the Crimean war was ended, and many a hero, elevated by the verdict of contemporaneous eulogy to a temporary pedestal in the Temple of Fame, has since been dethroned by the calmer and more honest judgment of a later generation. When the Emperor Napoleon called us a "*nation of shopkeepers*," he, perhaps, intentionally, paid us a compliment; for peace, commerce, and prosperity, have, as a rule, I venture to hold, been more regarded in our islands than projects of violence, warfare, or conquest; and this with us has ever been an honourable characteristic of the Spirit of our present Age.

But as Sir Bartle Frere, one of England's greatest, wisest, and most humane administrators, was well aware, the great and time-honoured law of self-defence sometimes compels a State, like an individual, to resort to arms, and the Appeal of Battle, when all peaceful modes of arrangement have been vainly tried, becomes occasionally unavoidable. Then, and perhaps only then, we may be allowed, even by the Peace Society and the Acolytes who trim the lamps for Mr. John Bright, to take an interest in and feel proud of the disciplined courage, the love of honour, and the sense of duty of which we read in the campaigns, where those who are near and dear to us have fought and fallen under the British flag. Then the commanders we may have known as subalterns, but whose names are now in all circles as veritable "Household Words"; whose careers we have watched with proud, yet kindly sympathy, and whose triumphs we have seemed as countrymen to share; whose powers of intellect and prescience array, regulate, and wield at will the grim and stern materials at command; whoso daring, and yet coolness in the midst of death, acts like a talisman upon the rank and file—whose providence, when one path fails, is ever ready for fresh resources and designs—are not these the men of whom we may say with Tacitus,—

Ratio et consilium propriae Ducis artes?

and of this class, I venture to think, were Lord Chelmsford and his lieutenants. And when we are ourselves in the "sere and yellow leaf," or have joined, mayhap, that "larger majority" which Gladstonian tactics and energy cannot hope to rival, our children and children's children, when they read of such names as Bartle Frere, Chelmsford, Wood, Pearson, Buller, and Piet Uys, may look back to English History and see that our "island mastiffs" have not become degenerate, either in courage or generosity, since the days of Harold, the Black Prince, or that knightly Sydney who fell at Zutphen!

Some experience of the Kaffir tribes and their characteristics, of the physical and geographical difficulties which attend upon a campaign in South Africa,—dating, indeed, as far back as a score of years ago, and the interest which I have since taken in colonies where, as an adjutant, I passed some very happy years among Boers, Bôk, and Kaffirs, had at the commencement of the late war prompted me to follow its various phases, with a view to write the story of the campaign. In this purpose I was encouraged by the offers of many old comrades who were about to start with their regiments for the seat of war, and who promised me by each available opportunity the assistances of their several journals, notes, and sketches.

But one I would select from that proud throng,

★★★★★★

And partly that bright names will hallow song,
And his was of the bravest."

And to those who have known that most accomplished gentleman and gallant soldier, young, brave, cheery, and *débonnaire*, Edmund Wyatt Edgell, I need not say how delighted I was at his undertaking to correspond with me, and, as far as time and opportunity permitted, to keep me au courant with the march of events. From the time of his arrival at Natal to the fatal day on which he fell, he fulfilled that promise, and if any merit be due to the narrative I now present to public notice, it will, I believe, come through those descriptions which I received from my dead comrade and friend—*Sit tibi terra levis!*

Another motive, or perhaps more than one, "pricked the sides of my intent," and invited me to wield the pen upon a soil where erst I had drawn a "regulation" sword. In the "unvexed silence of a student's cell," *i. e.* London chambers, I could only watch the progress of the campaign, without hoping to share in its toils or its dangers. I might envy, but I could not participate—

For who can view the ripen'd rose, nor seek
To wear it?

In default of this, I could, however, follow in spirit the adventures, by flood and field, of more than a score of old comrades and companions in arms, who were winning honour and renown in a land not unfamiliar to me. In the hasty and, with all deference I say it, somewhat ignorant criticism of those amateur mentors who tell us how battles ought or ought not to be won, and who, from the calm solitudes of Fleet Street, would make or mar a military reputation, I venture to believe, was much injustice done to the commander-in-chief of our forces in South Africa.

A man must serve his time to every trade
Save censure. Critics all are ready made.

And I was the more convinced of this partisan and hostile feeling from the knowledge that, west of Temple Bar, and especially in the regions where veterans do most congregate, in the clubs and haunts alike of *vieilles moustaches* and military neophytes, from the "Senior" to the "Naval and Military," criticism was far less pronounced, and experience, as it invariably is, was more moderate in stricture and charitable in argument than elsewhere.

9

Lastly, the tragic fate of England's young chivalrous and knightly guest, which formed such a terrible episode of the war and draped our colours with mourning, even in the hour of victory, made a deep impression upon my mind, and caused me insensibly to marvel at the unworthy sentiments to which a large portion of the English public and the English press at that time gave utterance. Political feeling seemed then, as it now seems in poor Ireland, to override all sense of manly honour, generosity, hospitality, or common decency. The slaughter, for it was nothing less, of the princely and noble lad, who came to the shores of his country's hereditary foe, as a messenger of hope, alliance and future friendship, who had been taught by his father to love and study our English laws and customs, and who, in his abandonment in that fatal donga, must have felt shame for the comrades to whom his safety was entrusted; the sacrifice, I say, of this pure and devoted spirit, seemed to me to call for some record, less evanescent than a passing note or a newspaper article.

If I have spoken strongly of the living in my sorrow for the dead, as a soldier I can but plead in vindication, that, in all my remembrance of the records of our English Army I can recall no instance, save the one I have quoted, where an officer wearing our royal uniform and holding a royal commission, galloped away in front of his escort, and allowed a comrade to be done to death in unknightly fashion! In conclusion I may say that this little work, although written *con amore* and from details furnished to me by my friend, Captain the Hon. E.V. Wyatt Edgell, and others, lays no claim to historical value, but assumes to be merely the *impressions de voyage* of those who were actors in the scenes described.

Waller Ashe
Hare Court, Temple,
Nov. 1880.

CHAPTER 1

Origin of Zulus

The Emashlabatini country was originally occupied by a small tribe called the Abanguni; of its more ancient kings little is known beyond that they seem to have been of peaceful habits, making no wars, but breeding cattle; also that the name of one was Zulu. In their own country the appellation of Abanguni in course of time died out, though still used by their neighbours, and for it was substituted Abakwa-Zulu (sons of Zulu), Zulu and Undabezita. The tribe was composed of several families or clans, each having its own chieftain. In the time of Cetywayo's reign the names of these clans and their respective chiefs were as follows:—The Uhutilezi, a family having two branches; Umnyamana, Cetywayo's prime minister, was chief of one, and Umtyubane of the other; the Ubixela and Umgazi, who were divisions of one family, the former owning Umvumhlana as chief, the latter Sigodi—subsequently slain at Isandhlwana—whose predecessor was Panda's prime minister Masipula, and his successor Mapoko; the Umtombelo and Umblalosi, also two branches of one family, whose respective chiefs were Mabanda and Segetwayo; the Uquabe, whose chief was named Rouhlo; the Uzimgu, whose chieftain rejoiced in the appellation of Unfanawenklela; the Fakazi, whose chief was Umkasana; the Umtanzi, with a chieftain Umbono by name; and the Igazi, whose head was Umkanyile; the Amagungebe, their chief was the notorious Sirayo; the Ukanyile, whose chief was Upagatwayo; the Ulanga, their chief Umhlaka; the Umpingose, whose chief was Ganse; and the Umhloben, a scattered family having no head.

The word Zulu, or Undabezita, was invariably employed in addressing any member of these families, whatever his rank or station might happen to be.

The first king of whom any particulars are known was Senzaga-

11

cone, son of Ufaina. When this king began to reign he had no legitimate offspring: he had, however, a natural son by Unamdi, daughter of Umkeki, chief of the Langmene tribe, named Chaka (the bastard). He afterwards married this Unamdi, by whom he had a daughter Nuncoba, but no sons. She being his favourite wife, the king, according to the custom of the country, "gave her for a son," his natural son Chaka, thus legitimating him. When Chaka was fifteen, his father, thinking he might become troublesome, sent to kill him; but Chaka, being warned, fled to Dingiswayo, chief of the Umtwetwa, where he remained until the king's death, though on the occasion of his legitimation an invitation was given him to return to the paternal *kraal*.

Meanwhile Chaka had become an Induna of great influence and popularity in the land of his refuge; so when on the death of Senzagacone the Zulu tribe sent to him requesting him to be their king, and he consented, all the tribes through which he passed on his way to the Zulus accompanied him; and the whole of the Zulu clans assembled to meet him, and he was made king with great rejoicings. In the interim between Senzagacone's death and Chaka's accession, Umkaibye (paternal aunt of Chaka) ruled the Zulus and arranged for Chaka's return. It was now that the jealousy long smouldering between the Umdwandwe and the Umtwetwa, the two most powerful tribes in that part of Africa, broke into an open quarrel.

Uzwidi, chief of the former, attacked and utterly routed the latter, killing their chief, Dingiswayo, Chaka's friend and. protector. The worsted tribe naturally applied to Chaka for help. Thereupon Uzwidi immediately marched to attack the Zulus, and a great battle ensued on the south of the White Umvolosi. The result was that the left wing of either army was victorious; but both lost so heavily that they retired to their respective countries.

On his retreat, Chaka was attacked by the Langmeni, but failing in their assault, this tribe then deserted their own country and joined the Umdwandwe. Having defeated another coast tribe which assailed him, Chaka occupied both these countries, leaving the Emashlabatini district waste and uninhabited.

Uzwidi had now gathered a fresh army, which Chaka, by a night march, surprised and defeated between Kwagmagwasa and the Umhlatuzi River. He then retreated, but was rapidly followed up by Uzwidi, who had soon regathered his forces, and who succeeded in capturing much Zulu cattle and slaying a number of men, women, and children, surprised in their *kraals* by the swiftness of his advance.

He then again retreated. Uzwidi now made a great and final effort to crush his adversary. All the tribes around were pressed into his service, and the result was that he soon had an army—collected from ten tribes—far superior in point of numbers to the Zulu force, which represented only two tribes.

Chaka therefore retreated before Uzwidi's advance, and eventually occupied a strong position on the Inkankla range. Here he awaited his opponent's onset. In place of the old missile weapon, Chaka had armed his men with a shorter and stronger *assegai*, intended for use at close quarters; he therefore gave them strict orders not to throw their assegais but to charge the foe and fight them hand to hand. He also skilfully placed his force amidst broken ground, so that it was impossible for the enemy to attack in a compact and organised body. The battle, as usual, began in the early morn and continued till after midday. The Zulus, carrying out their leader's instructions, waited till the assault was delivered, and then charged so vigorously on the foe that they swept everything before them.

Chaka following up this defeat utterly dissipated the Umdwandwe army. Uzwidi fled beyond his own country, which Chaka annexed, and thus became the chief potentate in that part of Africa, levying tribute from all the tribes around him. Chaka now waged several wars. First he attacked and despoiled the Mangwani, a tribe on the Drackenberg; then he fell upon and extirpated the clan of Zulukanafu, a chief residing to the north of that range. Soon after he sent an army against the Pondos, which captured a considerable amount of cattle and then retreated. Again, in the following year, there was a similar expedition, and the Pondos sued for peace, which was granted.

By this time Chaka claimed to rule over the entire country, from the sea to the Pondola, to the Drackenberg, and to the land of the Pondos. His next object was to consolidate his power. Accordingly, the petty kings under his rule were no longer recognised as such, but became tributary chieftains; if any one of these was remiss in payment of his tribute, an "*impi*" was sent "to eat him" up. From time to time Chaka would also call up these chiefs to his royal *kraal*, where he would receive them with marks of distinction, and ask their advice on state matters. Another important step to weaken the power of the chiefs, and at the same time to augment his own, was the establishment of a standing army.

Military service was made compulsory on all males, each being told off to a certain regiment according to his age. Thus a man ceased to serve under the chief of his own clan, but belonged to a king's regiment, which was composed of men of all tribes. Similar divisions were also made amongst the females, who had to marry into regiments at the king's commands, though on a marriage cattle was still handed over to the bride's father or brother. Furthermore, regiments were not allowed wives till they were entitled to wear "head-rings," and this did not occur till men had reached forty years of age. Chaka's next war was against the Swazis, whom he defeated and made to pay tribute.

In the following year an immense expedition was despatched against the Sotshangana, a people dwelling across the Somba Mountains, beyond Delagoa Bay.

So large was this army that Zululand was almost denuded of warriors, an event which was taken advantage of by Dingaan and five more of the king's brothers, to treacherously fall upon Chaka, whom they slew, together with his chief councillor, Umxamana.

The benefits conferred on his people by Chaka can hardly be overestimated; he had raised them from a small tribe to a nation, and that nation a dominant one. As the Quirites were amongst the component tribes of the earlier Roman kingdom, so were the Zulus or Undabezita amongst the various tribes subject to the central Zulu authority, and curiously enough this resemblance extends still further; the Quirites were subdivided into *gentes*, or families, each with a distinctive name, and in a precisely similar manner, as has been before stated, the Undabezita were divided into sub-tribes or clans, each with its own gentile or family name. Nor were his people ungrateful to the memory of their first great king, for after the time of Chaka, the bastard, that name was never employed in its original signification, but to the present day a substitute, "*Umlandhwana*," is always used by a Zulu to express that idea.

That Chaka was not averse to civilization and white men was evinced by his treatment of Fynn and five others who were rescued from a shipwreck in St. Lucia Bay. He even went so far as to accompany Fynn the whole way to Durban, to see him embark on a ship sent round from Cape Town for him, and to send at considerable expenditure in the shape of cattle two envoys to England, which he contemplated visiting himself, if their report should prove favourable. But this latter project failed in consequence of the king's murder, and the messengers got no further than Cape Town.

A year or two after his departure Fynn returned, and with Chaka's sanction established a trading-station at Durban (1824) Once Fynn

14

and some white men, being called upon for aid, assisted Chaka to punish a refractory tribe. When Chaka' s army for the second time invaded the Pondos, it was through Fynn's representations that they would come into collision with the white men that the army proceeded no further.

On the army returning from the Sotshangana expedition. Panda, a brother of Chaka, was requested to assume the chief authority, but he declined, so Dingaan became king. Dingaan commenced his reign by killing all his brothers, except Panda, and all the late king's most trusted ministers. This caused great uneasiness amongst the chiefs, one of whom named Umquetu wishing therefore to withdraw from Dingaan's rule, departed with all his clan and cattle to the south. Coming into collision with the Pondos they were extirpated; hereupon Dingaan despatched an army to recover the cattle, which he regarded as his, from the Pondos. About the same time another chief, Umzilikazi, also revolted, and withdrew himself to the spot where Pretoria now stands. An expedition was in a similar manner despatched against him, and after capturing nearly all his cattle, returned therewith to the king.

Meanwhile the Boers had appeared on the scene at Natal, and they now claimed from Dingaan a considerable quantity of the cattle captured from Umzilikazi, alleging it had been originally stolen from them. To this Dingaan replied by bidding them recover some cattle that a petty chief had taken from him. Having done this and imprisoned the captured chief at Maritzburg, the Boers again applied for their own cattle, and a party under the command of one Peter Retief was sent to Dingaan. There now ensued a game of "diamond cut diamond," the Boers trying to outwit the king and capture him in his *kraal*, and Dingaan acting in much the same way to the Boers.

The exact course of events is unknown, but for certain in the result Retief and his party were surprised and slain (Feb. 5th, 1838). Dingaan then invaded Natal, slaughtered many of the Boers, and captured much cattle. His forces penetrated as far as Ladismith, whence, after a heavy repulse in an attack on the Dutch *laager*, they retired home. Encounters from time to time continued to occur between the Zulus and the Boers with varying success to either side, till at length a peace was patched up. Panda showed himself so active in this war as to excite Dingaan's jealousy, in consequence of which he, with all his people went over and joined the Boers. Soon after this (Jan. 1840) the Boers, in conjunction with Panda, invaded Zululand. The great fight occurred at Magongo, on the Umkusi River. Dingaan was utterly defeated, and retiring with a few attendants beyond the Bomba range, was killed by the Swazis. Panda now became king, and peace was made between the Zulus and Boers, the former ceding to the latter the Natal territory as far as the Tugela.

It was about this time that there occurred a struggle at Natal between the English and Dutch, in which the latter, being worsted, retired to the Utrecht district, where they received permission from Panda to dwell; Utrecht, it is said, being assigned as their outside limit.

Panda waged no more external wars, but lived peaceably in his *kraal*, breeding cattle. Most conspicuous amongst the sons of Panda were Cetywayo and Umbulazi; these two, having quarrelled, waged a sort of civil war one against the other, and in the result Umbulazi was defeated and killed. Amongst the army of Umbulazi were John Dunn and about thirty other white men armed with rifles. Cetywayo then quarrelled with another brother, and the same state of disorder continued till Panda's death, which occurred in October, 1872.

Cetywayo being thereupon accepted as king by the Zulu nation, applied to the English Government to recognise him. Accordingly, Sir Theophilus—then Mr.—Shepstone was sent as envoy, and publicly crowned Cetywayo at the Umlambongmenya *kraal*, on which occasion he spoke thus to the assembled Zulus:

Here is your king. You have recognised him as such, and I now do also, in the name of the Queen of England. Your kings have often met violent deaths at the hands of their people, but if you kill this one, we shall surely require his blood of you.

He then went on to say,:

. . . .that as the English had recognised him as king, they would expect him to give all men a fair trial before condemnation. Even a witch should be let off, and merely sent away to another district.

To this the Zulus returned that they would kill any man who went with the king's women, any man who ran away with another's wife, any thief of cattle, royal or otherwise; that a witch should not be put to death on a first accusation, but should any persist in witchcraft, he should be killed. And to this Shepstone signified his assent. The chiefs then rose in a body and said:

We will so govern the country under our King Cetywayo, and we look to England to support him as the king of the Zulu Nation.

16

Shepstone replied that he hoped the Zulus would live peaceably under the new king, whom England would expect to adhere to the terms to which he had just assented.

But these promises were broken on more than one occasion. Cetywayo having called up his army, and finding them tardy in response, and many absentees on the plea of illness, forthwith sent a regiment to slay all those thus absent, saying, "Sick men are no good; I will save the doctors the trouble of attending them." Again, one of the divisions of females being ordered to marry a certain regiment, objected that they were too few. Another regiment was named, and further objections raised. Then an *impi* was sent to punish these women, and a great number were killed. Great abuses in the practice of "smelling out" by witch-doctors also prevailed, though in this respect Cetywayo appears slightly better than his predecessors.

It is now time to turn attention to what is called the Boundary Question.

It has been previously stated that in Panda's time the Boers had settled in the Utrecht district. From time to time cattle undoubtedly was passed between the Boers and the Zulu king. The former assert that it was the price for the absolute ownership of the land they occupied, whilst on behalf of Cetywayo it is urged that it was merely a tribute from the Boers, whose outside limit had been fixed at Utrecht. Be this as it may, there kept occurring at frequent intervals outrages, robberies, and reprisals on either side, Sirayo, whose *kraal* was nearest the border, being the most prominent actor in these scenes.

Umbelini also now appeared, to further complicate matters. Originally a Swazi, he had fled from his native land, and settled in Zululand, together with his uncle Umbeliani and his people. This uncle joined the Boers, taking his cattle with him. Land was assigned to Umbeliani by the Boers close to where Umbelini was dwelling. No sooner, therefore, had the former built himself a *kraal* than the latter attacked and destroyed it. Thus ensued a contest between the Boers and Umbelini, The Boers drove Umbelini from his stronghold, but failed to capture him. He, retreating, erected a new *kraal* on the Dumbe range, north of the Zlobani, whence he continued to make raids into Swaziland and the Transvaal, which had now become British soil.

At Cetywayo's coronation this vexed question of the boundary had been referred to Mr. Shepstone, and he, in accordance with a promise then given, subsequently met the Zulu envoys at Conference-hill to hear their claims in this matter. They then claimed the Buffalo River

17

as their original and proper boundary. In reply, Mr. Shepstone said that he considered this was asking too much; but that a fair line would be the Blood River and the old hunting road running close by the Kambulakop to the Pongola or Zulu side of Luneberg. He would, however, examine the question more closely before coming to a final decision, which, when arrived at, would be communicated to them.

During all this time the Zulu Army had been growing more and more restless, and the younger men especially were clamorous for an opportunity of "washing" their spears. For this sole purpose they contemplated a raid on the Swazis, then in alliance with England. But on Cetywayo's applying to the British Government for its sanction to this project, it naturally declined to allow its allies to be thus wantonly attacked.

There also existed amongst the Zulu an intense antipathy to the Boers; and Cetywayo, after his capture, himself admitted that had the Transvaal not been annexed, it was a mere question of time how soon a war broke out between his people and the Dutch settlers; nor can this afford much ground for wonder when the characteristics of a Boer are had well in mind. The typical Boer is doubtless a pattern of hospitality, simplicity of heart, fondness for his home and family, and of those general domestic attributes which are so dear to an Englishman. But in his relations and contact with the native races and real owners of the soil, the Dutch Boer seems to lose all sense of reason and justice, and to remember only those early and bloodstained annals of pioneering, when the white man and the black neither gave nor asked for quarter in their struggle for supremacy in the land.

Indeed, his intolerance of a native is so intense that he cannot be induced to look upon him as a human being, but he regards the unfortunate aboriginal as a wild beast to be hunted and shot down. But the Boer has his fairer side, although his type has as yet been unchangeable. As he existed when he ruled in Cape Colony in 1808, so he now exists in the present day in his settlements in the interior. He is uneducated, uncultivated, unprogressive, and obstinate; but he develops qualities under adverse circumstances which must command English respect.

He is certainly domestic as far as his own family circle is concerned, but, at the same time, the reverse of gregarious in regard to the world in general. When he first commences to farm and settle he likes to possess not less than 6000 and not more than 20,000 acres of good undulating "*veldt.*" When he has obtained this, he starts in his waggon

18

with his wife, his children, his scanty supply of goods and chattels, his cattle and sheep, and his only literature, the family Bible.

He selects a good spring of water, being careful that no neighbour is located within at least ten miles. He builds his house with one large central hall, with the kitchen in rear, and four or five bedrooms opening out of the hall, all on the ground floor, and sometimes with a wide verandah outside. *Kraals* for his cattle, fences to his garden, and enclosures of 50 or 100 acres, are quickly run up; and so fertile is the soil and so favourable the climate, that in four or five years his garden will be full of oranges, lemons, citrons, peaches, apricots, figs, apples, pears, and vines. His herds and flocks multiply, his wheat and Indian corn thrive, and thus he lives in a rude but grateful abundance. His sons arrive at manhood and marry; his daughters are sought as wives, and if the land is good and plenty they remain and farm near, and for each generation and new family a new house is built a few hundred yards from the original.

More acres with each generation are brought under the plough, and the man who is a good farmer, good father, and good husband cannot be brought to see that he must not covet his neighbour's land when that neighbour happens to be a black man! Without sentiment, without tenderness, and without a particle of enthusiasm, and with the most circumscribed intellectual horizon, he has a stubborn practicability which is admirably suited for the work of a pioneer, but which never develops into a power of civilization amongst savage tribes.

As has been shown in the preceding narrative the relations between the Zulu king and the English Government had been growing more and more tense. Two conspicuous outrages in the early part of 1878 at length brought matters to a climax. These two events were the Sirayo affair, and the Middle Drift difficulty. To understand the Sirayo business it is necessary to enter somewhat into detail. Sirayo and his tribe had a quarrel with one of the royal tribes—the Ischeni. This, like many another tribal dispute common enough in Zululand, never grew to an "*assegai*" matter, but encounters frequently occurred, in which sticks only were used, and the object of the rival factions was to drive off the opponent's cattle.

The result of this, and a "law-suit" between the parties, settled by the king, was that Sirayo lost all his cattle. Shortly after this, one of Sirayo's wives, who had already been put aside on account of having a son whose legitimacy was suspected, being again in the family-way, fled with her paramour into Natal. Another wife, in a similar condi-

19

tion, also accompanied her. Nothing was done at the time, but Sirayo's sons subsequently learning that these women were in *kraals* close to the border, having collected an armed band, crossed the River Buffalo in broad daylight, seized one of the women, recrossed the stream, and then killed her. The Natal Kaffirs armed and threatened a rescue, but made no attack on Sirayo's party, who, on the same night, made another incursion, and the second woman suffered the same fate as the first.

Thereupon the English demanded the surrender of Sirayo's sons. Cetywayo sent to Sirayo advising him to hand over cattle instead of his sons. Sirayo replied that in consequence of the Ischeni dispute he had no cattle; that he was aware that his sons had transgressed; and that he was sorry. Again the English insisted on the surrender of the two young men. To this Cetywayo replied that they were very young, and therefore their conduct should be excused, and mercy shown to them. He added, that beyond all doubt they had done wrong; that the English had good cause for anger, and that he himself was displeased with Sirayo for not sending either his sons or cattle.

The Middle Drift affair occurred thus:—At the very beginning of 1878 the English were constructing a road from Kranz Kop to the middle drift of the Tugela. The men at work on this were interrupted, and driven away from their task by the Zulus living in the district, and Smith, the road engineer, who had landed on the island at this drift, was seized, stripped of all his clothing, and much maltreated by the same people. Reparation was demanded by the government for this outrage. Furthermore, from June, 1877, it was evident that Cetywayo was instigating Secocoeni to hostilities; and even allowing that part of this chiefs claim for compensation was just, it was necessary that the former chief should be made to understand that while arbitration was going on the law could not be broken by either side. With great tact, Sir T. Shepstone kept the peace until the Galeka and Gaika War was over, when Lord Chelmsford and his forces were freed, and it became possible to support words by action. Such were the events which led to the sending of an ultimatum by Sir Bartle Frere.

In the beginning of December, 1878, therefore, Messrs. John Shepstone, Brownlie, Walker, Fynn, and Fyney were selected to be the messengers to Cetywayo, to whom they were to communicate a message, of which the following was the purport:—The boundary-line was to be drawn from the junction of the Buffalo and Blood Rivers to the Magedala Mountains, and thence on to the district of Roundhill and the source of the Pongolo. All the farmers on the frontier and disputed territory who could produce any tangible evidence of damage or loss due to Zulu menace or warlike demonstration were to receive a moderate but fixed compensation.

A fine of 500 head of cattle and the surrender of the guilty members of the tribe was imposed upon Usiray's (Sirayo) people, and twenty days only allowed for the payment of the penalty; 100 head of cattle to be paid for the outrage upon Lieut. Smith; Umbelini, who had given so much trouble, to be handed over to and dealt with by the Transvaal Government; the whole of King Cetywayo's large army at once to be disbanded; freedom of marriage to be allowed when the parties thereto were of age; justice to be impartially administered; missionaries to be allowed to return to the Zulu country; British Residents to be appointed; all disputes between Europeans to be referred to the king and the resident; and, finally, no expulsion from Zulu territory to be carried into effect without the distinct approval of the resident.

It was further intimated to the king that unless he showed his compliance with these terms, on or before December 31st, then on January 1st, 1879, the British Army would commence the invasion of his land, and would enforce them at the point of the bayonet. The advance, it has been said, originally was to have been made on the 1st; but his Excellency the High Commissioner, allowing for the possibility of letters being delayed by the swollen state of the river, the Tugela being then in flood, extended his term of grace to the 11th. A *Gazette* extraordinary was published on January 6th, containing a declaration from Sir Bartle Frere, demanding from Cetywayo unqualified submission, stating that the general would after the 11th instant demand redress, and that the Zulu people were to be protected. The following was its form:—

Notification by his Excellency the High Commissioner.
In July last two armed bodies of Zulus, retainers of the Chief Usirago, led by his sons and brothers, entered Natal and took away by force refugee women, who were claiming protection from the resident magistrate of Umsinga. These women were dragged across the border, and, it is believed, murdered. These acts of outrage were promptly brought to Cetywayo's notice by his Excellency the Lieutenant-Governor of Natal, but no explanation or redress could be obtained from Cetywayo. twenty-one days were allowed to the Zulu king to surrender the three sons and brother of the Chief Usirago for trial, and as this term

expired on 31st December, 1878, the High Commissioner entertains no hope that it is the intention of the Zulu king to afford the redress which Her Majesty's Government has a right to demand.

Therefore I hereby make known, for the information of Cetywayo and all the Zulu people, that I have placed the further prosecution of this and all other demands for redress and reparation in the hands of his Excellency the Lieutenant-General Lord Chelmsford, commanding Her Majesty's Forces in South Africa, with the request that he will take such steps as he may find necessary to protect the British territory from further aggression, and to compel the Zulu king to comply with all the demands made on him for satisfaction due to the British Government, or for the greater security of the British territory, or for the better and more peaceable government of the Zulu people.

Lieutenant-General Lord Chelmsford will carefully notify to all Zulu chiefs and people who may come within his reach that the commands of the British Government are made on Cetywayo, as much in the interests of the Zulu people as of the English Nation, and that till the 11th January the lieut.-general will be willing to receive and to transmit to me any intimation of the unqualified acceptance by Cetywayo of all the terms offered to him.

If such intimation of unqualified and complete acceptance be received by the Lieut. -General before the 11th January no further hostile movement will be made, unless rendered necessary by the action of the Zulu forces, and up to the above date Lord Chelmsford will be ready to consider any steps which the Zulu king may propose for the purpose of giving real and permanent effect to the demands of the British Government. But unless all these terms be fully complied with by the above date, the Lieut.-General will no longer be bound by the terms of the 11th December, but will take such measures as the forces under his command will permit for compelling the submission of the Zulu king; always bearing in mind that the British Government has no quarrel with the Zulu nation, and that the future good government and well-being of the Zulus is as much an object of the steps now taken as the safety and protection of the British territories of Natal and the Transvaal.

And I do hereby warn all residents and inhabitants of Her Majesty's possessions and colonies in South Africa, of whatever race, to be guided by this, my notification, and I do strongly charge and command all Her Majesty's officers, ministers, and subjects, and all others whom it may concern, to govern themselves and to act accordingly, and to take due notice of and to pay due regard to the tenor thereof.

H. B. E. Frere,
High Commissioner.

Pietermaritzburg, Natal, Jan. 4, 1879.

During the whole of December Lord Chelmsford had been indefatigable in collecting and organising the military forces at his command. The result was that at this date (Jan. 11th) the return in the order-book was as follows:—

General State of the Field Forces.
No. 1 Column (Headquarters, Thring's Poet, Lower Tugela)

Commandant—Colonel C. K. Pearson, the Buffs.

Naval Brigade—170 bluejackets and marines of H.M.S. *Active* (with one Gatling and two 7-pounder guns), under Captain Campbell, R.N.

Royal Artillery—Two 7-pounder guns and rocket battery, under Lieut. W. N. Lloyd, R.A.

Infantry—2nd battalion 3rd Buffs, under Lieut.-Col. H. Parnell.

Mounted Infantry—100 men under Captain Barrow, 19th Hussars.

Volunteers—Durban Rifles, Natal Hussars, Stanger Rifles, Victoria Rifles, Alexandra Rifles. Average, forty men per corps, all mounted.

Native Contingent—1000 men, under Major Graves, the Buffs.

No. 2 Column (Headquarters, Helpmakaar, near Rorke's Drift)

Commandant—Colonel Glyn, 1st battalion 24th Regiment.

Royal Artillery—N battery 5th brigade Royal Artillery (with 7-pounder guns), under Major A. Harness, R.A.

Infantry—Seven companies 1st battalion 24th Regiment and 2nd battalion 24th Regiment, under Lieut.-Col. Degacher.

Natal Mounted Police—Commanded by Major Dartnell.

Volunteers—Natal Carabineers, Buffalo Border Guard, Newcastle Mounted Rifles. All mounted; average forty men.

Native Contingent—1000 men, under Commandant Lonsdale, late 74th Highlanders.

No. 3 Column (Headquarters, Utrecht)

Commandant—Colonel Evelyn Wood, V.C, C.B., 90th Regiment. Royal Artillery—11th battery 7th brigade R.A. (with four 7-pounder guns) under Major E. Tremlett, R.A. Infantry—1st battalion 13th Regiment and 90th Regiment. Mounted Infantry—100 men, under Major J. C. Russell, 12th Lancers. Frontier Light Horse—200 strong, under Major Redvers Buller, C.B., 60th Rifles.
Volunteers—The Kaffrarian Vanguard, Commandant Schermbrucker, 100 strong.
Native Contingent—The Swazis, our native allies, some 5000 strong.

An idea of the numbers and nature of Cetywayo's force may be gathered from the report of the Government Intelligence Department made at this time.

The Zulu Army, as at present constituted, is drawn from the entire male population, as every male between the ages of fifteen and sixty-five is called upon to serve, without any exemption. The military force consists of fourteen corps or regiments, divided into wings right and left, and the latter into companies. The companies, however, are not of equal strength, but vary immensely, even from ten to 200, according to the numerical strength of the corps to which they belong. In fact, the companies and regiments would more correctly be termed families or clans, and each corps possesses its own military headquarters, or *kraal*, with the following hierarchy, namely, one commanding officer, chief, or Iduna-Yesibaya; one second in command, major, or Iduna-Yohlangoti, who has charge of the left wing; two wing officers, and company officers according to the need of the battalion.

As a rule, all these officers are in command of men of the same ages as themselves, and the method of recruiting is as follows:— At stated and periodical intervals, generally from two to five years, a general levy takes place, when all the youths who happen at that time to have attained the age of fifteen are formed into a regiment and undergo a year's probation, during which time they are supposed to pass from boyhood to manhood. As

24

the regiment becomes disciplined and seasoned it receives large drafts from other corps, so that as the elders die out young men come in to fill up the ranks. The entire Zulu Army consists of thirty-three regiments, married and unmarried.

No one in Zululand, male or female, is allowed to marry without the king's permission, and this permission is never granted until the men are about forty years of age. They then have to shave the crown of the head, and to put a ring round it, and carry a white shield, in contradistinction to the unmarried regiments, who do not shave their heads and carry coloured shields. Many of these regiments are too young for active service, others are too old, consequently it is estimated that only about twenty-five regiments would be able to take the field, and these would muster perhaps 40,000. Of these 4500 are between fifty and sixty years of age; 3400 are between forty and fifty; 10,000 between thirty and forty; and 22,000 between twenty and thirty. We have heard a great deal about the drill of these, but their movements, as far as we can learn, are few and very simple, but very quickly performed in their own way. They form circles of regiments in order to outflank the enemy. From this formation they break into columns of regiments or companies, and from these into skirmishing order, with supports and reserves. The sole commissariat of the Zulu Army consists of three or four days' grain, carried by the lads who follow each corps, and, if necessary, a herd of cattle driven with each column.

GENERAL PLAN
OF THE
OPERATIONS IN ZULULAND, 1879.

Scale of Miles.
5   0   5   10   15   20   25

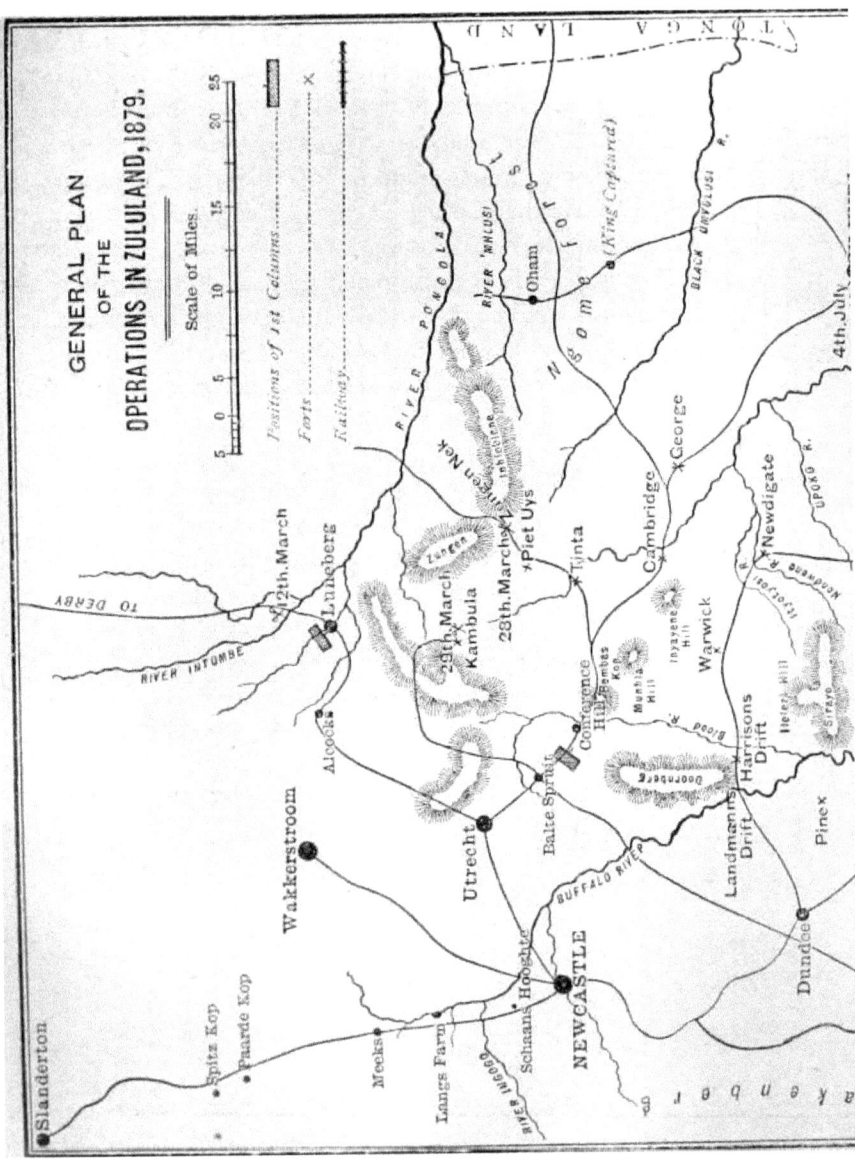

Positions of 1st Columns ....
Forts .... ×
Railway .... ━━━━

TONGA LAND

Pongolo of Some

Oham

(King Cetywayo)

BLACK UMVOLOSI R.

RIVER PONGOLO

RIVER UMLUSI

George

Umshitina inhlobane

TO DERBY

12th March
Luneberg

RIVER INTOMBE

Zungen

Cambridge

Newdigate

UPOKO R.

29th March
Kambula

28th March
Piet Uys

Tinta

Alcocks

Inyezane Hill

Warwick

Nondweni R.

Itelezi Hill

Umshia Hill

Conference Hill

Baile Spruit

Utrecht

Doornberg

Blood R.

Harrisons Drift

Wakkerstroom

Landmanns Drift

Buffalo River

Pinex

Slanderton

Spitz Kop

Paarde Kop

Meeks

Langs Farm

RIVER INGOGO

Schuans Hooghte

NEWCASTLE

Dundee

4th July

Drakensberg

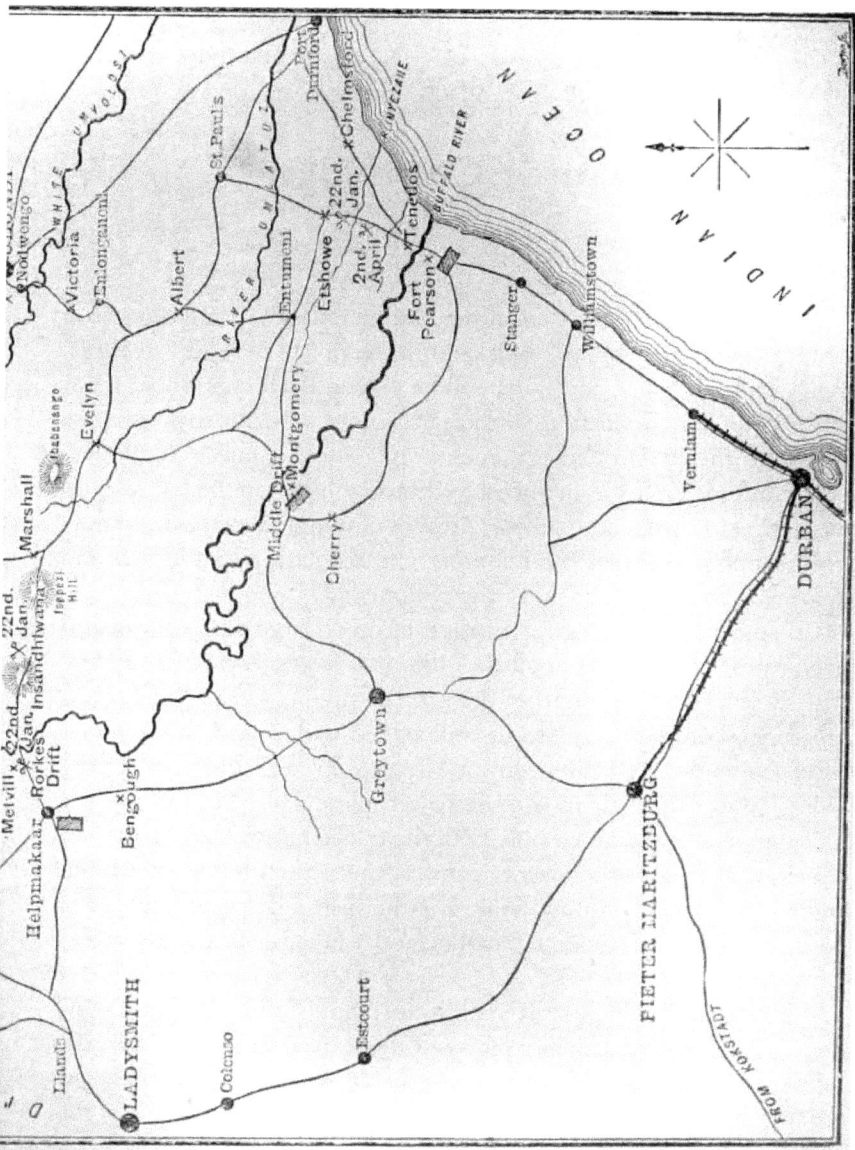

CHAPTER 2

Plan of Campaign

The plan of the campaign now commenced was to advance into Zululand in four columns, each column complete in itself, having its own artillery, cavalry, and independent leader. Each column was also to keep up communications with the columns on flank, thus creating, as it were, the effect of an advance in one extended line.

By this means it was intended to thoroughly sweep the entire Zulu territory, and at the same time to prevent any large body of the enemy from slipping between the columns, and so getting to the rear and delivering a counter-attack on the colonies.

In addition to the regular European forces, large native levies had been raised, amounting in all to 7400. It is a great error to suppose that these were without arms, dress, or discipline. On the contrary, a great many of them came to us well armed with serviceable-looking rifles, evidently of Birmingham or Sheffield make, while some of the older-fashioned fire-arms had the Tower mark.

Nor were they clothed only with the conventional blanket. On the contrary, their uniform was neat, and, at the same time, workmanlike, and consisted of a corduroy tunic, or rather patrol jacket, and breeches, with long boots of untanned leather, and a broad-leafed *sombrero* as a head-dress.

Several native corps were rapidly formed, in the following manner:—The commandant and his staff officers were British officers, the captains mostly retired British officers, colonists, or settlers; the non-commissioned officers, white settlers of different nationalities, and the privates usually Kaffirs.

Among the English officers who received commands in this native contingent were Captain Nolan (Pioneers), Major Bengough, Captain Russell (Rocket Battery), Captain Ulich de Burgh (5th West York Militia), Captain Cherry (32nd Foot), and Lieutenant Hon. H. Gough. Colonel Durnford had command of the whole column, which was to be entirely native so far as the rank and file were concerned, and to be composed of all the three arms—artillery, cavalry, and infantry.

There was also a considerable contingent of European Volunteers—more especially of mounted men, whose total reached close on 1000. Conspicuous amongst these were the Volunteer Hussars and Alexandra Mounted Rifles, the Durban Mounted Rifles, Captain Raaf's Diamond Field and Free State Horse, and a contingent of mounted Boers under Piet Uys, who gallantly responded to Colonel Wood's spirited and soldierlike appeal. These Boers were a splendid body of men, most of them crack shots with the rifle, and although somewhat fierce and uncompromising towards their ancient enemies, the Zulus, proved of invaluable service through their knowledge of localities.

The following "special service" officers, sent out from England, had also arrived and entered on their respective duties—Captain Cherry (32nd Light Infantry), was placed in command of the 3rd battalion Natal Contingent; Captain Gardner (14th Hussars), was sub-director of transports at headquarters, as well as Captain Huntley (10th Regiment), who was posted to the River Mooi; Captains Essex (76th), and Hon. H. Campbell (Coldstream Guards), were also directors of transports. Major Hopton had this duty at Pieter-Maritzburg. Captain Brunker, of the Cameronians (26th), had the command of a squadron of Light Horse. Captain Barton (7th Regiment), was staff officer to Colonel Durnford; Captains Pelly Clark (103rd Regiment), Spratt (29th), and Lieutenant Lawrence (18th), were all employed on transport duty at Durban, where, as most of the ammunition and stores were landed, their office was no sinecure. Captain Macgregor (29th Regiment), was staff officer to Colonel Pearson, and Captain Hart (31st Regiment) was on the staff of Lord Chelmsford.

Meanwhile Cetywayo's term of grace had expired; the 11th of January had come and gone without any sign from the Zulu monarch. On the following day the war had begun, and the Tugela was successfully crossed. By four o'clock on the 12th the Buffs, four companies of the 99th, the Victoria Mounted Rifles, the native Sappers, the 1st Natal Native Contingent, and the Naval Brigade were well over the Lower Tugela, near Fort Buckingham. The pontoon worked remarkably well, making three trips an hour. Four small boats were also employed. A herd of cattle was brought into the camp by the vedettes, who also reported that a large Zulu force was in position about twenty miles off, and also at Ondini. It has been mentioned that four columns would be formed from out of the three (whose details have been given above), and these four were now advancing into Zululand in a line which partly described a crescent, of which the left extremity rested on Luneberg and the Pongolo, the right upon the Lower Drift of the Tugela, close to the sea, while the inner half of the circle was represented by the boundaries of Natal and the Transvaal.

The centre may be considered as being at Fort Pearson, where there was a strongly entrenched camp on the summit of a rising or bluff overlooking the River Tugela. The column moving from Fort Pearson consisted of 1600 regular infantry, that is to say, eight companies of the Buffs, under Colonel Parnell; six companies of the 99th, under Colonel Welman; one company Royal Artillery and two 7-pounder guns, drawn by mules under Lieutenant Lloyd; one Naval Brigade of 276 bluejackets and Marines, under Captain Campbell, from Her Majesty's ships *Active* and *Tenedos*, with three Gatlings; 200 Mounted Infantry, under Captain Barrow, and 200 Mounted Volunteers (Durban Mounted Rifles), under Captain W. Shepstone; the Alexandra Mounted Rifles, Captain Arbuthnot; Victoria Mounted Rifles, Captain Saner; Slangar Mounted Rifles, Captain Addison; the Natal Hussars, Captain Norton. Colonel Pearson, of the Buffs, was in command of the column, and had to co-operate with him a native contingent of 2000 men, under Major Graves, as well as two companies of the 99th posted at Slangar and Durban. The total strength of Colonel Pearson's column may, therefore, be set down at 2200 Europeans and 2000 natives.

The second or right centre column moved from Kranz Kop, a most formidable position, supported by Fort Buckingham. This was the scene of operations in 1861. The heights are commanding and look over a wide field of country. The position is unassailable except from the Natal side, and this was strongly fortified. Colonel Durnford, R.E., commanded this district and attack, and had with him now the 1st Regiment Native Contingent, which then consisted of three fine battalions, with three rocket tubes, under Lieutenant Russell, and 250 mounted natives, making altogether 3300 natives, officered by 200 European officers.

Following the line of advance to the left, and occupying about fifty or sixty miles of frontier, we come to column three, the left centre attack, commanded by Colonel Glyn. Take any good map and you will remark how the boundary winds serpentine fashion in its length from

Fort Buckingham to Rorke's Drift and Helpmakaar. Helpmakaar made an excellent base to Rorke's Drift. Being situated on a lofty plateau, it formed an admirable place for a permanent encampment. It also had depots at Greytown on the one side and Ladismith on the other. Colonel Glyn had with him seven companies of the 1st battalion 24th and eight companies of the 2nd battalion 24th, six 7-pounder guns with Kaffrarian carriages under Colonel Harness, a squadron of mounted infantry under Captain Browne, the Natal Mounted Police (150 men), the Natal Carabineers under Captain Shepstone, the Buffalo Border Guard (Captain Robson), the Newcastle Mounted Rifles (Captain Bradstreet), also the native contingent (2nd Regiment), 2000 strong, under Commandant Lonsdale, officered by 200 whites.

From Rorke's Drift, about five miles over the river is Ungusdana, and thence on the traveller comes to the Intalalala River, which is about fifteen miles inland. The country all about the district is rugged and broken, and calculated to afford positions of great defensive strength. Colonel Glyn was, if possible, to bear a little to his left flank after crossing the boundary with a view to communication being opened with Wood's right flank. To effect this connexion, however, there was a sad need of cavalry.

We now come to the extreme left of the advance, whose headquarters were Utrecht, and which was thus composed:—Colonel Evelyn Wood, V.C, C.B., 90th Light Infantry, commanding No. 4 Column; Staff Orderly Officer, Lieutenant Lysons, 90th Infantry; Principal Staff Officer, Captain Hon. R. G. E. Campbell, Coldstream Guards; general Staff duties. Captain Woodgate, 4th Regiment; transport duties. Captain Vaughan, R.A.; senior commissary officer, Commissary Hughes; commissary of ordnance, Assistant Commissary Philimore; sub-district paymaster. Paymaster McDonald; senior medical officer, Surgeon-Major Cuffe. Corps—Royal Artillery, six 7-pounders, Major Tremlett, R.A.; lst-13th Light Infantry, Lieutenant-Colonel Gilbert, 13th; 90th Light Infantry, Brevet Lieutenant-Colonel Cherry, 90th; Frontier Light Horse, Brevet Lieut.-Colonel Buller, C.B., 60th; Wood's Irregulars, 700 men, Commandant Henderson, In addition, a few Boers were coming in, and more were expected.

Utrecht is the most southerly part of the Transvaal, and lies upon the border of both Natal and Zululand. It is separated from the former by the Buffalo river, and, after crossing the Blood River, a few marches bring one to the territories of King Cetywayo. From the lowest, or most southerly portions of Utrecht, just where the Buffalo and Blood

Rivers form a junction, to the port of Durban, on the coast of Natal, is but 100 miles, and the capital city is about thirty miles from Newcastle, the most northern of Natal towns. The two districts are connected by a tolerably fair road and a drift over the Buffalo River. Utrecht, in a strategical point of view, wedged in as it were between Natal and Zululand, cannot be equalled by any position of a similar nature. The interior of this district extends away to the summit of the Drakenberg range, one of which reaches an altitude of 4000 feet.

Most of the Utrecht land lies in what is called the "terrace country," and has the advantage of the most splendid bracing air, added to which are mountain ridge and peak, precipice, wooded gorge, and grass-land, and scenery whose characteristics are of a grander and nobler nature than that of the Cape Colony. The portion of the Drakenberg which runs through Utrecht has its eastern front and glacis looking towards the sea, which is about eighty miles distant, and as each terrace or range slopes down the character of the country changes, presenting many of the features of the upper portions of the Cape Colony, that is to say, broad undulating downs in one part and immense flats covered with bush on the other.

All the principal rivers and streams of Utrecht and their tributaries flow eastward to the Indian Ocean. On one boundary there is the Pongola, and on the other the Buffalo, while the Blood River passes through it with a south-eastern flow, and the Pifan does the same, but with an inclination to the northeast. From the wild highlands between these two streams issue the headwaters of the Umoolosi, which traverses Zululand and empties itself into St. Lucia Bay.

Wood's column marched from Utrecht on the 7th, so as to be on the borderland in order to operate with the right-hand column on the appointed day. General Lord Chelmsford had given orders that Colonel Wood was to be at a certain point on the 10th, and consequently arrangements were made to carry out these instructions. It was known that Sirayo would probably oppose the crossing of Colonel Glyn at Rorke's Drift, and Colonel Wood had been told, if possible, to get sufficiently near to operate on the enemy's right and rear should such an attempt be made.

Leaving a small guard at his camps at Sandspruit, the rest of Wood's force paraded in the lightest possible order at 1.30 p.m. on the 10th, and marched from two that afternoon until six p.m. A halt was then made until 1.30 a.m., when by the light of a glorious moon the advance was pursued. A mounted advanced guard was thrown out, flanking patrols were organised and told off, and the troops moved in the greatest silence, not a word in the ranks being allowed to be spoken. At 3 a.m., a short halt took place, and the chief ordered forward a reconnaissance, consisting of Buller's Light Horse, two 7-pounder guns under Major Tremlett, and twenty-four picked shots from the 13th and 90th Regiments respectively. These men were to be carried in some of the mule waggons, and were accompanied by the 700 irregulars, horse and foot.

Colonel Wood accompanied this advanced force, leaving the remaining (main) body in charge of Colonel Gilbert, who was ordered to follow at a fixed time. The advanced body arrived within ten miles of Rorke's Drift at 7.30 a.m., and by eight the camp fires were lit and the men comfortably having their breakfasts on the banks of a small stream; the mounted men having at once off-saddled, the infantry piled arms, and the horses and mules turned out to graze under a strong guard.

About nine o'clock the general, Lord Chelmsford, cantered up to the camp, accompanied by his staff and an escort of 100 mounted infantry and some Natal mounted police. The general seemed delighted at the celerity with which his orders had been carried out, as in eighteen hours Wood's party had covered twenty-seven miles, and the men and horses were as fresh as paint. A long consultation took place with the general, and then the order was issued for the return to the main body; but this was not found necessary, as Colonel Gilbert met them after about ten miles.

In this day, or rather twenty-four hours, the men had marched thirty-one miles, and were not fated, on camp being pitched, to enjoy the fruits of their labour and toil, for soon after they were settled for the evening a heavy thunderstorm came suddenly over the tents, and in a quarter of an hour they were up to their ankles in a perfect river of water. The tents went down in all directions, and in many cases poles were snapped. The next day, however, a patrol of Buller's Horse was paraded soon after daybreak, as scouts had brought in information that a large number of cattle were to be seen in the neighbouring *kloof*. Soon after leaving camp Buller's men were fired upon, but the Zulus did not stand their ground, and by the afternoon they had brought in nearly 1000 cattle.

Captain Barton, who had gone out later in the day with another party, marched twenty miles in the direction of Umkanga's *kraal*, where in the skirmish which resulted 560 cattle were taken, and seven

Battle of Rorke's Drift

of the Zulus were killed and wounded. On the following morning a strong reconnaissance was made in the direction of the Bushee Valley. The Zulus were in considerable force, and their general tried to induce the English skirmishers to follow him to ground of his own choosing. Colonel Wood, however, kept his men well in hand, and contented himself by sending forward two companies of the 13th Light Infantry, Colonel Gilbert's fine corps, and menacing the Zulu flank with some score or more horsemen, who, galloping to a favouring eminence, made capital practice at the Zulu main body with their rifles at 700 and 800 yards.

The Zulus still continued to creep up in rear, getting what cover they could from the bushes, and a sharp fire was kept up on both sides. As the men in skirmishing order pushed the enemy gradually before them, the mounted force harassed them on either flank, sometimes galloping round to the right and left to obtain vantage-ground and cover, and then dismounting in sections, and acting as infantry, while the main body was kept carefully out of sight in the dense mimosa which was found in the rear. The bush, as they advanced, gradually became more dense, and the path scarcely allowed them to move in fours by a steep descent into a wooded valley. Instinctively it was guessed that here would be the main body of the foe, and this turned out to be the case, for away to the left front, on a tall "*copjie*" or circular hill, about twenty mounted Zulus were to be seen, evidently the commander and his staff giving orders and directing the operations of the columns in the plain.

The firing had now become general, but the soldiers were not allowed to waste their ammunition, and nearly every shot told with fatal effect. Colonel Wood had taken the precaution to strengthen his flanks as he advanced, and as the enemy could not tell how strong he was, the main body being still invisible, they were completely puzzled by the daring of the mounted men, who seemed ubiquitous. The guns were found rather a nuisance; one of the carriages broke down, and the limber had to be left behind, while the gun itself was secured. The head of the first line of skirmishers had now made good their way through the *kloof* with slight loss, and the Zulus attempted in vain to get round to its rear, but found all hopes of such a manoeuvre utterly futile—as the flanking parties were on the *qui-vive*.

It was now Wood's turn to push them, and he used the opportunity. Two more companies were advanced at the double to force the centre of the Zulu line, and in a few moments we had cut it in two.

In the meanwhile, one of the light field-pieces had obtained a favourable position, and had got the enemy's range exactly, but the execution done was not what could have been obtained with a good honest nine or twelve pounder. The pursuit was carried on for about a mile, and the Zulus were scattered in all directions, but the commander was too wary to allow his men to go too far, and the recall was sounded, and in a short time brought back the excited fellows, puffing and blowing, to rejoin the main body.

For some days this column continued to advance steadily without meeting any serious opposition. Having moved on from the Blood River, Wood's force encamped at Bemba's Kop till the 20th January. The country over which they had passed since they left Utrecht may be described as a succession of large rolling plains, interspersed in all directions by watercourses (*dongas*), which radiate from the bases of the table-topped mountains rising at intervals throughout this part of the country. These watercourses are as a rule about twelve to fourteen feet deep, and serve to irrigate the country, which seems prosperous and well-populated. What would be called a road in England does not exist in Zululand.

The tracks made by the traders with their waggons answer the purpose. These tracks are, however, tolerably good, and experience proved that artillery could be moved almost anywhere, except in wet weather. Waggons could pass each other at almost any part of the main road from Utrecht to Ulundi, except at that portion leading across the Inhlazatye Mountain, which runs along a narrow ledge, and where it ascends the Intendeka table-land. Wherever the troops moved they came across numerous *kraals*, each *kraal* containing from eight to fifteen huts, and each hut ten to fifteen men.

From Bemba's Kop they moved on the 20th to Wolpoint, as nearly as possible seven miles west of the White Umbolosi, and thence went on to Tunguin's Neck, where a *laager* was planned and completed. After a reconnaissance made by Colonel Wood on the 22nd, in which his troops had a slight skirmish with a small body of Zulus, suffering no casualties, and inflicting a slight loss upon them, he halted on the 23rd, and sent out strong patrols in the direction of the Ingwazini River. These men rode over an open plain admirably suited for cavalry operations, but found nothing but some deserted *kraals* and the dead bodies of some Zulus, who, it was subsequently discovered, were wounded at Isandula the previous day.

On their return the party were fortunate enough to discover the whereabouts of a strong body, some 4000 to 5000 Zulu warriors, who, it was imagined, were merely the nucleus of a force intended to surprise Wood's column. They were posted in a well-chosen position at a place called Tintas Hill, and when they moved down in his direction the following day, Wood had concealed a portion of his force so well, that he got them between two fires, and in about half an hour had killed about sixty or seventy of them, his own casualties being only two men wounded.

It was during this action that information was brought by Captain Alan Gardner, who gallantly rode without any escort from Helpmakaar to Utrecht, notifying the terrible disaster of the 22nd, and the destruction of No. 3 Column. This news caused Colonel Wood to change his plans, and after a halt of a couple of hours, he turned back towards the Umbolosi, where his little force arrived at seven a.m. on the 25th. On Sunday (26th) he moved on to Ugaba Ka Hawana, where good camping-ground and a defensive position were chosen, and where the minor essentials of wood and water were in plenty.

Colonel Pearson, who commanded No. 1 Column on the extreme right, had also been prosecuting his advance with the greatest vigour, and the results were in every way satisfactory, though already the tremendous difficulties of commissariat and transport had made themselves unpleasantly evident. This force assembled near Fort Stanger, and crossed the Lower Tugela on the 12th, having as nearly as possible 1500 regular troops, consisting of eight companies of the old Buffs, under Colonel Parnell; six companies of the 99th, under Colonel Welman; one company Royal Engineers, and two 7-pounder guns. A naval brigade, however, which might be considered as a little army in itself, went with them, and were under Colonel Pearson's command.

This force consisted of 270 bluejackets and marines, under Captain Campbell, of Her Majesty's ships *Active* and *Tenedos*, with three of the new-pattern Gatling. Two hundred mounted infantry and 200 colonial mounted riflemen also formed part of the column, while the whole force was supplemented by Major Griffiths and about 2000 men of the Native Contingent. The crossing of the river was at first impeded by the rains, and another delay occurred at the lower drift, where the river was at least 400 yards wide, but all these difficulties were overcome, and after a week's delay a flying column was sent forward on the 18th in the direction of Ekowe, which is a mission-station not quite forty miles inland, and distant nearly seventy from the king's *kraal* at Ulundi.

It was the intention of Colonel Pearson to establish here an entrenched post as a *point-d'appui* to the invading army. On the following day the colonel was followed by the rear division, escorting the heavy baggage, necessary though inconvenient *impedimenta*, as it contained stores and ammunition. The column of waggons extended for five miles, and it took the officers in charge all their time and the services of three horses each during the day to supervise its progress from inspan till outspan. Again, two days later, came the commissariat, and here imagination fails to describe the difficulties encountered. The subject of transport is one that must be considered in any future operations in Africa. The waggons must be stronger than those employed; the animals should be proof against sickness caused by climate, the tulip plant, and the tsetse fly, and this can be avoided by choosing one's own season for marching.

The employment of mules would be much preferable to that of oxen, although in many books the converse is stated, the Dutch being infatuated in regard to the superior qualities of the latter. Mules, for instance, have this advantage over oxen. They can travel twenty-five miles a day with ease, while twelve or fifteen a day with oxen is considered good work; but, on the other hand, it must be remembered that a mule costs twice as much as an ox, apart from the cost of feeding. The mule must, of course, be fed on forage carried for him or bought on the road, while the ox will feed on the *veldt*, except during the three winter months, when his services are not often required. Two kinds of mules can be procured about Pretoria—the Montevidean and the home-bred animal. The latter is generally preferred, although no doubt the former is most tractable.

There is an immense trouble in selecting oxen for campaigning, as none but those bred in the sour *veldt* of Natal or Zululand are of any use for such rough food and hard work; and, as a rule, these will live where others would die. The usual load is 7000 lbs., placed on a waggon weighing 3000 lbs., and drawn by sixteen or eighteen oxen. The cost for oxen averages about 9*l*. each, but during this war they went up to 18*l*., and even 25*l*. Each waggon, with *dissel*-boom and yokes complete, costs at least 180*l*. The cost of mules will average 20*l*. each, and mule waggons 100*l*., with harness at 5*l*. for each animal.

The road, after crossing the River Tugela, crosses no less than four streams, and before reaching Ekowe passes through a broken bushy country. On the 22nd, the day on which Isandula was attacked. Colonel Pearson had a sharp engagement with the enemy at a place called by the natives Inyezane, about four or five miles beyond his camping-ground of the 21st. Major Barrow had been sent forward along a fertile valley which led to the Inyezane, when Colonel Pearson received a despatch from him, saying that he had selected a tolerably good place for camping, which he had carefully guarded by vedettes.

On receiving this information, the colonel at once rode on to the spot, and although he did not quite approve of the ground, as being too full of bush for an outspan, he decided to allow the waggons to be outspanned for two hours on account of there being no water near at hand. This was done to rest and feed the oxen, and to allow the men to have their morning meal. About eight o'clock, just as the waggons had begun to park, and while the officers were busy in directing the posting of pickets, scouts, and sentries, the advanced company of the Native Contingent, which had been scouting in front under Captain Hart, discovered the Zulus in force rapidly advancing over the slopes and attempting to gain the bushes on both flanks. They came on in skirmishing and extended order in the finest style, rushing from bush to bush in a steady but stealthy manner until within 100 or 150 yards of the outposts. Captain Hart's men, being in the open, had to bear the brunt of a heavy fire, and not without casualties, as they lost one officer, four non-commissioned officers, and four privates almost at once.

These poor fellows, it is feared, were sacrificed, inasmuch as they did not understand the order to retire and seek cover, and concluded that it was their duty to remain in the open. The Naval Brigade was now ordered into action, and most ably they acquitted themselves. Two 7-pounders and two 24-pounder Naval Brigade rockets were smartly brought into action on a knoll at the base of the pass, but commanding the valley from which the flank attack was made. Meanwhile two companies of the Buffs and A and B companies of the Naval Brigade opened a heavy and well-directed fire upon the enemy, and effectually held him in check. This coign of vantage was occupied by Colonel Pearson, whence he directed the movements of his troops during the fight.

All this time the waggons continued to park, and while the fire was kept up by Commander Campbell, Lieutenant Lloyd, with his guns, and Lieutenant Martin with the Buffs, two other companies of the same regiment which had been employed in guarding waggons were moved down, ready to clear the bush as soon as it was well shelled and swept with rockets and musketry.

Colonel Pearson selected Captain Macgregor to undertake this duty, with the assistance of Captains Harrison and Wyld, who, getting their men into skirmishing order, and bringing their shoulders gradually forward as steadily as if manoeuvring at a field-day, sent the Zulu braves flying discomfited before them, and exposed them once more in the open to the hail of shot and shell which swept the plain. Colonel Welman, 99th Regiment, now took advantage of this favourable moment, when the enemy was demoralised, to send forward Captain Wynne and Major Barrow with the infantry. These, with skirmishers and flankers on the left, and supported by two half-companies of the Buffs and 99th, now moved forward at a steady pace.

The Zulus, however, were not beaten, though evidently puzzled, and Campbell, who was in charge of the Naval Brigade, saw that they were making a flank movement on the left. This officer at once obtained permission from Colonel Pearson to take a portion of his men and drive out a body of Zulus who had obtained possession of a *kraal* about 400 yards from the knoll. Captain Hart, with part of his Native Contingent, gallantly supported this movement. They managed to obtain possession of the high ground to the left of the Ekowe road, and effectually checked the enemy in their movement on the British left.

But the gallant sailor Campbell was not satisfied with this partial success, and sent for further permission to follow up his *coup* by driving on the foe to a more respectable distance. Colonel Parnell, of the Buffs, who up to this time had been acting as a sort of reserve with Captain Foster's company at the foot knoll, where Colonel Pearson remained throughout the action, had now an opportunity of mingling in the fray. Smartly deploying his men, he advanced at the double, and forming up on the right of the bluejackets, swept the heights beyond the *kraal* which a few moments before were crowned with savage warriors. This decided the action, as the Zulus, thoroughly distracted, fled in all directions, the guns making capital practice wherever a group collected. The last round from the rocket-tubes seemed to carry destruction and confusion amongst them, and was fired a little before ten a.m.

Colonel Pearson and Colonel Parnell both had their horses shot under them, and several officers remarked that the fire of the Zulus was principally directed at the English leaders. The regiments opposed to Pearson were composed of the Umxapu, Umdhlanefu, and Ingulubi, and as near as could be judged, and from the information subsequently received, numbered about 5000 men. Of these at the very least 300 were slain, while the number of wounded, as a rule carried away into the bush, could not have been less than double that. Pearson's loss was eight killed and sixteen wounded, and of these were six officers and non-commissioned officers of the Native Contingent.

The following day two companies of the Buffs, two companies Native Contingent, and a few mounted men were sent off to the help of Colonel Ely, 99th Regiment, who with three companies of his regiment was bringing up a convoy, much wanted, of seventy waggons of stores and ammunition, while on Saturday, the 18th, Major Coates started with fifty extra waggons to bring up more supplies. On the day after the Inyezane engagement Pearson arrived at Ekowe. The position was a strong one, and he immediately set to work to make it still more formidable. Water was close to the fort, and well under its fire.

At this juncture news of the Isandhlwana disaster reached Colonel Pearson. After consultation with his officers, he decided to remain where he was, feeling confident that even without further supplies or reinforcements he could hold his position for at least a couple of months. All his waggons came in safety to the fort except five, which broke down and had to be abandoned. The mounted men and Native Contingent were sent back to save food, and there thus remained 1200 British troops, having 320 rounds per man.

The first failure in the carrying out of Lord Chelmsford's plans occurred to No. 4 Column, and proved the initial step to the crowning disaster of Isandhlwana. The right centre column, which should have operated simultaneously with Colonel Wood's force, was unfortunately composed almost entirely of natives, and these fellows did not succeed in getting over at the point directed in orders. As this column could not be brought over the river, a portion of it was left behind to keep open communications and guard the frontier, while the remainder, under Colonel Durnford, was moved up to Rorke's Drift to reinforce Colonel Glyn's command.

The following day (12th) Colonel Glyn had his first brush with the enemy. Lord Chelmsford had joined this column, and after crossing the Tugela ordered out a reconnaissance by the Bashee Valley and along the road leading to Izpizi. Glyn took with him three companies of the 1st battalion 24th and one battalion 3rd Regiment Natal Native Contingent, while the mounted men, crossing the valley, went rapidly along the road leading over the Ngudu mountains, where high cliffs close in the gorge for more than three miles. Cattle and armed Zulus were seen on the heights, and some of the 24th and the natives were ordered to bear round to the right flank and cut them off. The

Kraal

Kraal

To Rorke's Drift

Mealie bags

Heap of Mealie bags

Biscuit boxes

Commissariat
Store House

Garden

Road

Bush

Wall 3 ft. high

Wall of Mealie bags 4 ft. high

Wall of Mealie bags

Rock ledge

Mealie bags

Wagons

Ditch
Bank 2 ft. high

Cook House

Hospital

Ditch
Bank 2 ft. high

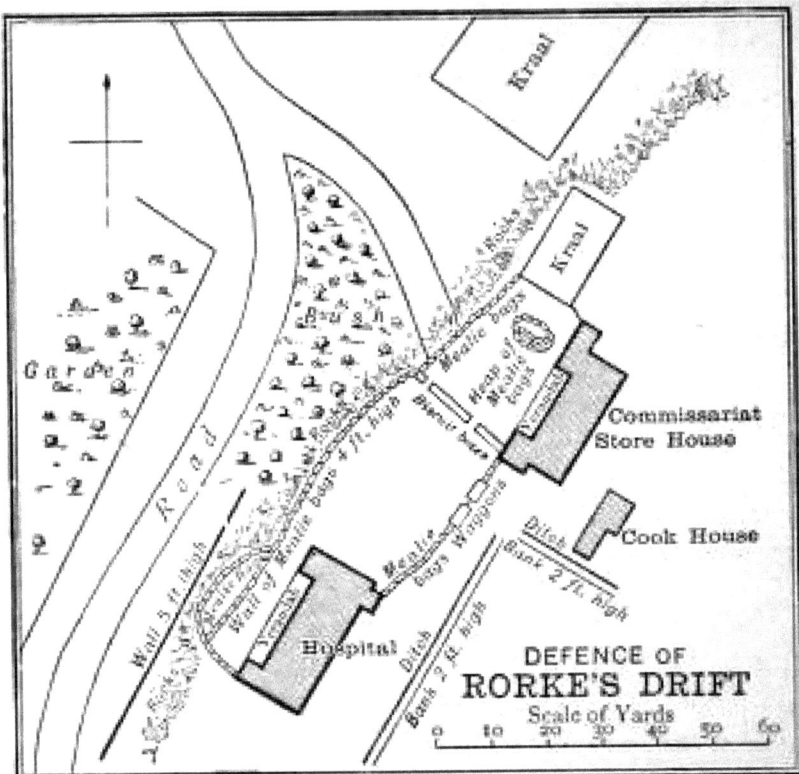

DEFENCE OF
RORKE'S DRIFT

Scale of Yards

0   10   20   30   40   50   60

skirmish which followed lasted about twenty minutes, and was a very smart affair.

It resulted in the taking of the fastnesses and the precipitate flight of the Zulus, who suffered a loss of ten killed, three wounded, and nine prisoners taken, together with a quantity of cattle, horses, and sheep. Colonel Glyn's loss was two privates Natal Contingent killed, one officer of the same. Lieutenant Purvis, severely wounded; Corporal Mayer, Natal Native Contingent, severe wound in thigh. Four companies of the 2nd battalion 24th, and four companies of the 2nd battalion 3rd Regiment Natal Native Contingent, under Colonel Degacher, were now ordered by the general to advance up the Bashee and attack Usirayo's *kraal*, a place called Loxie, about two or three miles farther on. This place, situated in a wild and mountainous gorge or *krantz*, interspersed with caves, guarded by huge boulders, was completely explored by these men.

In the meantime, Russell and his mounted men had ascended to the summit of the Ngudu mountain, where they were fired upon at a distance of 90 or 100 yards. Sixteen of the Zulus were killed, and a very heavy thunderstorm came on during the fight. No signs could be observed of any Zulu force in reserve, and this was explained by the subsequent news that Usirayo had made a precipitate flight in the direction of the king's *kraal*. On the following day communications were opened between Wood's column and that of Colonel Glyn. The general's movements from the first appear to have been hampered by baggage and transport arrangements, and a similar reason delayed Colonel Pearson.

Lord Chelmsford was present with this column when it moved from Rorke's Drift, and saw the site which was chosen by Colonel Glyn at Insalwana, ten miles on the road to the Indeni forest. He then left Colonel Glyn in charge of the camp, and on the same day moved, with a portion of the force, ten miles further on, to reconnoitre the country in front. Returning to camp that evening, without having had time to fully explore, the general, the following morning, sent out two separate reconnoitring columns, under the command respectively of Major Dartnell, who took with him the Mounted Police and Natal Volunteers, of which he is commandant, and Commandant Lonsdale with two battalions of his Native Contingent. Dartnell went along the same road as that explored by the general the previous day, while Lonsdale moved along the southern slope of the Inhlazatye range, towards a hill called Malaka's Kop.

If possible a junction between these two bodies was to be effected; and, as soon as information could be obtained as to the situation of the enemy and the strategical features of the locality, both were to return to the headquarter camp. By some extraordinary oversight, neither of these reconnoitring columns seems to have been supplied with rations, while it was usual on such expeditions for the men to take preserved meat and three days' biscuit in their haversacks, supposing that mule transport cannot be had. On the afternoon of the Tuesday Major Dartnell sent an officer to the headquarter camp, to inform the General that he could not advance beyond the Insangu River, a small stream near Inkankla Mountain, as the Zulus were posted there in force.

Dartnell, therefore, sent an orderly to call up Lonsdale with his Native Contingent, and sent to Lord Chelmsford to request a reinforcement of regulars to enable him to attack the enemy. His lordship did not consider it advisable to comply with this demand, as the daylight was almost gone, and the distance was long. A supply of biscuit was, however, sent out to the exploring party, who bivouacked at the foot of the Inhlazatye. During the night, however. Major Dartnell appears to have become aware of his critical position, and at half-past two on the morning of the 22nd (Wednesday), Colonel Glyn received a letter from him, saying that the Zulus had been strongly reinforced, and were now in his front in great strength. Instead of recalling the column, or at once pushing forward troops to its assistance, a delay took place, and a staff officer was despatched to ask Dartnell what he wished done.

After some further lapse of time the general ordered Colonel Glyn to march to Major Dartnell's assistance with the 2nd battalion 24th Regiment, consisting of six companies, the mounted infantry, and four of Harness's guns. As this detachment would considerably weaken the camp, the general at the same time sent off two expresses to Colonel Durnford, who had been left at Rorke's Drift, telling him to move up at once to Isandula with his 500 native troops, 250 of whom were mounted. The general then decided to accompany Colonel Glyn's force, and Lieutenant-Colonel Pulleine, 1-24th, was left in charge of the camp, with orders to defend it, pending the arrival of Durnford's natives. The actual fighting strength of Pulleine's force consisted of 2 officers, 78 men, and 2 guns R.A.; 1-24th Regiment, 15 officers, 334 men; 2-24th Regiment, 5 officers, 90 men; mounted Europeans, 5 officers, 204 men; Native Contingent, 19 officers, 391 men; Natal Pio-

RORKE'S DRIFT

COMMISSARIAT STORES
HOSPITAL &c.
defended 22nd Jan. 1879.

From *W.Russell*

To *N. Beaumont*
1st September 1829
Pietermaritzburg

To the pontoon & ferry

To Helpmakaar

Garden

Fence

Ditch

R O A D

B u s h

Wall 5'

Wall of Mealie Bags 6' high

Rough Stone Kraal

The Buffalo River

Ver.ah

HOSPITAL

Mealie Bags

Wagons

Heap of Mealie Bags

Kraal

Well built Kraal

Door above and below

COMM?. STORE

 R o c k

door
window

Ditch
Bank 2'   Oven

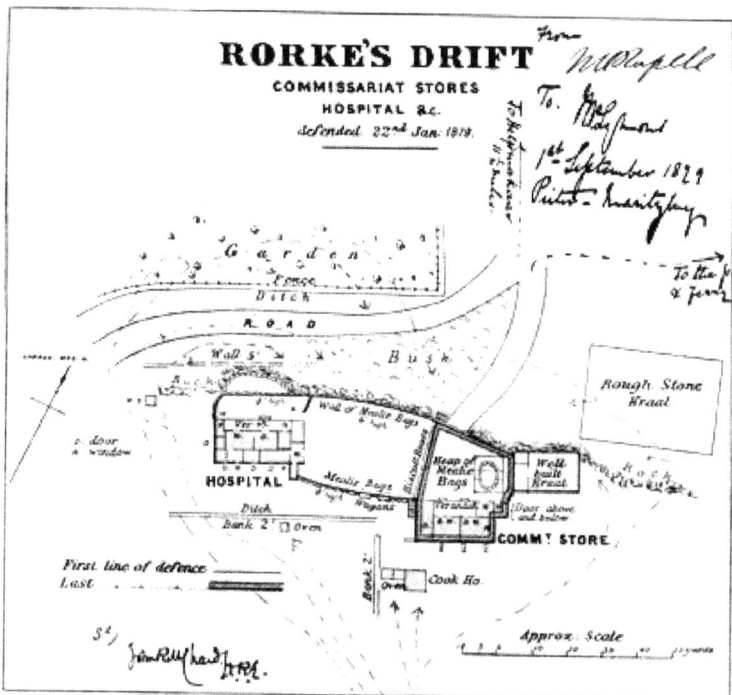

First line of defence
Last

Biscuit Boxes

Oven   Cook Ho.

Approx. Scale

St.
John R. M. Chard R.E.

Zulu advance

Hill

Direction Isandhlwana

Lith? at the Intelligence Branch 2? in? Guard Dept. 1879.

neers, 1 officer, 10 men; while Durnford, when he arrived very soon after, brought with him 18 officers and 450 men, thus making an aggregate of 772 Europeans and 850 natives, or in all 1622 combatants. On his arrival at the camp. Colonel Durnford, being the senior officer, of course immediately assumed the command.

To the right understanding of what follows it is necessary to give a somewhat detailed account of the situation. The leading feature of the plain on the southern slopes of which the English camp was placed is the Isandhlwana, or Lion Hill. To the west it rises abruptly, forming the head of the crouching animal it resembles in shape; after forming the back it descends sharply to the east. At both ends are necks or ridges connecting the hill with the smaller undulations of which the more level part of the country consists. The road from Rorke's Drift passes over the western ridge, while on the north facing the camp was a deep ravine and watercourse.

To the immediate right was a small *kopse*; beyond this the ground was much broken, irregular *krantzes* and hills all covered with huge boulders continuing as far as the Buffalo River. To the left of the camp, at the distance of rather more than a mile, ran a long ridge towards the south, connecting it with the great Isandhlwana hill, having on its summit a plateau which, towards the east, opened on to an open and extensive valley.

On the extreme left of the camp, looking towards the ridge, were pitched the tents of the Natal Native Contingent; between these and the next two battalions intervened a space of rather less than 300 yards; occupying the centre were the British Regular Infantry, just above whom came the headquarters camp of Lord Chelmsford, and in close proximity the headquarters of the column. On the right were the guns and mounted corps lining the edge of the road. Soon after it came over the neck at the back of the camp the ground rose considerably, until the bottom of the precipitous Isandhlwana was reached: the camp therefore literally had its back to a wall.

At six a.m. on the 22nd, a company of the Natal Natives was ordered to scout towards the left, the enemy having appeared in that direction. Whilst these were away Durnford arrived, about nine o'clock, with a rocket battery under Colonel Russell, R.A., 250 mounted natives, and 250 native foot. News was now brought in that the Zulus in very large numbers were driving the pickets before them. A later messenger—a native without uniform, supposed by some to be a Zulu purposely sent with false intelligence—brought the news that the Zulus had divided into three columns, one of which it was supposed was about to attack Colonel Durnford's baggage, still on the road from Rorke's Drift, the other to harass Lord Chelmsford and Colonel Glyn's party in their rear, whilst the third was to hover round and watch the camp.

Finally came the news "Zulus retiring in all directions." Colonel Durnford thereupon asked Colonel Pulleine to lend him a couple of the 24th companies, but he declined, saying his orders were to guard the camp, and he could not, under the circumstances, let them go without a positive command. Durnford then determined to go on with his own force, which he divided into three, one part being sent up the hill to the left (east), one to the left front, and the third to the rear, in the direction of Rorke's Drift, to act as an escort for the baggage not yet arrived. The rocket-battery was of the party that proceeded to the front under Colonel Durnford in person, to a distance of four or five miles from the camp, but being unable to keep pace with the mounted force was soon left behind.

The body of troops despatched to the left became engaged with the enemy almost immediately, and firing was soon heard all along the crest of the hill. In about an hour Durnford's mounted men reappeared over the hills, hotly pursued by swarms of Zulus; at the same time the horsemen to the front were also driven back. These, after retiring steadily in skirmishing order for about two miles, came upon the remains of the rocket battery, which had been cut off and broken up, whilst a hand to hand engagement was going on with those who remained.

It appears that Russell, whilst advancing with his battery, perceived a body of the enemy on his left, he fired three rockets with some effect; then the Zulus fired a volley, upon which the Native Contingent of infantry retreated, the mules were frightened, and disorder ensued. Taking advantage of this, the enemy charged down the hill, a *melee* ensued, and Russell was killed. As the mounted men retired towards them, the Zulus retreated to their cover, and they, after making a final stand in a *spruit* about a mile and a half in front of the camp, were eventually driven in.

As the cavalry on the left was being pushed rapidly back, Captain Mostyn was ordered to advance with two companies of l-24th on the eastern neck of the Isandhlwana, where at a distance of about a mile and a half the Zulus were advancing in large numbers along the north of the Isandhlwana, to outflank the camp on the right, and with this

MILITARY SURVEY
of the
COUNTRY AROUND ISANDHLWANA

No. 2.

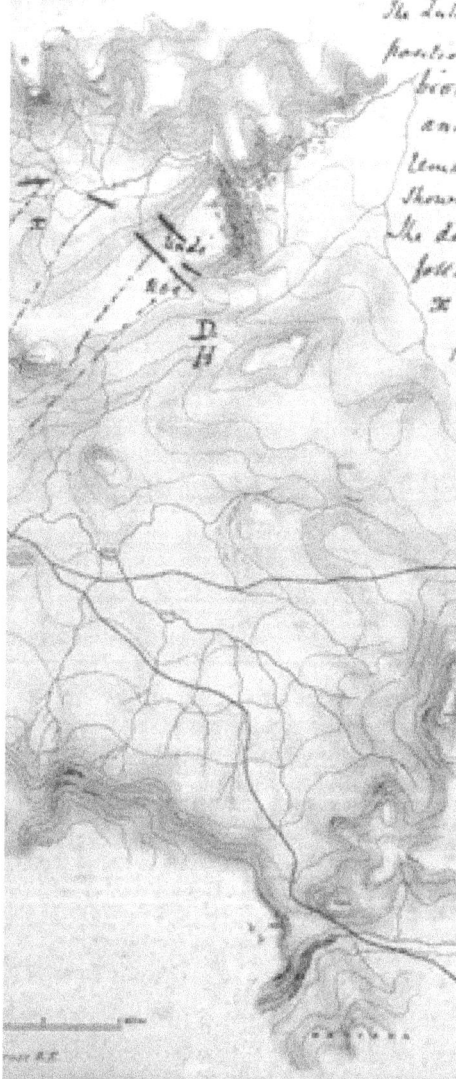

The Zulu pointed out exactly the
position of the head orange on
bivouac — near a mealie garden
and indicated generally the
remainder. The thick line × a
shows the intended movement
The dotted lines that actually
followed

× I believe about where
the Basutos fired on the
Umcityu.

The Zulus attacked locally
as they bivouacked —
all in line of Regiments
except the Undi Corps
which was ½ a mile
in rear of Ngabamakhosi
in bivouac and in
action

D.H. Approximate
position of Colonel Dur-
ford when the firing hearing
the firing of Umcityu and
other contingents of Basutos
persuaded him to retire

wing of the foe they at once became engaged.

Meanwhile the Zulu left rapidly, and the centre steadily, though more slowly, pushed forward, despite the artillery fire poured into them. Orders were now given for three companies of the 1-24th to occupy ground near the Native Contingent camp, facing the hill over which the Zulu force was streaming. These three companies were supported to their right front by the Natal Native Contingent.

Immediately to the right of the Native Contingent tents came the guns, at a distance of about four hundred yards from the left, and rather more from the right, which was composed of two companies, 24th Regiment and the Mounted Corps, and which occupied the extreme right of the camp and rested on the road. The infantry, in extended order, were by this time engaged along the whole line, and were firing rapidly and steadily. Though the enemy fell in hundreds they kept advancing in apparently undiminished numbers.

As rank after rank of the foremost were swept down others pressed on, till at length the companies of the 1-24th above mentioned had been driven back to within 300 yards of that portion of the camp occupied by the Native Contingent. A number of the native infantry now began a hasty retreat to the camp; their officers endeavoured to restrain them, but without effect. Captain Essex pointed this out to Colonel Durnford, who ordered him to take men to that portion of the field, and endeavour to hold the enemy in check.

But before this could be executed the natives rushed back in the utmost disorder, thus laying open the right and rear of the companies of the first battalion of the 24th on the left and rear, and the enemy dashing forward at once poured in through this part of the line. In a moment all was disorder, and but few had time to fix bayonets before the Zulus were amongst them, using their *assegais* with terrible effect. Then followed a scene of utter confusion; horse and foot, black and white, English and Zulu, friend and foe, in a struggling, fighting crowd, pushed gradually through the camp towards the road, where the Zulu right already barred the way.

Every man endeavoured to escape towards the Buffalo River, but this was almost an impossibility even for mounted men. The ground was rugged, broken with water-washes, boulder-strewn ground over which an active native Zulu could progress even faster than a horse. In front ran the river, swift, deep, and fordless, sharp rocks, and deep water alternating. Not half of those who escaped from the camp succeeded in crossing this obstacle: many were drowned, many *assegaied,*

50

some few shot, and so the pursuit continued right into Natal. The guns moved from right to left across the camp, and endeavoured to get on the Rorke's Drift road. This being occupied by the enemy, they turned off to the left, and coming to grief in a *donga* had to be abandoned. Major Smith, though wounded, managed to reach the Buffalo, but was there shot.

Lieuts. Melvill and Coghill, seeing all was lost, made an attempt to escape on horseback with the colours of the 24th. Coghill succeeded in getting safely across the Buffalo, but Melvill was struck by a shot just as he was reaching the far bank of the river. Coghill, with heroic devotion, turned back to assist his less fortunate comrade—alas only to share his fate. Their bodies were subsequently discovered in close proximity, and around them a group of dead Zulus. The colours which they had so desperately defended were also found in the bed of the river, saved from the degradation of capture and contamination by the hands of savages.

In this sad affair there perished twenty-six Imperial officers and 600 non-commissioned officers and men. The loss of the Colonial forces was not less terrible; twenty-four officers being included in the list.

The following is a detailed list of the victims of that sad day:—l-24th, Col. Pulleine, Major White; Captains Degacher, Wardell, Mostyn, Younghusband; Lieuts. Hodson, Cavaye, Atkinson, Daly, Anstey, Porteous, Melvill, Quarter-Master Pullen, and five entire companies: 2-24th, Lieuts. Pope, Austin, Dyer, Griffiths, Quarter-Master Bloomfield, and ninety men. Royal Engineers, Colonel Durnford, Lieut. McDowell, Captain G. Shepstone (political assistant to Col. Durnford), Lieut. Coghill, A.D.C. (to Sir Bartle Frere), Surgeon-Major Shepherd. The Mounted Police Carabineers and Volunteers lost forty-three out of seventy-one, including Captain Bradstreet, Lieut. F. J. D. Scott, and Quarter-Master Hitchcock. The Mounted Infantry lost thirty out of thirty-four. The N Battery 5th Brigade, Royal Artillery, under Major Stuart Smith, was destroyed (Lieut. Curling escaped), as also the Rocket Battery under Major Russell, R.A. 1st Battalion 3rd Regiment, N.N.C., lost in officers, Captains Robert Krohn and James Lonsdale, Lieuts. Avery, Holcraft, and Jameson; Surgeon F. Bull, Quarter-Master John McCormick. 2nd Battalion 3rd Regiment, N.N.C., lost Captains Erskine, Barry, and Murray; Lieuts. Pritchard, Young, Gibson, Standish Vereker, and Rivers, Quarter-Master A. Chambers.

The loss of material is put down at 102 waggons, 1400 oxen, 2

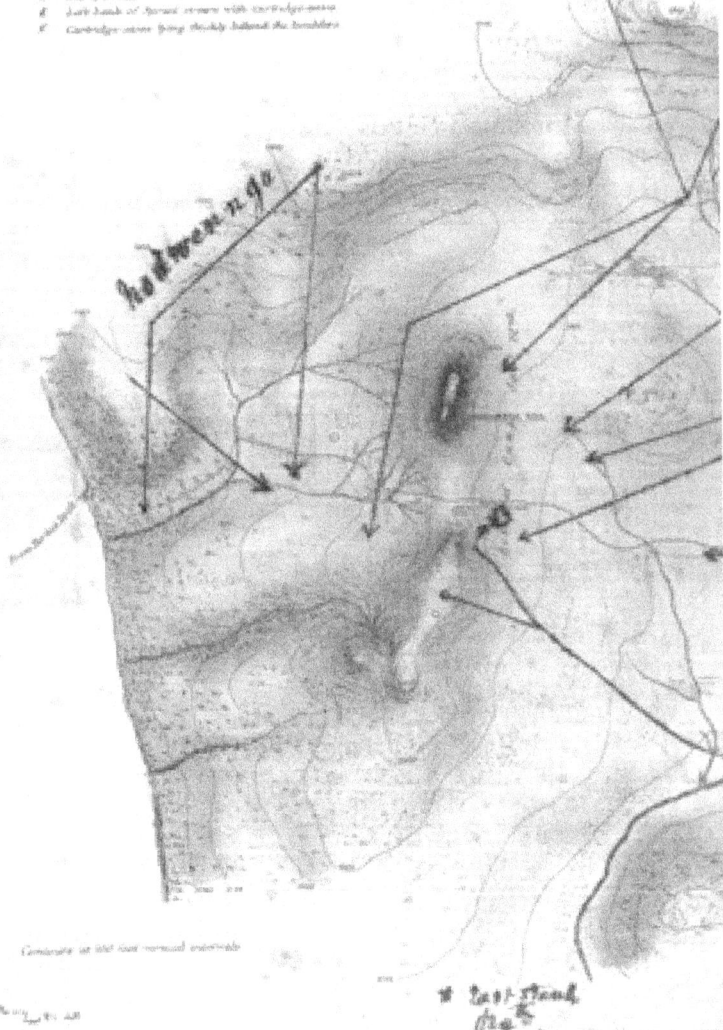

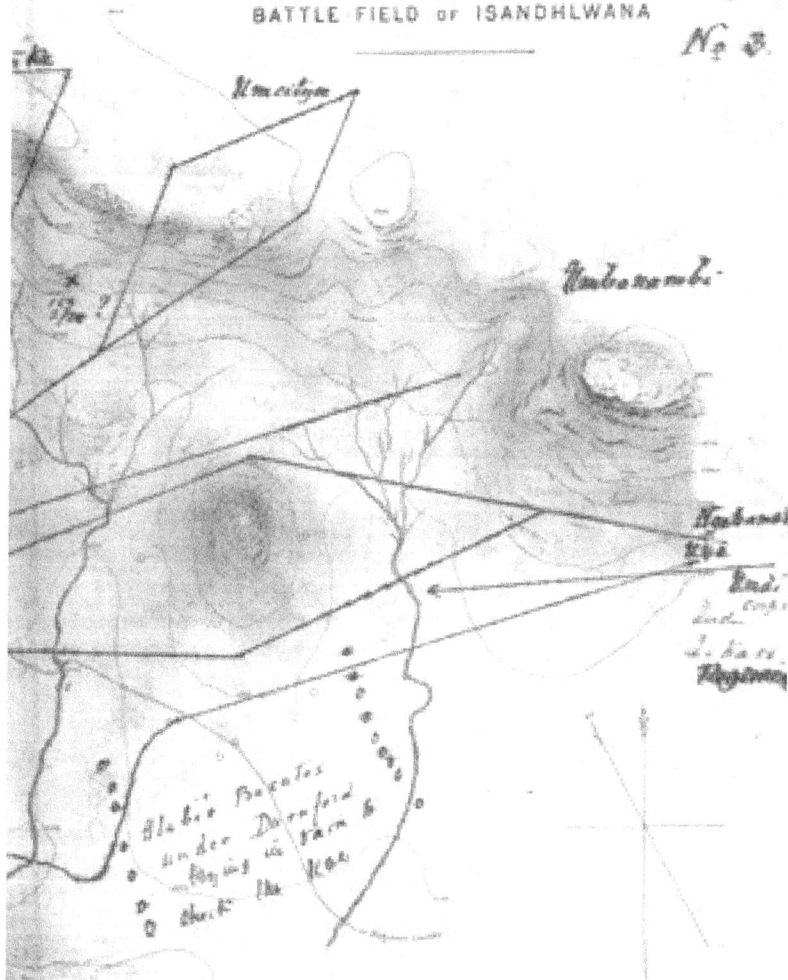

MILITARY SURVEY
of the
BATTLE FIELD OF ISANDHLWANA

N.º 3

guns, 400 shot and shell, 1200 rifles, 250,000 rounds of rifle ammunition, 60,000*l*. worth of commissariat supplies, a rocket trough, and a number of tents.

Four special-service officers, *viz*. Captain Alan Gardner, 14th Hussars and Essex 75th Regiment, and Lieuts. Smith-Dorien, 95th, and Cochrane, 32nd, together with Lieut. Curling, R.A., succeeded in escaping, and rode away to Helpmakaar, where a *laager* was immediately formed. The same night, as no other messenger could be found, and it was feared Wood's column might be cut off in rear, Captain Gardner started to give him timely warning. Riding all night, he reached Utrecht about four o'clock next day, thence despatching a messenger to Colonel Wood, he himself returned to Helpmakaar.

The following account is of great interest as having been given by a Zulu deserter:—

The Zulu Army, consisting of the Ulundi corps about 3000 strong, the Nokenke 2000, the Nkobamakosi, including the Uve, 5000 strong, the Umcityu 4000 strong, the Nodwengu 2000 strong, the Umbonambi 3000, and the Udkloko 1000— a total of 20,000 men in all—after an address from the king left the Nodwengu military *kraal* on January 17th, and proceeded on their march towards Rorke's Drift. On the 20th they halted for the night close by the Isipezi hill, and on the 21st, keeping to the eastward, they occupied a valley running north and south under the spurs of the Ngutu Hill, which concealed that of Isandhlwana, distant about four miles nearly due west.

The order of encampment was—on the right, the Nodwengu, Nokenke and Umcityu; in the centre, the Nkobamakosi and Umbonambi; on the left, the Ulundi and Udkloko corps. On the morning of the 22nd there was no intention of making an attack on account of some superstition as to the state of the moon, and they were sitting down resting when firing was heard by the Zulus on the right. This was at first supposed by them to be an attack on the centre, but a move being made in that direction this proved not to be the case; and it was soon found out that this was the whites engaged with Matyana's people some ten miles off to the left front. Just after the Zulus had resumed their position, and again sat down, a herd of cattle came past their line driven down by some of their scouts from the right. Just when these were opposite the Umcityu regiment a body of mounted men on the hill to the west were seen galloping and evidently trying to cut them off.

When several hundred yards off, seeing the Umcityu, they dismounted, fired a volley, and retired. The Umcityu at once jumped up and charged. This example was followed by the Nokenke and Nodwengu on the right, as well as by the Nkobamakosi and Umbonambi in the centre, whilst the Undi and Udkloko formed a circle—as is customary with the Zulus when a force is about to engage—and remained in their position. With these were the two chief officers Mavamingwana and Tyugwayo, who after a short pause led away these centre troops in a north-westerly direction, and keeping to the north of the Isandhlwana performed a turning movement, unseen by the English through the nature of the ground.

Thus the original Zulu left became the extreme right, the right the centre, and the centre the left. The two regiments forming the latter—the Nkobamakosi and Umbonambi—made a turning movement along the front of the camp to the English right, but became engaged before they could complete it. The Uve battalion of the Nkobamakosi had to retire till reinforced; and the Umbonambi suffered heavily from the artillery fire. Meanwhile the Zulu centre, consisting of the Umcityu (left centre) and Nokenke and Nodwengu (higher up on the right) under the hill, were making a direct attack on the left of the camp.

The Umcityu suffered very severely from both artillery and musketry fire; the Nokenke from musketry fire alone; while the Nodwengu suffered least. When the camp was carried the regiments became all mixed up together; some pursued the fugitives to the Buffalo; the remainder plundered the camp: but the Undi and Udkloko made the best of their way to Rorke's Drift, in order to plunder the post there.

It is now time to turn attention to the remainder of the troops that had left the camp before this sad event occurred.

The force under Colonel Glyn, accompanied by Lord Chelmsford, moved off at early dawn, and had reached Major Dartnell by 6.15 a.m. The general at once took command, and ordered out scouting parties of mounted men to gain intelligence of the positions and strength of the enemy, who soon after showed in some force on the opposing heights parallel to the Inhlazatye Mountains. A general advance of the

FORT ESHOWE

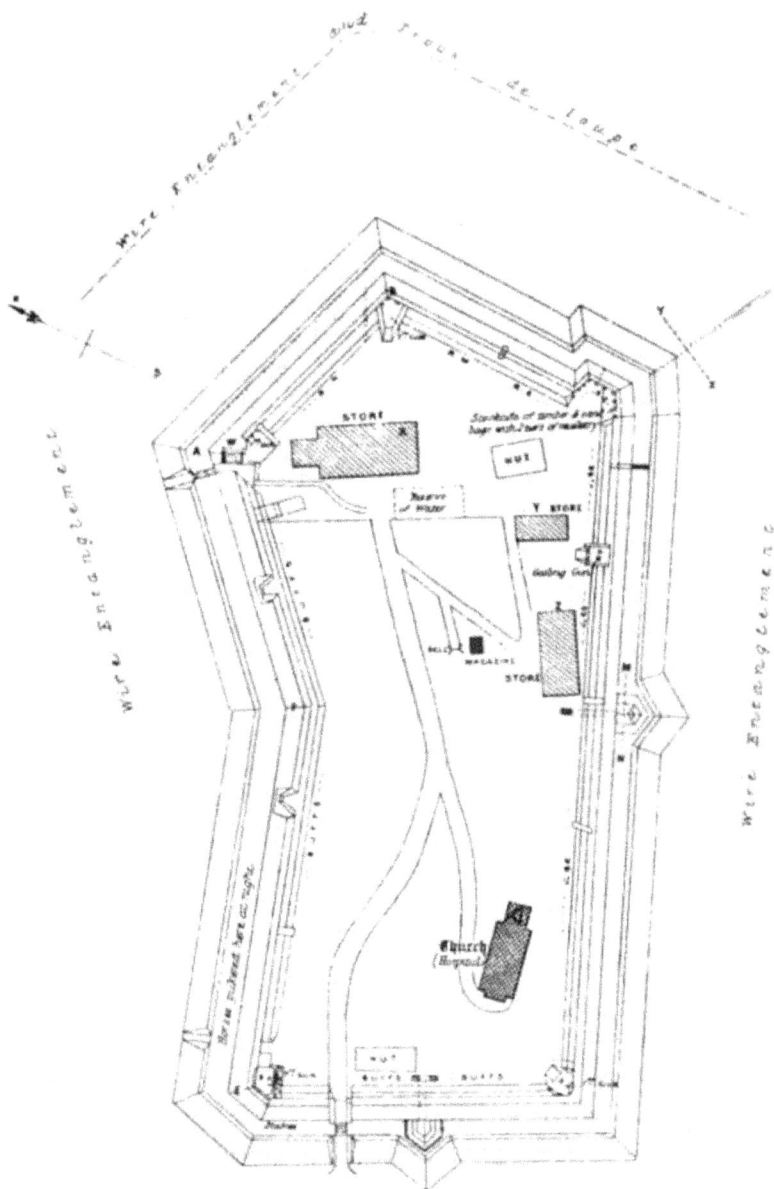

troops was made, and the enemy retired slowly, but without firing. The guns and 24th Regiment meanwhile moved up the valley, their left being protected by the Mounted Infantry, while the Mounted Police and Volunteers guarded the right flank.

The main body of the enemy drew back in regular order and took up a position with great skill on the spurs of the Isipisi Mountain, distant about six miles, but Captain Shepstone, with his Natal Carabineers, managed to cut off about 300 of the stragglers and destroyed fifty of them. At nine a.m. a messenger, whose horse was panting and covered with foam, arrived before Colonel Glyn with a brief despatch from Colonel Pulleine, notifying that musketry firing was heard on the left front of the camp. Lord Chelmsford at once sent a staff officer, Lieutenant Milne, to an eminence from whence the camp and valley of Insalwana could be seen, and it seems that a delay of an hour took place while this officer was vainly scanning the horizon. The actual scene of conflict where Colonel Durnford was engaged with the Zulu Army was five miles away, and hidden by some hills intervening between Lord Chelmsford's position and the British camp. The general, therefore, seems to have felt no apprehensions in regard to the safety of the camp, and continued his operations against the supposed main body of the Zulus.

About two o'clock Lord Chelmsford was on the banks of the Amange Stream, selecting a fit spot for a camp, he having already in the morning sent Captain Gardner back to Colonel Pulleine with an order to that officer to forward the camping materials of the party out on reconnaissance. While thus engaged a native on horseback galloped down from the opposite ridge saying that an attack was being made on the camp, and that he had seen heavy firing and heard the big guns. Lord Chelmsford immediately hastened to the crest of the hill, whence through a glass the camp could be plainly seen.

All, however, seemed quiet: the sun was shining on the white tents; no signs of firing were seen, and the bodies of men moving about in the camp were put down to be English soldiers and friendly natives. Knowing how careful were his dispositions and how positive his orders for the defence of the camp, one and all of Lord Chelmsford's escort came to the conclusion that an attack had been made and repulsed. It was then decided that the headquarters camp should move to the spot selected on the Amange Stream, whilst the general himself, who was anxious to know the details of the attack, should proceed back to camp. The Carabineers and the Mounted Infantry accompanied him:

the 1st battalion 24th Regiment, the four guns, the Mounted Police and 2nd battalion of 3rd Regiment Native Contingent were left to form the new camp.

During the first seven miles of the journey nothing occurred to excite the general's suspicion. Certainly some of the tents had disappeared, but then this was in accordance with the orders given in the morning. When about four miles from the camp he fell in with the Natal Native Contingent, which had been ordered to return many hours previously, but which seeing the camp attacked by forces superior to its own had wisely halted. In about half-an-hour they were met by a solitary horseman coming at a foot pace from the direction of the camp. Commandant Lonsdale, for it was he, rode up to the general and uttered the astounding words:

The camp is in possession of the enemy.

It appears that Lonsdale, who had been ill, being very tired was quietly returning from Glyn's column to the camp. He had crossed the small water-wash to the south of the camp and was jogging slowly along in a sort of lethargy, from which he was roused by the discharge of a rifle close to him. Looking up, he saw a native, who had evidently just fired, and him he imagined to be one of his own contingent indulging in reckless firing; so he pursued his way. Sitting in and around the tents were groups of red-coats, so he still kept on till within a bare ten yards of the tents. He then saw a great black Zulu come out of one with a blood-besmeared *assegai* in his hand.

Gazing more carefully, he saw that black men, and black men only, were the wearers of the red-coats. The truth flashed on him: turning his pony sharp round he galloped off before the enemy knew what he was about. Not less than 150 shots were fired at him as he did so, but, providentially, he escaped to warn the general, who, without such warning, his staff and troops with him, would have walked unsuspiciously into the trap, and the whole force would probably have perished to a man.

The general at once sent back to hurry up Colonel Glyn and his force, while Colonel Russell was sent on to reconnoitre the camp, which was found to be as Commandant Lonsdale had reported. On Colonel Glyn's arrival the whole force was disposed in fighting order, and moved rapidly across the plain, but could not arrive in the vicinity of the camp until after dark. All was found a wreck—corpses, broken tents, dead horses, oxen, and other debris were strewed around; and the men, most of whom were without ammunition, and had not tasted food for forty-eight hours, were ordered to bivouac amidst the crowd of blood-stained relics which marked the day's slaughter. Our soldiers had covered more than thirty miles on the previous day without food or ammunition, and if resolutely attacked by the entire force of Zulus might have shared the fate of their comrades. The next morning, therefore, before daylight a sad retreat was effected to Rorke's Drift, where the first glad tidings were heard of the glorious defence which had been made by Chard and Bromhead, with their handful of men.

It came about thus. Lieutenant Chard, with one sergeant and six men, had been left in charge of the ponts over the Tugela at this point. Close by was a commissariat depot in charge of Lieutenant Bromhead and a company of the 24th Regiment. About three o'clock on January 22nd news of the disaster at Isandhlwana reached this officer, together with a note, saying that the enemy were advancing in force against his post, which was to be held at all costs. Chard immediately withdrew his small party, and in concert with Bromhead arranged for the loopholing and barricading the store-building and hospital, and for connecting the defences of the two by building walls of mealie-bags.

At 3.30 an officer of Durnford's Horse with about 100 men came in, and was asked to send them out as vedettes; these, when pressed, to fall back and assist in the defence of the buildings. At 4.30 this officer returned with the news that the enemy was close at hand, that his men would not obey orders, but had galloped off to Helpmakaar. About the same time Captain Stephenson and his detachment of natives also withdrew. It was at once perceived that the line of defence was now too extended for the small force left, and an inner entrenchment of biscuit-boxes was made, and this had been completed to a wall two boxes high, when suddenly 600 of the enemy turned the hill to the south. They advanced at a run against the southern wall, and notwithstanding a tremendous fire reached to within fifty yards of it. Being here encountered by a cross-fire from the store they were stopped.

Taking advantage, however, of some shelter afforded by the cookhouse and ovens, they kept up heavy musketry volleys thence, whilst the main body moved on to the left round the hospital, whence they made a rush upon the north-west wall and breastwork of mealie-bags. Meanwhile the mass of the advancing foe lined a ledge of rocks and filled the caves overlooking the English position at a distance of 100 yards to the south, whence they too kept up a constant fire. Another party to the left occupied a garden in a hollow in the road, and also

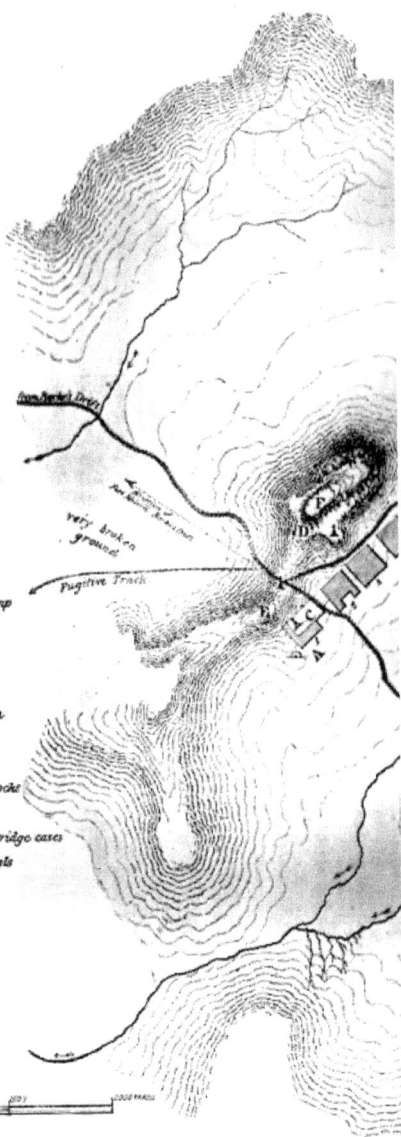

REFERENCE TABLE

A to B Site of Camp 22ⁿᵈ January 1879.

    1   1-24ᵗʰ Regiment.

    2   Mounted Camp { Mounted Infantry, N.M.P.
                           { N. Carabineers and N.M.R.

    3   Col. Harness's Battery.

    4   2-24ᵗʰ Regiment.

    5   N.N.C.

    6   N.N.C.

C   Col. Durnford R.E. Capᵗ Wardell 1-24ᵗʰ Regᵗ,
      Lieut. Dyer 2-24ᵗʰ Regᵗ, Lieut. Scott N. Carbʳˢ,
      Lieut. Bradstreet N.M.R., Quartᵣ Hitchcock N.M.R.,
      1 Officer 24ᵗʰ Regᵗ unrecognisable and about 150 men
      (mostly 24ᵗʰ Regᵗ) buried here

D   Capᵗ R. Younghusband 1-24ᵗʰ Regᵗ, 2 Officers 24ᵗʰ Regᵗ
      unrecognisable and about 60 men (24ᵗʰ Regᵗ) buried here

E   Black's Kopjie

      About 100 white bodies buried on nek below, close to road,
      also many single bodies along road which runs at head of camp
      as far as B.

F   Isandhlwana Rock

G to H Signs of heavy fighting and determined stand having been
      made here
      Kraal at G full of dead Zulus.
      Color Serjᵗ Wolf and 20 men (24ᵗʰ Regᵗ) found amongst rocks
      just above G.
      The southern crest line from G to H strewn with empty cartridge cases
      Guns of R.A. were firing for some time from point H to kraals
      at I which were afterwards found full of dead Zulus.

   Cairns

   Kraals

SKETCH MAP
of
ISANDHLWANA
showing the positions
of the
Graves of those who fell & were buried

by Lieut: Mainwaring.

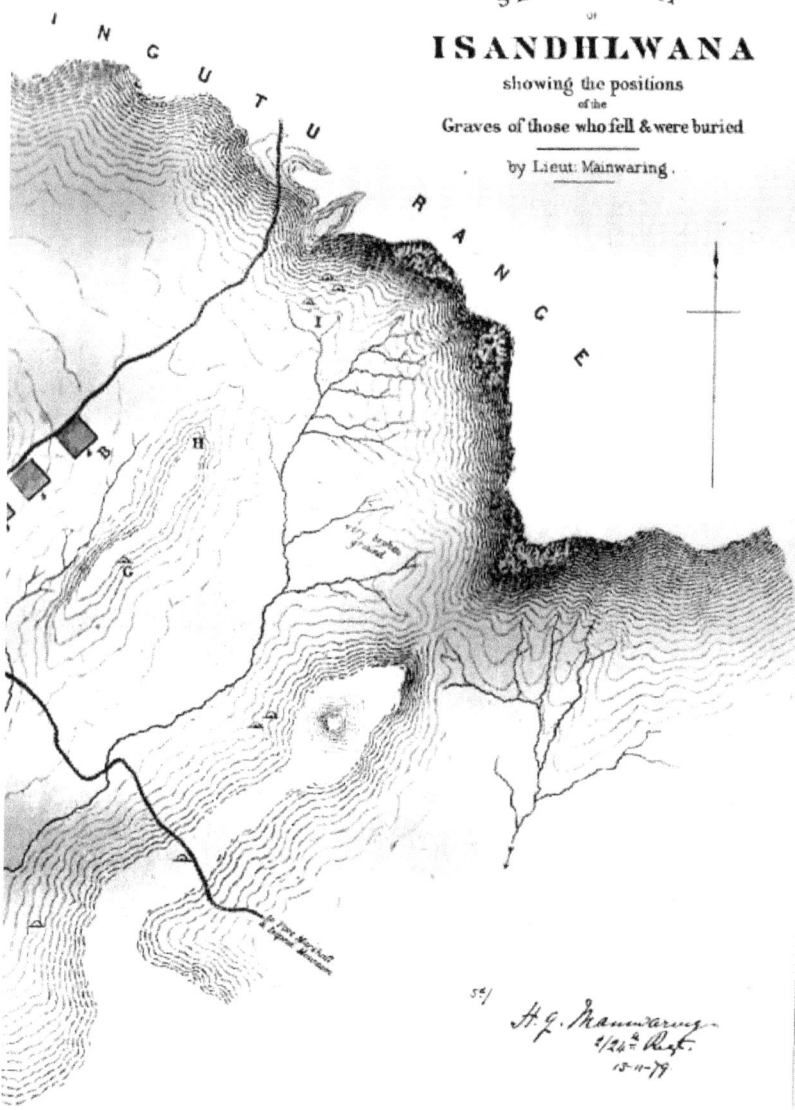

I N G U T U   R A N G E

H.G. Mainwaring
1/24ᵗʰ Regt.
15-11-79

h beyond, which time had not permitted to be cut down.
my could thus advance close to the English works, and were
... possession of one whole side of the wall, whilst on the other in a line extending from the hospital all along the wall to the bush they made a series of determined onsets. But each attack was met and splendidly repulsed with the bayonet, Corporal Schiess (N.N.C.) especially distinguishing himself. The fire from the ledge of rock and caves at length became so galling, that it was necessary to retire behind the inner line of biscuit-boxes.

All this time the enemy had been trying to force the hospital, and at length they did set fire to the roof. The garrison defended the place room by room, bringing out all the sick who could be moved before they retired. Privates Williams, Hook, K Jones, and W. Jones, 24th Regiment, were the last to leave, holding the doorway against the Zulus with their bayonets, their ammunition being quite expended. Five sick men, owing to the smoke and want of interior communication, had unfortunately to be left to their fates. Two heaps of mealie-bags were now converted into a sort of redoubt, and a second line of fire was thus obtained all round.

Darkness now came on, and after several more furious attacks had been repulsed the defenders had ultimately to retire to the middle, and then to the inner wall of the *kraal*, east of the position they had at first held. The attacks continued all night, the soldiers firing with the utmost coolness, and never wasting a shot. At four a.m., January 23rd, firing ceased, and by daybreak the enemy were disappearing over the hill to the south-west. The ground was then patrolled, the arms of the dead Zulus collected, and the position strengthened as far as possible. About seven a.m. a large body of the enemy was again seen on the hill to the south-west, and a friendly Kaffir, who had come in shortly before, was sent to Helpmakaar to ask for assistance. However, about eight am. the British 3rd column began to appear, whereupon the enemy, who had been again advancing, fell back as the troops advanced, and Rorke's Drift Post had been saved.

The number of English engaged in this action was eight officers and 131 non-commissioned officers and men; of these fifteen were killed and twelve wounded, two subsequently dying of their hurts. The attacking Zulu force consisted of two regiments—the Undi and Udkloko—in all a total of something less than 4000. Of these 370 lay dead around the post on the morning that Lord Chelmsford so opportunely arrived.

Surgeon Reynolds, Acting Commissary Officer Dalton, and Assistant Commissary Dunne were throughout conspicuous for their gallantry and coolness. Lieutenants Chard, R.E., and Bromhead, 24th Regiment, subsequently received the thanks of both Houses of Parliament for their heroic conduct, and were advanced to the rank of majors.

So much has been said and written as to the cause of, and so many people have been held responsible for the Isandhlwana disaster that the subject cannot here be passed over in silence.

The living no less than the dead have a claim to a full share of justice and truth; but remembering that the mouths of one party—*"les morts qui ne reviennent pas"*—are closed, we should be extremely careful in drawing any conclusion from acts which, could the testimony of the fallen be obtained, it would not only explain and excuse, but amply justify.

The court of inquiry held at Helpmakaar found itself unable to form from the available evidence any positive judgment; but the facts disclosed point irresistibly to a negative conclusion. Had the troops acted on the defensive, the camp would not have been lost.

Still there may have been cogent—nay irresistible reasons which caused Colonel Durnford to push forward his forces. Were Colonel Pulleine alive, he might give equally good reasons for acceding to Durnford's urgent request and sending out the reinforcements.

The British regular infantry advanced successfully, retired slowly and in unbroken order; they were still firing rapidly, coolly, and with great effect. Things though desperate were by no means hopeless. Suddenly the native levies, "though their officers tried to restrain them, rushed back in the utmost disorder," thus exposing the flank and rear of the regulars. "Few of the men had time to fix bayonets before the enemy were amongst them, using their *assegais* with terrible effect."

Here is the answer to "How did it happen?" The natives on one side—the Zulu—were regarded too lightly; on the other, fighting for the English with too great confidence. "Why," it will be asked, "were not the waggons l*aagered?* Whose duty was it to see this done?" Lord Chelmsford had issued a standing order at the very commencement of the campaign, that this was to be the first consideration in all camps. Lord Chelmsford, accompanied Colonel Glyn from Rorke's Drift, saw the site chosen at Isandhlwana, and then immediately started on a reconnaissance which lasted till after nightfall. Doubtless Lord Chelmsford supposed Colonel Glyn had done what was necessary.

On the following morning with the first streak of dawn Colonel Glyn was ordered to proceed to Major Dartnell's assistance, and Lord Chelmsford determined to accompany him, after despatching an express to Colonel Durnford ordering him up "to strengthen the camp." Doubtless Colonel Glyn supposed that Colonel Pulleine would see to *laagering* the waggons. Colonel Pulleine was in command of the camp a bare three hours, and doubtless, knowing how brief his tenure of office was to be, preferred to let things remain as they were till his successor's arrival. Colonel Durnford had not been a single half-hour in camp before the action was commenced.

It is asked why did not the troops form squares? Hastings, we are told, had Harold's men only remained in their position, would have been a Saxon victory—Torres Vedras a disgrace instead of a glory had the British troops been rashly taunted into leaving their trenches: and Waterloo a more glowing theme for Beranger's lyre had Napoleon been able to entice the patient English squares to forsake their adamantine formation. But why was Colonel Durnford to form squares? How was he to imagine that such an immense force was arrayed against him when the commander-in-chief had with him a superior force to that left in the camp avowedly to operate against the enemy's main body? For such his information and personal observation led him to believe was the force against whom he and Major Dartnell were acting.

Colonel Durnford was no novice in South African war; like Caesar, he had the gift of the pen no less than the sword; he had both written and fought well. Colonel Pulleine was an experienced officer of no mean reputation, and by whatever device they were deceived, we may be sure that it was no ordinary one, and that few would have stood where they fell.

Again, who could have anticipated the attack? We have it from the lips of a Zulu that the onset was unpremeditated, and the result of accident. With all humbleness, let it be confessed that—

Our indiscretion sometimes serves us well
When our deep plots do fail; and that should teach us
There's a divinity that shapes our ends
Rough hew them as we will.

Another question, often asked, is, "Why did not Lord Chelmsford, immediately on his return, make a counter-attack on the enemy?" First of all, he had to wait for Colonel Glyn and the main body to come up to him. Meanwhile darkness had come on. When Glyn arrived he did advance with his troops formed up for action, and with the intention of retaking the camp, which he had every reason to suppose was occupied by the enemy. The event proved they had abandoned it. Was not this a good reason for striking a blow? Let the facts of the case be well borne in mind.

Lord Chelmsford knew that there was a large force in his rear; the force that had sacked the camp was supposed, and reasonably enough, to be on the right flank. In front were the bright watchfires of another force, and the blazing hospital at Rorke's Drift, which, together with Helpmakaar, there was every ground to believe had been captured and looted by the foe; in a word, his force was surrounded. The men had only fifty rounds of ammunition apiece; they had been twenty-four hours without food; they were physically exhausted by eighteen hours' continuous marching, and no less morally by the loss of their camp; their probabilities of escape were distant. How could a general lead troops in such a condition against a foe flushed and elated with spoil and recent victory?

CHAPTER 3

Ekowe Described

We must now return to Pearson, whom we left entrenching himself at Ekowe.

The position is a most commanding one, being almost on the summit of the Tyoe range, and more than 2000 feet above the sea level; and for beauty of site could scarcely be surpassed. To the north, about a mile and a half, is the Umlalazi River, at that time rather full from the late rains, and beyond this stream are long undulating grassy plains, almost devoid of bush, with the exception here and there of a few wild and dwarf date-palms, and lichens in the hollows. Behind, to the south, is the Umkukusi range, and a hilly but open country, while on the west is a very broken and difficult country, bounded by the Hintza forest.

Away to the east, right to the coast at Port Durnford, is about forty miles of undulating and here and there hilly country. About 1200 yards to the south-east there is a rocky eminence at least 600 feet higher than the fort, and from this place a magnificent view of Port Durnford and the mouth of the Umlalazi can be seen. The sea is not more than twenty-two miles off, in a line as the crow flies. The original building was formerly a Norwegian mission station, and when the present war began it was abandoned by the missionaries and plundered by the Zulus. The buildings, when Pearson arrived, consisted of three moderately-sized brick erections, thatched originally with straw, but subsequently covered with a less inflammable material. In addition to these buildings, which were utilised as stores, there was a small church, built of the native-made sun-dried bricks, and covered, as most of these edifices are in that country, with corrugated galvanized iron.

The church was turned into an hospital, while the tower made a capital look-out, from whence could be seen the next post, and which

66

afterwards proved of such service in the way of signalling. Pearson now began to suffer the inconveniences of a regular siege; his communications were cut, and it was found that of the twelve messengers belonging to the Natal Native Contingent sent from Ekowe with letters during the first week in February, only one arrived, the others having been intercepted and killed on their way. The fort soon completely changed its character under the incessant labour bestowed upon it by Pearson's men, under the vigilant supervision of their chief.

It now became a six-angled enclosure, about sixty yards wide, having a ditch eighteen feet in depth, while its breadth was twelve feet. At the bottom it was studded profusely with *assegai* heads securely planted, and the parapets, carefully riveted, were proof not only against any musketry fire, but field artillery. From its southern angles ran out two well-built curtain walls, enclosing a fine *kraal* for cattle and horses. These curtains were well protected by the fire of the angles from which they sprung, while the *kraal* itself had its own massive gateway and drawbridge. At the end of the *kraal*, or cattle enclosure, furthest from the angular fort, was constructed from the remains of a dilapidated magazine, a kind of irregular redoubt, which also had a deep ditch and thick mud walls, defended by a quantity of powerful thorns laid along the parapet.

It was most fortunate that this force brought with them a large supply of well-selected entrenching tools, consisting of shovels, picks, spades, billhooks, axes, and crowbars. Day by day, whenever their time could be spared from patrol and outpost duty, the men were employed in making entanglements of rows of felled trees, as well as constructing fascines, filling sandbags, turning out gabions, loopholes, and *abattis*. All these obstacles possessed the usual requisites. They were under the close fire of the fort, were covered from the enemy's fire, and gave him no cover; while they were all made so substantially that they could not be cut down or removed without immense difficulty.

The piquet duties were rather severe, and each piquet had to furnish two or three double sentries in reliefs, patrols, and links. They were posted under the best circumstances obtainable, being sheltered from the enemy, having a good range in front, with every advantage in retreating if attacked in force. Each face or front of the fort was cleared up to 800 yards; shelter trenches were made for the first line of defence; cover was left for the supports and reserves; ranges were marked and measures taken for the artillery and rifle fire, and all precautionary arrangements made in regard to the supply and storage of provisions, forage, water, and ammunition.

The water was good, and not brackish at that time of the year. It was taken from a bright stream well under the fire of the fort, and fed by a capital spring, also under fire of one of the seven-pounders. The church and the storehouses were also carefully loopholed, and sandbags furnished to make the defences more secure. These three strong loopholed buildings, forming part of the enceinte, were rendered more formidable by double planking, backed crossways by iron barrel hoops, while fine, damp, heavy sand from the neighbouring hill was employed in filling bags, made from old provision sacks.

Every man in the fort had his proper place assigned to him, and at exercise it was found that with three minutes' notice each detachment was in its place. The Buffs were told off to the two northern faces, on which side there was a well-made *caponnière* thrown up in the re-entering angle. At the west angle of this fort one gun and a detachment of the Royal Artillery were posted, while on the east salient were two guns and a somewhat stronger number of men. Here there was a small outlet for water-parties, guarded on the flank by a little loopholed building, and commanded in the rear by a strong building with a thatched roof.

The rocket tubes were placed under charge of the Royal Marines, on the south-west front, and could, if necessary, sweep the trek oxen laager, and slaughter oxen *laager* outside the fort on that side. The principal gateway was on the west face, and was guarded by a company of the Buffs, who loopholed the church tower in their rear to fall back upon, and to act as a commanding flanking fire. The front, facing due south, was served by the 99th, with one gun at the salient angle, a *caponnière* in the centre, guarded by a Gatling, and with a thirteen feet stockade at the opposing angle.

Another strong building, also thatch roof, commanded this front. Not a day passed but some improvement was made in strengthening these works, and this as much for prudence against possible attack, as to keep the men occupied and free from the lassitude attendant upon long confinement. It should also be mentioned that torpedoes had been laid down by the bluejackets for three miles along the bed of the Tugela, so that if the Zulus attempted to cross near any of the posts of observation they might be somewhat astonished.

The ration daily used to be two pounds of beef—fresh killed and tough as leather—a couple, of commissariat biscuits—hard as flint—a very small complement of coffee or tea, sugar, and one spoonful of

Ume juice, which every man had to take whether he liked it or not; preserved potatoes, compressed vegetables, and an occasional ration of beans, made a little variety now and then. During the last days of the siege the meat and biscuit ration was reduced.

A day's routine was as follows—The men rose with the reveille at four a.m. for a parade of all hands and fatigue duties for a couple of hours, weather permitting: the breakfast bugle sounded at eight, and fatigues were again performed from 9.30 till noon; dinner bugle at 1.30, and rest and recreation till 4.30, and finally "retreat" at 6.30, when no one was to be outside the walls. The men amused themselves with quoits, cricket, and athletics, some of the Buffs being good "all round;" while all the officers, especially the colonel, encouraged these pastimes by example as well as precept.

After all, the life was not more monotonous than that on board ship. There was no lack of ammunition, as Colonel Ely on march to Ekowe had to abandon only ten waggons, and these were looted. The rest, however, arrived safely. The garrison also from time to time received valuable and most reassuring information regarding the disposition and whereabouts of their friends along the line of the Tugela, and in their rear. At Fort Pearson, which might be said to be the principal base of operations, and which commanded the river and lower drift from the Natal side, there were sufficient men of the Naval Brigade to work the two guns there. They had also the European officers and the non-commissioned officers of the disbanded native corps.

Then, to keep up communications, the Mounted Volunteers of Coast District were posted at intervals along the river, between Fort Pearson and Kranskop. Another fort on the Zulu bank of the Tugela was called "Fort Tenedos," in compliment to the detachment which formed its garrison. Major Barrow, with a squadron of mounted infantry, and Lieutenant Kingscote, with a smart body of marines and bluejackets, formed the defensive force.

At Rorke's Drift there were now five companies of the 2nd battalion of the 24th Regiment. A strongly entrenched position had also been formed on a commanding site called Macdonald's Farm, on a rocky eminence overlooking the Tugela. Ditches ten feet deep were cut, parapets seven feet high thrown up, the farmhouse itself strengthened, and all the garden walls loopholed. The garrison consisted of the Stanger Mounted Rifles, and some native auxiliaries, who proved most trustworthy as scouts and messengers. Captain Lucas, whose admirable powers of organisation were quite proverbial amongst the colonists, and whose frontier experiences were of long standing, was strongly posted at a bend of the river between the farm and Thring's Post, and had with him a useful body of natives. Thring's Post came next on the list, and here there were a couple of hundred of well-mounted and well-armed volunteers divided into squadrons, or corps of fifty men. Thring's Post is on the Imyamazana Mountain, and is about twenty-seven miles from Port Pearson. The volunteers, knowing the country well, were employed in keeping up by constant patrols communications with Fort Pearson and Fort Cherry.

News also reached them that Wood had been reinforced, and was more than holding his own. There was, therefore, little anxiety felt for the security of the frontier, and everything strengthened Colonel Pearson in his determination to remain in his position instead of attempting to cut his way out.

The health of the Ekowe garrison continued very good. The hospital, it has been said, was the old church of the mission-station. At the end of the second week in March there were only twenty-five men on the sick-list, and many of these almost convalescent. They had, however, lost two of their number lately, namely, poor Williams of the Buffs, and another great favourite, young Coker, the midshipman, who fought his Gatling so well at Inyanezi. Both these fine fellows were ill but a short time, and succumbed to fever. They were buried with the usual honours just outside the fort.

Lieutenant Rowden, 98th Regiment, who was nominated by Colonel Pearson commander of the mounted scouts, performed his difficult and dangerous task to perfection. He had by the end of February successfully explored the country in the direction of the Isangweni military *kraal*, which was not far from Ondini, and about three miles from Ekowe. He reported that there were 1500 men there, and more collecting. The 1500 were composed of the married regiment Isangu, whose averages-age is fifty-four, and whose services in former wars had been most distinguished. The country between the fort and Isangweni was an undulating table-land, running parallel to the forests on either side, and admirably suited for cavalry. Another brother of Cetywayo, named Dabulamanzi, had a fortified *kraal* not far from that of Isangweni, and Pearson determined to attack both those places as soon as he was in a position to move upon them.

The second week of March had now come to an end, and it was deemed advisable to vary the monotony of life in the fort by one or two offensive expeditions. The most important of these, both as to the

70

numbers engaged and its effects, was the foray on Dabulamanzi's *kraal*. The forces detailed for this expedition consisted of fifty men of the Buffs, the same number of the 99th, and twenty-five of the Naval Brigade, with their Gatling, and a small body of mounted scouts, under the active Lieutenant Rowden (98th).

Starting about five a.m., the party descended the slopes that led to the river, and continued its march along a valley running north-east, and gradually narrowing. The track in some places was crossed by difficult *spruits*, and was scarcely defined; but their guides were well acquainted with the landmarks, although the pathways were often obliterated by thorns and bush. The track was also frequently commanded by spurs and bluffs projecting overhead, but these were carefully explored by the mounted men, and no enemy could be seen. A considerable watershed was reached about eight miles from Ekowe, and here, in a favourable and secluded position, was made the first off-saddle for half an hour. The country about here was entirely denuded of fodder, but the horsemen had been fortunately directed to bring a few mealies for their mounts.

On resuming the march, they crossed the bottom of a deep sandy *nullah* with very precipitous sides, which they were forced to follow, as it was the only practicable track. About a mile and a half further on the advanced patrols sent back to inform the officer of the main body that there was a camping-ground or temporary *kraal* about three miles and a half north, where there was sufficient water and grass. The orders were therefore given to push on for this point, and in about forty-five minutes it was reached. It was now sundown, and their chief, having decided that it was inexpedient to march during the night, orders were issued for the usual precautions to be taken, and to bivouac till daybreak.

During the night, however, no one slept, as they had several alarms, and it became evident from certain indications known to the experienced in Zulu camping-out, that they were being reconnoitred by the enemy, though in all probability not in sufficient force to deliver an attack. As, however, it was quite possible that messengers would be despatched to the neighbouring *kraals*, it was deemed advisable to strengthen the position, in case of their being surrounded before the morning. Taking one of the guides, who said he knew the neighbourhood, from having frequently hunted here, one of the officers and a couple of men were sent to make a reconnaissance round the bivouac. This party at once started without making any noise, and entering on the old watercourse worked their way up towards the summit of the *kloof*.

Large, indeed enormous, blocks of stone were lying about in various directions, and the water during the heavy rains had so far worked its way among these rocks that several hollows were scooped out so as to form caves large enough to hold one or two human beings. These places had evidently been recently occupied, remains of mealies and the charred wood of a recent fire indicating the use to which the shelter had been applied. Ascending the *kloof* still farther, and keeping well under cover of the bush, these scouts walked along what at first seemed an old war-path, and this being examined it was evident that it had been worn by human beings, and not long since.

On following this path, it led to a small piece of table-land not much larger than an ordinary mess-tent or marquee, and this platform was formed by a solid piece of rock rising, not unlike the Pieter Bot at Mauritius, to a couple of hundred feet above where the explorers were standing. To the eye of a soldier the place was impregnable, and as the scouts scanned the country round by the fitful gleams of occasional moonlight they saw that twenty well-armed and steady men could hold the rock against an army. The face of the rock had been scooped out, and, either by time or human labour, a sort of cave or shelter afforded additional protection.

Upon leaving the rock and descending the ravine to carry the intelligence to the column in bivouac, these patrols were startled to see the outlines of several dark figures moving in the neighbouring bush. Making all possible speed, therefore, the messengers hurried back, and at the news received every man stood to his arms. They had not long to wait, for the enemy soon appeared, drawn out in clear relief against the grey of the early dawn, which was now coming on. Bodies of Zulus on the opposite ridges, which could not have been seen lower down, were now observed, while a few cattle were being rapidly hurried away in the distance. The Zulu scouts were evidently puzzled at the white men's proceedings, the more so as before leaving the *kop* one of the guides had tied his handkerchief to an overhanging branch, thus giving the enemy the idea that a detachment had been left to occupy the post.

This error on the part of their antagonists served the troops materially, as, by hurrying forward at a quick pace, they were enabled to gain the *kop*, and with some considerable difficulty get their Gatling to the summit. Their horses, of course, could not ascend, but halfway up there was an excellent position, where grass and water were found, and here the animals were tethered in the usual manner—by the head and knee. When daylight enabled them to examine the surrounding country with field-glasses, they could see the neighbouring *kraals* of the chief Dabulamanzie and his neighbour, Ungakamatue, and it was evident that the alarm had been given.

Several extraordinary movements attracted their attention. Armed bodies of natives were seen to be leaving the villages in various directions, as if going upon messages of importance. Aware of the celerity of movement of the Zulus, and the enormous distances their soldiers can cover in a few hours, this activity was not reassuring, as it was concluded that reinforcements were being sent for, for the purpose of intercepting the retreat to the fort of Ekowe. The English commander, however, was not long in choosing his plan of operations. It would never do to sustain a siege on the rock or kop, which, however defensible if provisioned, was sure to be taken by starvation in the long-run. The Dabulamanzie *kraal* had evidently been weakened by the absence of men harvesting, and it did not seem more than a mile from where the troops were.

One of the guides remembered a cattle-track which, by a circuitous route, led back on the eastern side to Ekowe, and as the road they had arrived by was certain to be now ambushed, it was deemed advisable to make a dash at the *kraal*, and return with what spoil they could obtain in the new direction. Having cut some long canes, some of the soldiers fixed them securely between the ledges of the rocks, and attached to them some coloured clothes, which they hoped would lead to the belief that they still occupied the kop. These precautions having been taken, the troops moved silently down through the dense bushes on the reverse side of the cliff, and succeeded in getting away without being observed by the Zulus, who evidently seemed principally anxious about their cattle.

Part of the mounted force went in front to explore the bush, while the rest remained in rear to follow and reconnoitre. On coming again to the valley, they moved still more rapidly until they came to a little rise, which, on surmounting, they found led to a deep *kloof*, the mouth of which was almost closed by the proximity of the hills, on either side rising to about 600 feet in height. These curious-looking hills appeared to be a series of ledges of rocks, with lines of dykes—probably of volcanic origin—cropping up, and forming the most natural-looking breastworks, behind which a determined party of men might destroy any attacking party. Having waited to collect the tail of the column, they descended the rise, and sending out a few men to scout on the ridge skirting the hill on their right, the commander led the main body under cover of this range towards the mouth of the *kloof,* which the guides said was the main entrance to the *kraal.*

When about 200 yards from the mouth of the gorge, the enemy commenced firing upon the advanced files from behind a formidable looking dyke, and seeing that one of the horses had been badly wounded in the quarter, an officer sent up a dozen men to the top of the range to extend as a covering party. These had barely been posted in a good position, when a perfect shower of bullets fell amongst the main body, the only casualty being, however, one man struck by an almost spent bullet. It being thus seen that they were out of range as far as any material injury could be effected, the men were directed to keep moving along the flank, while the Buffs advanced along the valley in a parallel line, closing to their centres as they neared the mouth of the *kloof.*

At the same time, the men of the Naval Brigade (twenty-five) were detached with their Gatling towards the foot of the left-hand hill, to see if there was a path by which the *kraal* could be taken in reverse. This left-hand hill seemed to be the key of the position, as it looked down upon the *kraal* itself. The 99th were all this time held in reserve to prevent the troops being taken in reverse should the enemy's reinforcements come up. While the English were effecting these movements the Zulus, whose forces did not seem to be augmenting, kept up what would have been a hot cross-fire had they been armed with Martini's, but which was perfectly innocuous at 700 yards.

A bugle-call now gave notice to the skirmishers to close in, and when this was effected the mounted men dashed through the *kloof,* followed by the Buffs and the 99th at the double. The Naval Brigade meanwhile was seen working its way in the most energetic manner round the left flank and ready to effect a junction with the others at the foot of the mound on which stood the outer defences of the *kraal.* A general stampede of men, women, and cattle now took place, the soldiers being specially warned not to fire at the two latter, and only at the former in return. In ten minutes the outer and inner circles of the *kraal* were fired, care having been taken to see that no living creature was hidden within.

As the Zulus generally store their mealies (Indian com) underground in the cattle enclosures, there was not time to look for any supplies, but they managed to carry off a few large packages which were found in two huts, as well as some millet (Kaffir corn). They also collected all the cattle they could find, not many having been left, and getting them together in the centre of the column, moved away by the path mentioned by their guides. These movements were conducted so quickly, that they were on the homeward march within half an hour of the time they had entered the *kraal*.

About half a mile from the *kraal* the *kloof* separated into two narrow gullies, the ledges of rock between them being inaccessible, and as it was known that these paths made a junction some two miles on, it was decided to use them both, to enable the troops to march more quickly. The Buffs accordingly took one trek, and the 99th detachment the other, both uniting again without any casualty later on. The English attack was undoubtedly a complete surprise, inasmuch as the bulk of the people belonging to the *kraal* were away, and could not be recalled in time to defend their village. Had the British column possessed a larger force of mounted men, they could have intercepted and carried back the cattle which they saw the attendants driving off. As it was, however, it was not safe or prudent to risk the chances of communications with the fort being cut off by delaying to pursue these animals.

The column had made good about ten miles of the return march when they discovered that their retreat had been found out; straight in front of them also were wooded *krantzes* and dark ravines, where an army of Zulus might have been concealed, but pioneers having been sent out reported that all was safe in that direction. Upon this they used the utmost speed to gain the friendly covert, as they saw that if pursued there was the best chance of eluding the vigilance of their enemies; or if unable to do this, they would have the opportunity of fighting them to the best advantage.

As the troops moved quickly on, they entered the forest and lost sight of the Zulus, who seemed in force, and were apparently retracing their steps for some mysterious object. They were not, however, kept long in doubt as to their proceedings, for upon sending on scouts to an eminence where they could see without being seen, it was found that the whole Zulu force, apparently some 2000 strong, was upon the crest of the hill over which they had passed. An advanced party of skirmishers were running very rapidly, their shields held aloft, and their *assegais* waving over their heads. They had discovered the trick played upon them, and the ruse of the coloured cloths planted upon the *kop*. When, however, they could not discover the spoor upon the direct trek by which the English party had come, they lost a considerable amount of time in casting about to make out their real direction.

At last, however, when crossing a bit of open *veldt*, the keen-sighted Zulus observed their cattle being carried away, at least five miles from them. The rage of the pursuers, and their contempt for the marching qualities of British soldiers—compared to their own speed and powers of endurance—no doubt made them confident of overtaking them; but the latter had little apprehension of the result, even if this were effected. They knew that as soon as their foes came within range, they could pick them off at 1000 or 1200 yards, and the little column had been specially furnished with several crack marksmen to whom this distance was no difficulty. They continued their march therefore steadily, and did not abandon the cattle, which, strange to say, gave little trouble, and were kept at a good pace by some of the mounted men, whose anticipation of a full beef ration on their return, from the spoil, made them doubly zealous in their duties.

In about an hour the Zulus had gained considerably upon them; they were imprudent enough to move in close order. The evening was, however, now drawing on, and in another hour the troops should be under the guns of the fort. A mist, which had been for some time hanging about the streams and the *kloof*, prevented the exact progress of the pursuers being seen, but the pursued were not long without intimation of their whereabouts.

The rear-guard were attracted, when about three miles from the fort, by what seemed to be dark objects moving between some rocks about half a mile on their left rear. So fitful was the view obtained, however, that the men were uncertain whether they were Zulus or some of the larger species of baboon, which often come out of their holes and caves to look at any human creature passing by. A steady watch was, however, maintained, and before many minutes they could plainly see that a large body of the enemy had, by the most tremendous pedestrian feat, succeeded in getting almost on a level with them, in a position to assail them in flank.

The column had not long to wait, for as they came to a portion of the trek they could not avoid, on account of the proximity of a deep morass on the right, the pursuers, deeming them within range, treated them to a volley which rattled up to about fifty paces short of their flank. Ten of the mounted men, all excellent shots, were now sent out to cover the attacked flank, and, as far as they could, to harass the enemy. The ground was difficult and broken, but this was no impediment to these gallant fellows, who, gaining a commanding position 500 yards from the Zulus, and where there was admirable cover, dismounted, and kept up such a galling fire that the Zulus retreated, as if waiting for their main body to come up. As the mist rolled away, they could distinctly be seen carrying off their dead and wounded with improvised stretchers of branches of mimosa. A running fire was now kept up, the English shot taking deadly effect, while no casualty occurred to their men. For more than half an hour this went on, until the fort was sighted, and as the Zulu main body had not come up, the flanking party drew quietly off.

The sun was sinking in the horizon as the returning soldiers received their well-earned welcome from their beleaguered comrades, who were beginning to be somewhat anxious as to their safe return.

Pearson's next raid was a most brilliant affair. It was found out from reliable sources that a body of Zulus had charge of a convoy of cattle, intended for the king's *kraal* at Ulundi. Deeming the Ekowe garrison as of no account for more than defensive purposes, the Zulu general had merely detailed 400 or 450 men to form the escort, which was known to be on its march not more than seven miles to the northwest of Ekowe, not far from the Inyezani River. Now here Pearson had an opportunity of achieving two objects at one stroke. He wished to explore the land and salient features of the country towards Inyezani, in order to see whether a road could be made by which the dense bush of Hintza could be avoided, while, at the same time, he could inflict a lesson upon the Zulus, and possibly obtain some cattle.

The foray was not to be on such a grand scale as that made on Dabulamanzie's *kraal*, but it was intended to be equally important for military purposes. Twenty men of the Naval Brigade, all the small force of acting engineers, forty of the Buffs, twenty of the 99th, and the mounted scouts were placed under orders to parade before daylight on Friday, 21st March. No Gatling was to accompany, as the utmost celerity of movement was required, and if the expedition did not succeed in its first dash an immediate retreat upon the guns was to be made. On leaving the fort at 3.30 a.m., the road by which the band advanced was found to be good, although here and there commanded from the neighbouring mountains.

About two miles from Ekowe a bluff runs out from the spur of the range of hills which had often served as a reconnoitring point, and this was immediately occupied by the mounted men, who had orders to keep up signalling both with the fort and the rest of the expedition. Continuing on its march, the column came to the Inyezani River, which for several miles runs between two remarkable mountains, the bases of which are clothed with luxuriant forest growths, while above spring sheer precipices 1000 and 1100 feet high. The formation seemed to be sandstone and limestone, affording excellent material for building purposes. Before reaching these dark solitudes the river passes through a country undulating and fertile, and the horizon is closed by higher hills, covered in the most part by forest. These forest-trees are of fine growth and of the most valuable description. The banks of the river are fringed by a quantity of bamboo-looking reeds, which serve as wattles in the district, and which are about the thickness of a finger, and some ten or twelve feet high.

Tracks of hippopotami are occasionally seen, and it is known that such are in the neighbourhood. The river here is about 200 yards broad, while the depth averages twenty-five feet. The expedition now noticed a few deserted *kraals* on the right bank, while those on the left were found to be in ruins, as if lately destroyed. At eight a.m. a herd of cattle was seen some two miles off, and rapidly skirting the base of a friendly hill the troops managed to cut in between these animals and a body of Zulus, who appeared to be bivouacking in front of some neighbouring caves, where fires were lit and cooking was going on.

The mounted men, who were observing these movements, now descended from the bluff where they had been watching, and coming up rapidly at a canter, made a dash at the Zulus, to cover the infantry retreat, which they effected with the capture of some thirty-five fine cattle. A desultory fire was kept up upon them from the hills during their return, and the enemy, who seemed to be gradually augmented, at one narrow gorge managed to get within range, slightly wounding two or three of the rear-guard. By noon on the same day the men with the captured cattle were safely discussing their frugal dinner, consisting of an extra half-ration in honour of the event, within the old fort, which they were already beginning to look upon as a friend from whom they were soon to part.

In spite of the rapidity of the raid, the necessary observations were made by the officers deputed for this duty, and a rough sketch of the ground passed over gave all the information requisite for the construction of the projected road. This work, which was forthwith taken in hand, had a most satisfactory effect upon the spirits of the garrison generally. The working parties were occasionally driven in, but not without inflicting loss upon the enemy, whose attention was much taken up in guarding and patrolling the main road by which Pearson came.

Wood, it has been mentioned, fell back upon receiving the news of Isandhlwana; but this retrograde movement was of short duration, and from that time till all was ready for the relief of Ekowe, his was the only column acting on the offensive.

From the 25th January to the 1st February his marches and counter-marches afford little matter of interest. On the 28th he moved on to a new camping-ground, called Potter's Store, and there obtained full particulars of the Maglisini or Baglusini Kraal. This place Colonel Wood had for some time known as one of the principal rallying-points and depots of supplies for the Zulu armies. Large quantities of "mealies" (Indian corn) and grain of other sorts were known to have been accumulated at this magazine, while cattle in large droves had been seen on their way to the depot.

Under these circumstances it was necessary to proceed with caution, as, had any ostentatious preparations been made for an advance in the direction of the magazine, it is more than probable Wood's object would only have been gained at a severe cost. In this view it was determined that a cavalry raid should be made by the mounted troops under Piet Uys, with his *burghers*, and Colonel Buller, with his dashing corps of Frontier Light Horse. From the camp near Potter's Store to the Baglusini stronghold was at least thirty miles. A plain suitable to the passage of cavalry intervened before the Manzana River was reached, and Colonel Buller saw no reason why the distance should not be covered in one day. The *kraals* of Umbelini and of Inyatini were also in the same neighbourhood, therefore the utmost caution and secrecy were necessary in making preparations for the attack.

The weather had been most unfavourable for some days, but fortunately cleared up, and became settled on the 1st of February. On that morning Colonel Buller, having selected on the previous day 106 of his best mounted men and thirty-three of the Dutch Contingent under Piet Uys, their commandant, paraded his men under the supervision of Colonel Wood, and explained to them clearly the feat they were about to attempt, not concealing the danger which they would have to incur in the performance of a most difficult and dangerous duty. The scene was a most dramatic one, as the camp lanterns lit up the faces of the bronzed and stalwart volunteers who formed the devoted band.

79

Each man was exceedingly well horsed, and no precaution had been neglected in the careful overhauling of arms, accoutrements, and saddlery. Biscuit and, for those who cared, a little ration of rum were served out, and with a hearty "God-speed" from their comrades, who half envied their chances of adventure, the little troop of 141 gallant fellows started long before the earliest streak of dawn. The utmost silence was ordered and maintained, while the ground for some miles was so favourable that the horses' hoofs were scarcely heard as they cantered over the light and springy *veldt*. Distances on horseback are so differently estimated out in South Africa and at home in England, that when the ground is favourable, very long, and to European experience almost impossible, marches are constantly made without distress to horse or rider.

In the present instance two short off-saddles only were indulged in; the first not far from the centre of the flat, and the next after the Manzana River had been safely crossed. The country now became more broken and the pace was reduced to a walk, but before the sun was well up the goal was in sight, and the herds of cattle were seen calmly feeding on the slopes. No suspicion would seem to have been excited, and it is more than probable that the very smallness of the attacking force, and its being all composed of the mounted branch, contributed to the success of the affair. The *kraal* was exceedingly well built, and seen from a distance of 1200 or 1000 yards it was doubtful whether it held a large guard or not. Cautiously yet swiftly advancing. Colonel Buller felt his way, with a few of his best shots thrown out as vedettes. These men soon encountered some scattered Zulus, who did not seem at all prepared for any hostile demonstration, but on retiring towards the hills they were reinforced by several other larger bodies, who had evidently been sent out to reconnoitre.

After a few shots had been fired, a sudden and simultaneous advance was made on two sides of the *kraal*, and almost without resistance on the part of its defenders the *kraal* was captured. Two hundred and fifty well-built huts were counted by Buller's men, who, losing not a moment, collected no less than four hundred head of cattle, and a large quantity of grain, and then set fire to the magazine. Six Zulus were killed in the capture of the place, and although more than one body of them were seen hovering about in the vicinity, numbering severally 100 to 200 and 300 men, no opposition was offered to the rear-guard or patrols.

Wood then again moved his camp to the White Umvolosi. His

position here was a remarkably strong one, and from it he commanded the passage of the White Umvolosi, the Pewana, while his day and night patrols held the disputed territory south of the Pongolo. A raid was next made in the direction of the Insulwa Kraal. The men got upon the road about seven a.m., and steady marching for about three miles brought them opposite the spot where, a few days before, a large force of Zulus had been seen engaged at drill. A scout who had been sent out on the right front came galloping back with the news that the Zulu cattle were in considerable numbers at the lower end of the valley, while he also added that the guard over these animals was not much larger than the English party.

Piet Uys at once concerted with a couple of his smart non-commissioned officers, and decided, as they were exceedingly well mounted, to ride for the *kloof* which formed the exit to the valley. To execute this manoeuvre was the work of ten minutes, during which they were hidden from sight of the Zulus by a tall ledge of scarped rocks which almost divided the valley. In the meanwhile, the remainder moved steadily on at a walk, so as not to alarm their prey. In rather more than half an hour they had so far gained upon the cattle that, they could make a tolerable guess as to their probable number, which was estimated at a couple of hundreds. The main body had now arrived at a place which Piet Uys and his Dutchmen seemed intimately acquainted with, and the Zulu cattle and guard could be seen on a ridge running parallel to the one they themselves were upon. Below was a deep *kloof* leading to the river.

Some of Buller's Horse were now sent round to the opposite side, to drive the enemy down the *kloof* to the main party, while they continued to march down the ridge to meet these men as they came on. But they had not advanced very far when, as was expected, a much larger force appeared on the neighbouring heights, but the cliff was so precipitous they could not join their comrades. The seven-pounder was now brought into action, and sent a couple of shells right in amongst them, one of the rounds being a capital shot. Advancing still, the English leader saw that the enemy lately on the heights had managed, by making a detour, to get to the cover of a dense mimosa bush on his left.

This move was answered by several rounds of canister, which it was afterwards found were not without effect. The foes were thus driven out into the open, and at one moment it seemed as though they were going to fight; the Boers, however, who had been detached to the neck of the valley now served their comrades by an excellent ruse. They had taken with them one of the bugle boys of the 13th, mounted on a wiry Kaffir pony, and the main party now heard coming across the valley the echoes of his bugle sounding the advance. The Zulus could not make out the meaning of this sound, and evidently imagined that the English commander had posted at least the wing of a regiment to intercept them.

The consequence was, that the moment the main body cantered forward with a bold front, the cattle were abandoned; and they were left masters of the field, taking 170 head and some few wounded prisoners. Two villages were left in flames behind the retiring troops, who, as the crackling and flashing approached the bush where the hills met the plain, could see individual forms of black warriors shouting and gesticulating from out of the dust and smoke, wild with impotent rage at the loss of their *kraal* and cattle. The ridges beyond the gulleys still afforded considerable shelter, and the English party were continually fired upon as they returned with their spoil; but it was evident that the Zulus had not any long-range weapons, as it could be seen from the splashes of dust how far short their bullets were falling. Ten of Buller's men were now sent on to cover the passage of the guns through the drift, and in about twenty minutes, and under the protection of the rear-guard, it was passed over in safety.

On the 15th, Wood was fortunate enough to destroy the great military *kraal* of Manyanyoba.

Several reconnaissances had been made by Colonel Wood's directions, and from the local knowledge of one of Piet Uys's men, Colonel Buller was enabled to carry out the instructions of his chief with a success fully equal to the most sanguine expectations. The stronghold in question was situated on the Intomba River, and had always been considered by Cetywayo and his *indunas* as a place of more than ordinary strength. At ten p.m. on the 14th the men were got under arms, and the column was composed of a strong detachment of Buller's Horse and fifty of the Burgher Volunteers under Piet Uys, whose services had on more than one occasion been most handsomely mentioned by Colonel Wood.

The men paraded without lights, bugles, or the slightest sound, and moved off silently into the bush, without even the jingle of a sabre or the clank of a chain. Their march was accompanied by one gun, the wheels of which were, however, carefully wrapped with cloth and bound with raw hide. This was not only a protection against sound, but a preventive to injury to spokes and axles from the sharp boulders and rocks in the bed of the drift. The column left the camp by moonlight, crossing the usual ford, and were fortunate enough to gain the shelter of the bush without being seen or heard in the neighbouring villages. After a couple of hours' marching they reached a wide plain, where there was a broad watercourse, but sufficiently shallow to be easily forded. Here the gun, as the early grey of the morning came on in the sky, was brought into position, and here the final instructions were given to the men.

As the daylight grew more marked there could be seen in front a long unbroken range of mountains, varying in height from 900 to 1000 feet. This range ran along the valley leading to the smaller *kraals* in the distance. Half the cavalry were now sent away by Colonel Buller to the left, with instructions to gain the bush, and wait dismounted until the shells were heard. They were then to dash forward at a swinging canter and cut off the cattle to be seen feeding on the slopes, which manoeuvre would, if carried out, drive them into the hands of Piet Uys and his men posted on the right. Just as the sun began to appear above the horizon the gunners managed to hit off the range to a nicety, and the second shell crashed and burst right into the centre of the interior circle where the cattle were placed at night, and which is usually surrounded by the beehive-shaped huts where the Zulus live. It was at once perceived that this shot had caused the wildest commotion, as it was immediately followed by smoke and flame, figures rushing about through the village, the bellowing of oxen, and the shouts of men.

As the horsemen advanced at a gallop towards the *kraal*, the enemy, firing a random and hasty volley, fled up the sides of the mountain, where cavalry could not follow. All the huts and stores along the base of the mountain were now destroyed without much resistance, although as soon as the Zulus got a little vantage-ground on the cliffs, they turned, and replied to the English fire. Four hundred head of cattle and a quantity of sheep and goats were brought off by Buller's men, who behaved with the most admirable coolness and steadiness. The fight had lasted about half an hour, when indications of reinforcements to the Zulus were observed. Seeing that nothing more was to be gained, and that he might lose the cattle, Colonel Buller gave the order to make good the retreat, covered by skirmishers and a rear-guard. This movement was skilfully effected without loss, and the column reached the camp early in the afternoon, having been about eight or nine hours in the saddle.

Meanwhile, to strengthen Wood's hands, the commander-in-chief had ordered Colonel Rowlands to join that general. Rowlands at this time had with him, at his entrenched camp at New Derby, only a wing of the 80th, a couple of guns, and 200 Swazis; Raaf's Horse and Weatherly's Borderers were, however, expected daily to reinforce him. In the meantime, Rowlands was not allowing the grass to grow under the feet of his men, for, on the same day that Wood destroyed the Manyanyoba Kraal he left his camp at Derby and marched on to the Talako range, where he knew the enemy were in the numerous caves hidden by dense bush. The operations were entirely successful. Five large *kraals*, some of them of great natural strength, were burnt to the ground, 197 cattle, seventy goats, and forty-five sheep were captured. Magalini, the chief, was killed, with ten of his men, while defending one of the caves. One Zulu prisoner was taken, and forty women and a number of children came in and claimed protection. Six of the Swazi allies, under Fairlie, were wounded, and one horse killed.

On a still more recent occasion Colonel Rowlands had shown even greater activity. On the 20th February intelligence was brought to his camp that a small force of Zulus had been left in charge of supplies at Makatees Kop, a natural fortress close to Elozo, and intended as a depot for future operations. The place was by no means easy of access, and apparently innumerable difficulties were mentioned to dissuade the colonel from any hostile attempt. On the date just named (20th) the detachment sent forward as a sort of advanced guard by Colonel Rowlands reached one of the mission-stations still left on the border. There was a laager consisting of a simple stone enclosure, bastioned, however, and loopholed, and situated on the bank of a running stream of bright and clearly sparkling water. In the dead of night, the sentries were heard to challenge, and the sergeant on guard at once called his men to arms. This alarm, however, proved to be merely the return of some mounted Boers who had been sent on to reconnoitre on the previous day, and the information they brought in was important.

The *kraal* which they had been seeking was about twenty miles off and supposed to be only held by about fifty Zulus, belonging to the regiment of Nkobamakosi, and part of the Undi or Royal corps. A large number of cattle were not supposed to be yet there, but some were coming in daily, and it was considered advisable to break this link in the enemy's communications. In the early morning, preceded by a few horsemen (many were coming in as volunteers to both Rowlands' and Wood's column), and marching with only their haversacks full of rations for two days, the little expedition started for a duty uncertain and believed to be full of risk. Eight European officers, 275 natives, partly Swazi allies, and some volunteer horse, the whole under command of Captain Harvey, staff officer, formed the reconnaissance; but, as it turns out, a smaller force would have sufficed.

From the post or *laager* at the mission-station the road lay up a narrow valley, from which, after an ascent of about 200 feet, it stretched out on to a wide grassy plain ten miles in length. On the left of this could be plainly seen a number of Zulus tending sheep and cattle on the hills. Crossing part of the Iwangovini district, and fording a drift on the Inpongo River, the Iembe mountain could be seen always to the right; while the Eloso, a rocky height, loomed in front. At the bottom of a steep, rocky, and heavily bush-grown gorge, fourteen miles from the *laager*, a halt and short off-saddle were made, and every precaution taken against surprise. From this point to the stronghold the pathway was most difficult, and the men had to proceed with the greatest caution, in case of an ambush, which was half suspected.

Two columns of smoke, one from a steep *krantz* on the left and another lower down on the right, were noticed, but these were afterwards found to be abandoned camping-grounds of the enemy, who fancied the British force was much stronger than it really was. On nearing the *kraal*, and on turning an angle of the gully, the column came in sight of the first village, which was as usual fortified in the Zulu fashion. As the foremost files dashed on, a couple of shots rang out and some *assegais* were thrown, causing a couple of casualties amongst the Swazis, who, however, showed a bold front, and, gallantly led by the European officers, carried the *kraal* by a rush. The results of this skirmish may not appear of great importance, but, taken in conjunction with Wood's recent successes, they had a most useful effect upon both the minds of the regular soldiers and those of the colonial volunteers.

The junction of Rowlands' column with Wood's was the next eventful incident in the history of the latter force. It was found, of course, impossible for Wood with so small a column and with so few cavalry to keep an efficient and reliable watch over the lengthy border he had to defend, and the result was that a Zulu force managed to effect a raid in the German settlements over the Pongolo. Commandant Schermbrucker had hitherto done remarkably well in keeping his line of defence intact, but his want of mounted men seriously hampered him, and enabled the Zulus to elude his vigilance. A serious raid happened on the 11th February: but Schermbrucker came up with the marauders as they were retiring with their booty, recaptured some of the cattle taken, and killed about a dozen of the enemy.

On the 13th a large Zulu force managed to cross the Pongolo, and steal past the fort and *laager* of Luneberg. This was in the dead of night, and by daybreak they had burnt a number of huts belonging to natives friendly to or in the employment of the Dutch. The savages rushed in thousands upon the *kraals* and single huts, setting the roofs on fire and massacring old people, women, and children who could not escape. They deliberately tortured to death about a score of old men, killed in the most brutal manner at least fifty women and an equal number of children, while they left several young women fearfully stabbed with *assegais*. All this took place within five miles of the fort; and as fire-arms were not employed, the attention of the sentries was not aroused.

Early in the morning one of the wounded managed to effect his escape, and brought this terrible news to the *laager*, and measures were immediately taken to follow and punish the band. Patrols were ordered out, and the utmost diligence exerted to overtake the enemy, who, it was known, was overladen with spoil. Before the Tombe River was reached, the leading patrol came up with a portion of the enemy's rear-guard, and a very pretty fight took place. The Zulus numbered about 460, but they were embarrassed by the cattle they had charge of, and this did not allow them to make a good stand. The consequence was that the Boer patrol killed twenty of their foes, put the remainder to flight, and won back a number of the stolen cattle.

The rest, however, managed to escape over the Tombe, and the patrol were wisely ordered not to pursue. These raids were principally due to the activity of both Umbelini and Manyanyoba, and were the immediate cause of the expedition to attack and burn the *kraals* of the chiefs on the Intombe River. It should be mentioned that Umbelini was a Swazi refugee, and not even a legitimate chieftain of that tribe, but was regarded by the real headmen as a mere adventurer and pretender. Manyanyoba's people, again, were not Zulus, but the debris or remnants of various tribes conquered by Chaka and Dingaan. They wandered about in a starving condition, landless, and without flocks or wealth of any kind, until Cetywayo, from compassion, allowed them to settle north of the Pongolo, and on the banks of the Tombe River. This very land was mentioned in the ultimatum sent by Sir Bartle Frere to the king, who had no right whatever to cede any portion of it.

ROUGH SKETCH
or
INTOMBE RIVER DRIFT

[Not drawn to scale.]

High broken
ground

Broken ground

Mealie Fields

Little Intombe River

Deep and muddy Spruit

Mealie Fields

the Convoy

Capt. Moriarty's tent

to Derby

Waggons

Commissariat Waggons

Camp

DRIFT

from Luneburg

Intombe River

147½

144½

Rear

Harness's party

Ammunition Waggons

Mealie Fields

Very broken ground

Wood next moved his camp to the Kambula Kop, and there entrenched himself in a position of great natural strength. There now occurred an event of considerable importance. Oham, brother of Cetywayo, had always declared himself opposed to war, had openly stated his opinion in Zulu's councils, and had ever since the outbreak of hostilities been making overtures of friendship to the British. These, however, had been but lightly treated, as suspicions of their honesty were entertained by the powers that were. How groundless were these suspicions the event proved. On the 2nd inst. Oham came into the camp of Captain McLeod, the political agent on the border of Swaziland, arrived at Derby on the 4th, and came on thence to Wood at Kambula a couple of days back, and declared his complete submission to Her Majesty's Government.

Immediately before leaving his *kraal* in Zululand the chief took the precaution to try and save some of his best cattle, and he subsequently sent a thousand head of his finest herds into the Swazie county; but they fell into Dutch hands, and some of the Boers, obtaining possession of them, had the audacity to brand them as their property before McLeod could arrive to claim them. Oham had with him between 300 and 400 of his people, and was accompanied by his eldest son, an intelligent lad of fifteen, who soon made himself an object of great interest in Wood's camp, and a favourite with the soldiers. Immediately on his arrival he had an interview with, and was received with great respect by Colonel Wood, who was informed by him that he would have surrendered some time back but for two reasons.

In the first place, he was under a system of espionage by the orders of the king, with whom he had never been on good terms since he openly, before the Indunas, spoke against the warlike attitude and aggressive tone of his brother; and, secondly, when he did make his first overtures for submission, he was told that he was not believed by the English, and would be cast into prison, and sent to Robbin Island as a convict.

Oham was a black *ikehla* (head-ringed man), resembling both his father, the late Mpanda, or Panda, and his brother Cetywayo, and although a large man, his body and muscles were firm, not flabby like those of so many other big Zulus. After the usual salutations he thus opened his interview with Wood:—

Sir, chief, and great warrior, whom I respect, because you fight against men, and do not kill women or children, I came here to

88

your camp from a desire to see you, and to ask you to intercede for me and my people, who have never wished to make war upon you, but to live in peace and goodwill, and hunt the wild deer together. I have left more than two thousand of my people ready and most anxious to come in and submit to you, surrendering their arms and cattle, and giving their sons as hostages, if you will guarantee their safety.

The chief, who had a dignified manner and an honest expression of countenance, was then informed that he and his people should receive every consideration, and as much protection as was consistent with the safe advance of the English troops into Zululand. He then assured Wood that the Zulu Army was considerably demoralised, and that, the people having gone back to their *kraals*, Cetywayo found it no easy task to collect a really effective fighting force. With some difficulty, indeed, the king had managed to get together a strong *impi*, composed of the Udhlambedhlu, or "Ill-tempered" Regiment, whose *kraal* was at Udhlambedhlweni, about six miles east of the Usixepe, to exercise a surveillance over Oham and his people.

This corps, however, was formed originally from a clan, or tribe, which were Dingaan's chief and favourite regiment, and although in a measure loyal to their then ruler, they were somewhat indignant at the duty imposed upon them, when they would infinitely prefer the chances of raiding and plunder, which the present unsettled state of the border presented.

Now, when Wood was at Utrecht the previous autumn, a letter was sent by the Landdrost Rudolph to the Secretary for Native Affairs, in which he mentioned the arrival of Gwegwana, the favourite messenger of Uhamo or Oham, with letters from that chief to the following effect, which Oham now repeated to Colonel Wood:—

I am sent back by Uhamo to hear what answer his father, Somtseu (Sir Theophilus Shepstone), has sent to his message brought by me on the 10th October last. Uhamo is very anxious to know what is going to take place in the land now that Cetywayo has called the whole of Zululand together, and Uhamo has refused liberty to his people to assemble at 'Ondi,' and will openly tell Cetywayo that if he (Cetywayo) makes war upon the English, he (Uhamo) will not join him, because Cetywayo's people, Sirayo and Umbelini, have, by their overt acts, brought the country into its present state of trouble and disgrace. Moreover, the building by Cetywayo's orders of a military *kraal* on the Pongolo, and the claims made by him of a portion of the Transvaal beyond the Blood River, which had been, as Uhamo repeatedly told Cetywayo, ceded many years ago to the Transvaal people, and other acts, had never received any countenance from Uhamo, who now asks. Why does Cetywayo want to quarrel with the English, who have ever been his friends, and who, indeed, placed him on his present throne?

In his second interview with Colonel Wood, Oham was still more explicit and demonstrative. He expressed himself with much indignation at his brother's countenancing such a despicable character as Umbelini, who, neither a pure Zulu nor a Swazi, had all the vices and none of the good qualities of either; and he added that the degradation which his brother had brought upon the race of Chaka by such an unworthy alliance has caused him to lose much of his former popularity. Oham also added that, in case of the continuance of the war, rather than be compelled to fight against his old friends the English he would at all hazards bring his people bodily over to that government, and under these circumstances claim their protection. "Uhamo loves peace as his father Panda did," said the chief in conclusion, and his open and honest-looking eyes seemed to corroborate this expression.

We now come to another sad event, which though less in magnitude, is in many points similar to the Isandhlwana disaster. Major Tucker, the chief officer at Luneberg, gives this account of the affair:—

Captain Moriarty, with a company of the 80th, was ordered to march from Luneberg on the 7th March, for the purpose of bringing in twenty waggons from Derby, variously loaded, which had arrived at the Intombi Drift. Earlier in the month Major Tucker sent down to the drift, which was not more than four miles off, a small escort to await the arrival of these waggons. Believing, however, the position a perilous one, owing to the proximity to Umbelini's *kraal*, on the 5th he ordered it to return.

On the 7th, however, the waggons, which had all but been captured on the way down, did arrive at the drift, and Moriarty was again sent with seventy men of his company to act as escort and assist in getting the convoy across the stream, which was considerably swollen by the continued rains. The drift was only four miles from the stronghold of the renegade Swazi freebooter, Umbelini, who had of late given so much trouble, and Moriarty had orders to neglect no precaution, and above all to laager his waggons and keep an incessant and vigilant look-out. It was ascertained from survivors that the waggons were actually parked, but in a somewhat loose and careless fashion, and that no earthworks were thrown up around the camp. For several days the river continued in strong flood, and consequently no crossing could be effected.

On the 11th it was reported by the native waggon-drivers that Umbelini's people were gathering in the neighbourhood. The camp was pitched in a most dangerous position, with its face towards some high ground, covered here and there with dense bush, while its rear was resting upon the swollen river, across which Lieutenant Harward and thirty-four men were posted. No particular precautions appear to have been taken, with the exception of a sentry being posted about fifteen paces from the front of the camp, on the Derby side.

When first warned by the drivers, Moriarty ordered the men to stand to their arms, but only for a short time. On the morning of the 12th, at four o'clock, a shot was heard from the unfortunate sentry, who had barely time to call "Guard, turn out!" when dense masses of the savages were seen not more than two hundred yards from the camp. Their front extended for several miles, and they could not, by the lowest estimate, have been less than 4000 or 5000 strong. Lieutenant Harward, who had been on the *qui-vive*, and who had carefully placed his thirty-five men under cover of his solitary waggon, at once called his detachment to arms, and made what dispositions he could to open fire upon the enemy's flank.

In less than ten minutes, however, the whole valley was swarming with the savages, who at once proceeded in their usual manner to surround and overlap the camp and waggons. In less time than it takes to tell, the camp was in their hands, and the majority of the soldiers were *assegaied*, many of them before they could leave their tents. The fight, or rather butchery, which ensued was soon over, and, in spite of a well-directed and well-sustained fire from the Luneberg bank of the river, the enemy followed up the men, and *assegaied* them as they endeavoured to swim the river. Harward, seeing the enemy crossing the river in large numbers, gave the order to his men to retire slowly.

Then, jumping on the back of his horse, he galloped away at full speed to Luneberg, where he reported what had happened. The savages continued to cross the stream, and coming on in dense masses, for a short time a hand-to-hand fight took place, ending however in the little band being broken up.

Eight men, and the sergeant of Harward's detachment, by taking advantage of shelter afforded by an old and dismantled *kraal* wall at some little distance from the stream, and by their cool and determined shooting, succeeded in saving their lives and getting to Luneberg. Ten men only were saved from Moriarty's party, while he, with a civilian, Surgeon Cobbin, was slain.

The camp was evidently wrongly placed, and was clearly taken by surprise. Major Tucker went out from Luneberg in person, with a small party of horsemen, followed by 150 of the 80th, to see what could be recovered, and the bodies of the dead were brought over the river and buried, while twenty-five of the enemy's dead were discovered, and a couple of wounded taken prisoners. From these men it was ascertained that Umbelini himself was in command, having with him some men belonging to our old antagonist Manyanyoba.

Mcame, a powerful *induna*, had been asked to join in the foray, but refused. When Tucker and his handful of horsemen arrived on the banks of the river, the enemy were seen to be retreating, but they could not be followed until the infantry came up. Curious to remark, the waggons were not taken, and many of them were only half plundered by the savages, who seemed most anxious to decamp with what spoil they had secured.

For his conduct in this affair Lieutenant Harward was subsequently tried by court-martial. The ground of complaint was his having galloped off on his horse—the only one present on the scene—leaving his men engaged in a desperate engagement. The loss of the camp, or anything of a similar nature, was in no way charged against him. His defence was that he had ridden off to obtain assistance from the nearest point—that this was his duty—and that he could not send a soldier in his place, as none of them could ride. In the event the Court acquitted him. But in May of the ensuing year (1880), the Field-Marshal Commanding-in-Chief issued the following special general order relative to a court-martial recently held on an officer in South Africa:—

At a general court-martial recently held, an officer was ar-

raigned upon the following charges,—First. Having misbe-
haved before the enemy, in shamefully abandoning a party of
the regiment under his command when attacked by the enemy,
and in riding off at speed from his men. Second. Conduct to
the prejudice of good order and military discipline in having at
the time and place mentioned in the first charge, neglected to
take proper precautions for the safety of a party of the regiment
under his command when attacked.

The court recorded a verdict of 'Not Guilty' on both charges.
The main facts of the case were not in dispute. The officer rode
away from his men to a station distant four and a half miles, at
a moment of extreme danger, when to all appearance the small
party under his command were being surrounded and overwhelmed by the enemy.

The charge alleged misbehaviour—that is, cowardice in so doing; the defence averred that it was to procure reinforcements,
and either by their actual arrival, or by the imminence of their
arrival, to ward off destruction. In acquitting the prisoner, they
have found that he was not guilty of cowardice. The proceedings of the Court were submitted to the general commanding,
who recorded the following minute:—'Disapproved and not
confirmed. Lieutenant . . . to be released from arrest, and to
return to his duty.'

The confirming officer has further recorded his reasons for
withholding his approval and confirmation in the following
terms:—'Had I released this officer without making any re-
marks upon the verdict in question, it would have been a tacit
acknowledgment that I concurred in what appears to me a
monstrous theory, *viz.*, that a regimental officer who is the only
officer present with a party of soldiers actually and seriously
engaged with the enemy can, under any pretext whatever, be
justified in deserting them, and by so doing abandoning them
to their fate. The more helpless the position in which an officer
finds his men, the more it is his bounden duty to stay and share
their fortune, whether for good or ill.

'It is because the British officer has always done so that he occupies the position in which he is held in the estimation of the
world, that he possesses the influence he does in the ranks of
our army. The soldier has learnt to feel that, come what may,
he can, in the direst moment of danger, look with implicit faith

to his officer, knowing that he will never desert him under any possible circumstances. It is to this faith of the British soldier in his officers that we owe most of the gallant deeds recorded in our military annals; and it is because the verdict of this court-martial strikes at the root of this faith that I feel it necessary to mark officially my emphatic dissent from the theory upon which the verdict has been founded.'

In communicating to the army the result of this court-martial, the Field-Marshal Commanding-in-Chief desires to signify his entire approval of the views expressed by the confirming officer in respect of the principles of duty which have always actuated British officers in the field, and by which His Royal Highness feels assured they will continue to be guided. This general order will, by His Highness's command, be read at the head of every regiment in Her Majesty's service.—By Command, H. Ellice.

It was about this time that Oham, whose actions had now clearly proved his sincerity, and the value of his friendship to the British, having made an earnest request to Colonel Wood that his wives and family might be rescued from the power of Cetywayo, the colonel sent off about twenty of the chief's men to collect them. To carry out the remainder of the project, some days after, (on the 14th), a strong detachment of Buller's men and the Burghers under Piet Uys, with 200 of Oham's people, left the camp at daybreak, and guided by James Rorke and Calverly, marched to the caves of Nhlangwine, which were situated rather more than twelve miles east of the source of the Un-kassi, and not less than forty-five miles from Kambula. The caves were reached at 9.30 p.m. the last of the march of seven miles being very difficult travelling, and taking three hours to surmount.

A few Zulus in charge of cattle were shot, and the animals which had belonged to Oham were taken possession of. As has been said, it was scarcely daybreak when the little column started. They rode along for a considerable time in complete silence, the men being allowed to smoke their pipes, but not to speak above a whisper. At first they followed the spoor of some cattle, which indicated the road by which Oham and his people had come to the camp, and then turning more in a northerly direction, followed the course of some small streams which flowed from the hills upon the left. The moon shone brightly, and enabled them to see clearly for some distance before them.

Many strange sounds were heard, the growl of some beast of prey or the scream of the night-birds disturbed by the clank of the horses' hoofs, or the occasional rattle of a chain. The rapidity with which the column cantered over the soft and springy *veldt*, the dead and ominous silence maintained by all hands, and the steady and business-like mode in which they pursued their course, neither turning to the right nor the left, gave the journey a singularly weird character.

As soon as the first morning's light began to appear the guides, who rode in front, turned into a ravine covered with dense brushwood and trees, and, having ascended this for about three miles, they found it was possible to ride out of it in three different directions, besides the one by which they had entered, and thus a retreat could be effected if any attack were made. Here it was decided to make the first off-saddle and partake of breakfast. At a signal from their leader, and without any word of command, the horsemen dismounted, slackened girths, and took off saddles, while the bits were removed from the horses' mouths and the animals allowed Cape fashion, to take the customary roll in the grass.

This luxury to a Cape horse seems indispensable, and without it he will rarely enjoy his grass or corn. No sooner, however, had the steeds rolled than each was again saddled, and, with the exception of the still slackened girths, was ready to be mounted in half a moment. Rifles and revolvers were carefully examined, to see whether the night dew had done any mischief, and then, having made a careful sweep round the horizon with his field-glasses, the commander gave the order for the morning meal, which consisted of a little cold tea, some bread, and "*beltong*" (sun-dried game).

After half an hour's rest they again started as silently as before. The day had broken with all the splendour of an African morning. The day before had been rainy, and the showers had refreshed the ground and filled the various pools with water, and all kinds of wild animals were busy and cheerful in the plains. A number of parrots and monkeys were screaming and chattering with content, and the sportsmen of the party were much exercised at hearing the pleasant double whistle of the quail sounding from various patches of long grass. Figures which it was first thought were Zulus were seen on the summits of the rocks, but Piet Uys declared that they were merely baboons, whose early morning custom was to come from the heights to search for and dig up roots, which seemed to grow here in abundance.

Vultures, sweeping aloft, were circling in the air above where there had evidently been a skirmish, for the carcasses of some horses still remained uneaten and poisoning the pure air. Here and there a black-breasted and magnificent eagle sat on some withered branch, and, seeming quite indifferent to the soldier's presence, scanned the ground below him as if to select the daintiest morsel for his morning meal. Mounting to the head of the *kloof* the party came to a splendid prospect and panorama stretching out below. The plains seemed to roll away to the north-east as far as the eye could see, while the bright, glowing tints of the rugged foreground were mellowed away into the middle distance, until, quite far away, the bold outlines of the mountains assumed, not a purple, as in Europe they would have done, but a rich blue tint, yet standing out in fine clear relief against the distant sky, the dry atmosphere failing to give the subdued effect of distance usually observed in other climates. These mountains were the Tobomba range, which run northward, and almost parallel to the coast-line.

Amidst small groves of what seemed in the distance to be acacia, and near the banks of many tiny streams that wound along the plain, were groups of game. Herds of various kinds of *bok* were there, and here and there some solitary and not gregarious animal was to be seen, now bounding away from some imaginary danger, and now calmly browsing on the sweet *veldt*. What a place for an encampment!—wood, water, cover, commanding heights, which, properly occupied and entrenched, could be held against an army; and a climate where fever could scarcely penetrate, so pure and bracing was the air. Away up a smaller valley on the right lay the path that had to be followed, and, leaving the bright and smiling landscape in front, the column once more plunged into the gloom of the bush. Two more outspans brought them to sunset, and now precautions had to be redoubled, as they were nearing most dangerous ground.

The chances were more than probable that Cetywayo, on hearing of his brother's defection and flight, had sent a party of his warriors to take possession of his wives and cattle, both vendible commodities in the land. If this were the case, it would inevitably result that a vigilant watch would be kept to prevent their escape to Oham. Strange to say, these anticipations were only partly verified, for as the troops neared the caves they could see that they were watched, but only by scattered and weak bodies of Zulus. These fellows had evidently discovered that the white man's intention was hostile, and they probably thought his object was cattle, and not to recover or rescue Oham's wives and children, for they ran rapidly along the heights above, taking no precaution for concealment, and seeming only anxious to drive away their herds. As the horsemen approached the caves at a canter, flankers were extended on either side to prevent surprise. The excitement of Buller's men could hardly be restrained, while the calm and stolid Dutchmen, who glided silently and grimly on, offered a wide contrast to their more hot-blooded comrades.

As they came nearer and nearer the place seemed inhabited, and it was evident that the natives sent on a few days previously had apprised the people of Buller's advent and friendly intentions. Then Oham's people came crowding out of their caves, jostling each other in their anxiety to greet the English soldiers, grasping their assegais, and giving vent to a succession of guttural clicks, which it would baffle any known combination of vowels to reproduce. They did not cheer; such was not their custom, but they waved their spears aloft, as if they felt them entering the enemy's body.

Rorke, having now been sent on with a small escort to explore the caves, was not long in reporting that all the women and children had been collected, and a bivouac having been formed with outlying pickets in every direction, and sentries posted, that night was passed without molestation. At nine a.m. the following morning a compact column was formed, consisting of the rescued allies or prisoners, the few cattle collected in the centre, and the whole party started for the homeward march. It could scarcely have been hoped that the retreat would have been unmolested, yet only at the Inklepgwene, a difficult defile, were they fired upon by a body of Zulus, evidently hastily collected, and numbering some thousand men. The detachment reached the camp, with the rescued families, at one p.m. on the 16th.

Wood had for some time purposed taking the initiative against Umbelini, and from information obtained from Oham's people came to the conclusion that Umbelini's place on the Mhlobana Mountain, which was not more than five and twenty miles from Kambula, was capable of being successfully surprised. He had heard from headquarters that Lord Chelmsford would probably start for Pearson's relief on the 28th, so he determined to take that opportunity of making a diversion towards Mhlobana.

On Wednesday, 26th March, Colonel Buller and Piet Uys were summoned to Colonel Wood's tent, and told that information had come in to the effect that a large quantity of fine cattle had been seen on the Zlobani range of mountains, some ten or twelve miles from Kambula. This Zlobani range could be seen from the camp, and in most places was steep and precipitous, well wooded, and full of large caves, places of concealment, and natural fastnesses.

Several reconnaissances had been previously made by Colonels Wood and Buller, who had both made themselves well acquainted with its natural features and its various difficulties of attack. It was well known that scattered bands of predatory Zulus, guarding large quantities of cattle, had been for some time concealed in these rocky recesses, and that, in compliance with the king's orders, these bands had been consolidated and reinforced by regiments sent by Cetywayo from Ulundi. Colonel Wood had, however, other information, from some of Oham's people, that all the regiments indicated had not yet come in, and that want of ammunition was detaining them in their own *kraals*. This, as it turned out, could not have been quite correct.

After some conversation. Colonel Weatherly and Commandants Raaf and Schermbrucker were also summoned to the colonel's tent, and it was unanimously decided that it would be advisable to take the initiative and strike a blow before the Zulus concentrated to attack the camp, as Wood was on all hands assured they would do. Before any operations on the Zlobani are described, it should be mentioned that Wood had been enabled from the additions to his column to establish a chain of communications between Kambula, Utrecht, and Dundee. He had also organised a strong outpost between his camp and the Transvaal border, and another at Doom Kop, or Thorn-hill. To this place Captain Schermbrucker and a party of his men were sent, but had been temporarily recalled to assist us at Kambula.

After the council of war held by the colonel on the 26th, arrangements were at once made for the reconnaissance to the Zlobani. The force selected for this expedition consisted of the Imperial Mounted Infantry, 160; the Frontier Light Horse, 125; Raaf's Contingent, 50; Piet Uys's Boer Contingent, 50; Weatherly's Horse, 80; and Schermbrucker's Horse, 40, making a total of 495; and each man was supplied with three days' rations and 100 rounds of ammunition.

All the horses intended for the expedition were carefully inspected on the 26th, and the colonel rejected several that did not seem in good form. They did not, as a rule, average more than fourteen hands two inches in height, but all were stout, short-backed, well ribbed up animals, and up to far more weight than their appearance would lead a novice to suppose. All these animals were trained to remain perfectly quiet when the men dismounted to fire, and many of them would actually come to their rider at a whistle. Piet Uys's men were especially well mounted, and it was necessary that they should be, as your Dutch Boer is, as a rule, by no means a feather-weight, being usually over thirteen stone. They are also very powerful men, and until forty or forty-five not unwieldy. After that age, they generally get heavier. Most of the old-fashioned Boers still retained the long *"roer"* or smoothbore, but all the younger generation had taken to the latest pattern rifles. A revolver and stout cutlass also formed part of their equipment, and a single blanket strapped in front of the saddle carried all their kit.

At three a.m. on the 27th, the first little band of gallant horsemen under Colonel Russell were quietly paraded in the moonlight, and after being carefully inspected were addressed in a few well-chosen words by Colonel Wood, who had finally decided to accompany the party. The whole party made up altogether 495 sabres, every one of whom was a good swordsman and a picked marksman. The horses, although somewhat rough in the coat, were in good wind and excellent condition, and every one of these animals was well trained to stand fire. They moved off quietly from the camp, and passing along the track, which descended towards a sandy and deep *nullah* with most precipitous sides, debouched into an open space, from which the Zlobani range could be seen in the intervals of moonlight, now and then obscured by the passing clouds, which seemed to foretell a stormy day.

The track in many places crossed difficult *spruits*, and in parts was obliterated by thorn-trees and bush. It was frequently commanded by projecting spurs and bluffs, from which an enemy could have seriously annoyed the advance. At five o'clock the column halted, and after a careful reconnaissance, off-saddled for half an hour, while the men partook of a ration of cold tea and *beltong*. This halt was made near a large dried-up, sandy watercourse, in parts of which the sand was moist and by digging holes water was found in sufficient quantities for the horses to wash their mouths. The surrounding country was totally denuded of fodder, and as far as the eye could reach the most wild and barren prospect was to be seen.

Another advance of about five miles changed the aspect of the scene, and brought them to a slightly wooded ravine, amidst the rocks of which ran a clear stream, over a grassy or pebbly bed, behind which loomed a range of rocky hills, the summit of which seemed crowned by immense boulders, looking in the distance like huge slabs placed by giant hands in their present position. Away to the left was an undulating plain, upon which were detached clumps of bushes and trees.

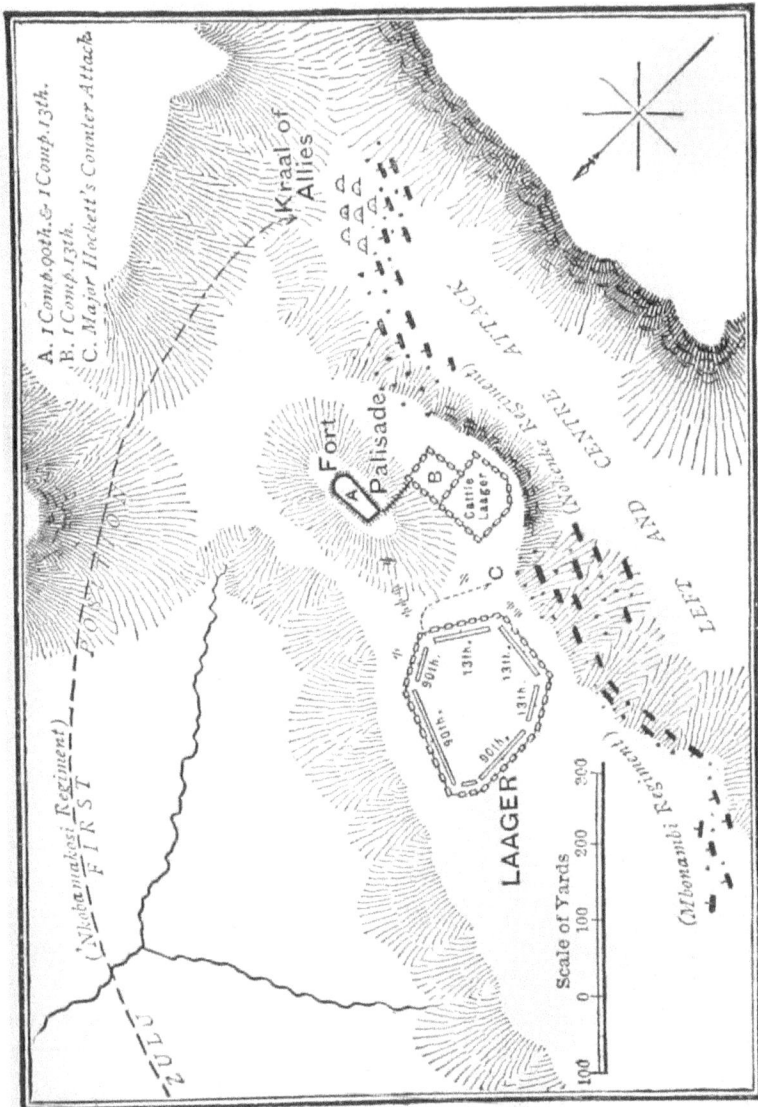

PLAN OF THE BATTLE OF KAMBULA.

A. I Comp. 90th & I Comp. 13th.
B. I Comp. 13th.
C. Major Hackett's Counter Attack.

Kraal of Allies

Fort

A

Palisade

B

Cattle Laager

C

(Nobamba Regiment) CENTRE ATTACK

LEFT AND

(Nobamba Regiment)

Notsheni Regiment

90th

13th

13th

90th

13th

90th

LAAGER

(Mbonambi Regiment)

(Nkobamakosi Regiment)
FIRST
ZULU
POSITION

Scale of Yards

100   0   100   200   300

Over this plain small mountain streams flowed in various directions, winding amongst trees, shrubs, and ferns of different variety. Here and there antelopes were grazing, ostriches were stalking, and now and then vultures were seen grimly circling round in seeming anticipation of a morning feast. A couple of miles further on they came to a large cultivated flat terminating to the right in a long, dark, and winding gorge, black with bush and skirted by huge precipices of sandstone and granite. They turned into this, and proceeded silently but quickly along the banks of a small rivulet, until they came to the foot of the mountain, and, after some little time, discovered a steep path, which seemed cut out of the solid cliff, and wide enough only for one horseman to pass. They were more than three-quarters of an hour scaling this path, which was most dangerous to horsemen unaccustomed to such tracks, and suited more to the bush *bok* seen here and there as the horsemen ascended higher and higher.

On nearing the top of the *krantz* the view was magnificent. Away to the extreme right was the purple range of the Ingive Mountains, behind which the sun was fast rising. The Ingonyama came next, and joined the Ntabatulu and Ingoma ranges, the latter of which overhangs the left bank of the Black Umfolosi, all along which are the most extensive forests and inaccessible *kloofs* and *krantzes*. The head of the column had no sooner gained the summit of the last ledge than the leading files noticed a large number of cattle grazing on the plateau. These were guarded by about 150 or 200 armed Zulus, who, however, did not see the advancing troops.

The range upon which the English party now found themselves extended about seven or eight miles, and was accessible only by a few most difficult footpaths leading from the plains below. Huge masses of scrub and boulders, *krantzes*, terraces, and ledges of rock, caves and immense fissures in the sides of the mountain, formed a retreat for the cattle, which, upon an alarm being sounded, were quickly driven from the grazing-ground above. The northern face of the mountain was a sheer precipice, perfectly bare of all bush or shrub. They were now halted, and ordered to bivouac. At about seven in the evening Colonel Wood rejoined them, having with him his usual small staff and personal escort, consisting of Captain the Hon. Ronald Campbell, his staff officer; Lieut. Lysons, 90th Light Infantry, his orderly officer; Mr. Lloyd, political agent (son of General Lloyd, of the Natal Legislative Assembly): eight mounted men of the 90th Light Infantry, and six stalwart natives under Umtongo, one of Pondo's sons.

101

Umtongo had by some means or other obtained information that the regiments named Naxeane, Umdomandi, Ucaridanburg, Macalsiene, Udmine, Ekotsamaclooser, and Macalvoore, under the Indunas Umgongo, Umsimoyao, and other noted chiefs, had left Ulundi three days before, on the 24th, and Umtongo was consequently most anxious that the column should at once return to the Kambula. This advice, however, could not have been followed without exposing Colonels Buller and Weatherly and Piet Uys, who were in front, to be cut off and surrounded, so that it was decided that a junction must be made with them at whatever risks.

At half-past three a.m. the commanding officer ordered the word to be quietly passed round for the men to stand to their horses and prepare to march. An occasional and straggling ray of moonlight helped them to follow the faint tracks of those who had gone before them, and before going very far they came upon unmistakable evidences of the advance having been opposed. A distant shot was now and then heard, away towards the bluff of the mountain on the north-east side; and soon after these indications of fighting was heard the sound of horses, and Colonel Weatherly, with his son, and about eighty of his troopers, met Colonel Wood, bringing him the news that on the previous night he had been unfortunate enough to miss his road.

As the morning was now breaking, and the warm sun commenced to light up the scene, Colonel Wood noticed, here and there on the path, a broken *assegai*, a damaged shield, rent with a Martini-Henry rifle-bullet, and further on the bodies of some Zulus and the carcass of a dead horse. These signs marked where Buller had passed and had been attacked. Campbell and Lysons therefore ascended the rocks above a huge cave, and, taking every precaution to screen themselves from observation, scanned the surrounding horizon with the field-glasses. Far away, almost upon the summit of an apparently inaccessible and gigantic cliff, the van of Buller's column could be seen slowly advancing, and driving some dark masses of cattle and Zulus before them. These officers came down at once to report, and Colonel Weatherly requested permission to lead his men on to Buller's assistance, while Colonel Wood followed with the remainder of his horsemen.

This permission being granted, Weatherly moved on by a terribly difficult path to the right, while the remainder kept to what seemed to be the main track. About half a mile farther on this party saw, a few hundred yards to the left, about 200 Zulus, who appeared to be armed with rifles. They were moving rapidly across the English front, stopping occasionally to take a shot at the leading files, who had, on account of the difficulties of the road, been compelled to dismount and lead their horses. The object of this detachment was now evident, it being their intention to get between the main column and Weatherly's little band. It was noticed that half a dozen gigantic warriors, each armed with rifle, shield, and bundle of *assegaies,* led the main body of these Zulus.

These men took it in turns to run in front, and were evidently acting as guides, often enabling the rest to make short cuts, and thus to get over the ground more quickly. They paused, however, now and then, as if to examine the spoor of the horses, on which the previous night's rain had fallen, and from this Colonel Wood concluded that some of his people were in the same direction. By means of some wild vine and creepers Lysons and one of the escort now descended from the opposite side of the plateau on which was the cave, and running rapidly along the top of the next ridge, made their way unseen to the edge of the bush. They thus commanded the plain below, and the serpentine pathway by which Buller had found his way to the summit of the cliff.

From this point Buller and his men could be seen scouring the mountains beyond the intervening *kloof,* and about halfway up the opposite ascent were observed a strong party of Zulus working forward as if to cut off the horsemen above. As Weatherly and Colonel Wood were now separated by a deep and impassable ravine, they could only hope that they should be able to effect a junction with Buller by different routes, and, if possible, in time to give effective help. Crouching down so as not to be seen by the main column were a few of the enemy on a narrow ledge of rock, about a hundred yards above their heads. Where these fellows had come from it was not easy to imagine, but they immediately opened a hot, but ill-directed fire, which the English troopers did not at first return, as they were too much occupied in guiding their horses over the dangerous places, where a single false step would have sent them to the valley below.

Meanwhile Umtongo and two of his men had climbed round by a higher portion of the cliff, and, guiding some of the English marksmen, they opened a fire upon the Zulu scouts, which soon cleared them from the path. Another half-hour's toilsome march brought Wood upon Weatherly's track, and they then could see the rear of Buller's column high above them to the right.

It would be difficult to describe the marvellously rugged and weird nature of the rocks around, and the ghastly features of the sheer precipices gaping on either side. Killed and wounded horses now were seen at every turn of the road, showing how stoutly the enemy must have held their ground, and how difficult an operation Buller had performed. Sending fifty men round to work on our right flank and to endeavour to take the Zulus in the rear, Colonel Wood kept his men for a few moments under cover of a friendly ledge of rocks to look to their rifles, girths, and ammunition, and then ascended rapidly to the front, passing the Border Horse, who had by this time got off the track.

The scene was at this moment intensely exciting. The firing was almost continuous, and the yells of the savages were re-echoed back by the loud and heart-stirring cheers of their gallant comrades, who had seen Wood's column coming and gave them this encouragement. It was not long before they came under more direct fire, and at this juncture Colonel Wood, who had been keeping his men cool and steady by his own presence of mind and good-humoured encouragement, left Colonel Russell in charge, and jumping upon his horse, as the ground was now practicable for riding, trotted through the skirmishers, and, closely followed by his staff and escort, pushed rapidly to the front.

This party, with a dozen of the Border Horse, galloped to within a hundred paces of the summit of the cliff, where they saw that they were in the thick of the fire, raining upon them both from front and flank, and proceeding from a mass of Zulus skirmishing in the most artistic and workmanlike manner from their caves, crevices, and enormous boulders which formed the natural fortifications of the mountain plateau. At this moment Weatherly, with his gallant and noble-hearted boy, aged only fifteen, and who insisted on fighting by his father's side, were cheering on their men, dashing boldly into the caves, and closing in mortal strife with the Zulus.

"Take a dozen men over to the cave to the right front, and rattle out the fellows who are firing so well, Colonel Weatherly," said Colonel Wood, as his horse staggered under him from a deep *assegai* wound in the chest, and a savage from behind a boulder fired at that officer at ten paces' distance. The bullet missed him, and Llewellen Lloyd, seeing the man loading quickly again, at once rode to cut him down, and was shot through the head. Wood, seeing this officer fall, dashed spurs into his wounded horse and galloped up to catch him, closely followed by Ronald Campbell. Two other Zulus from the cave now fired simultaneously at the colonel, whose horse at this moment

104

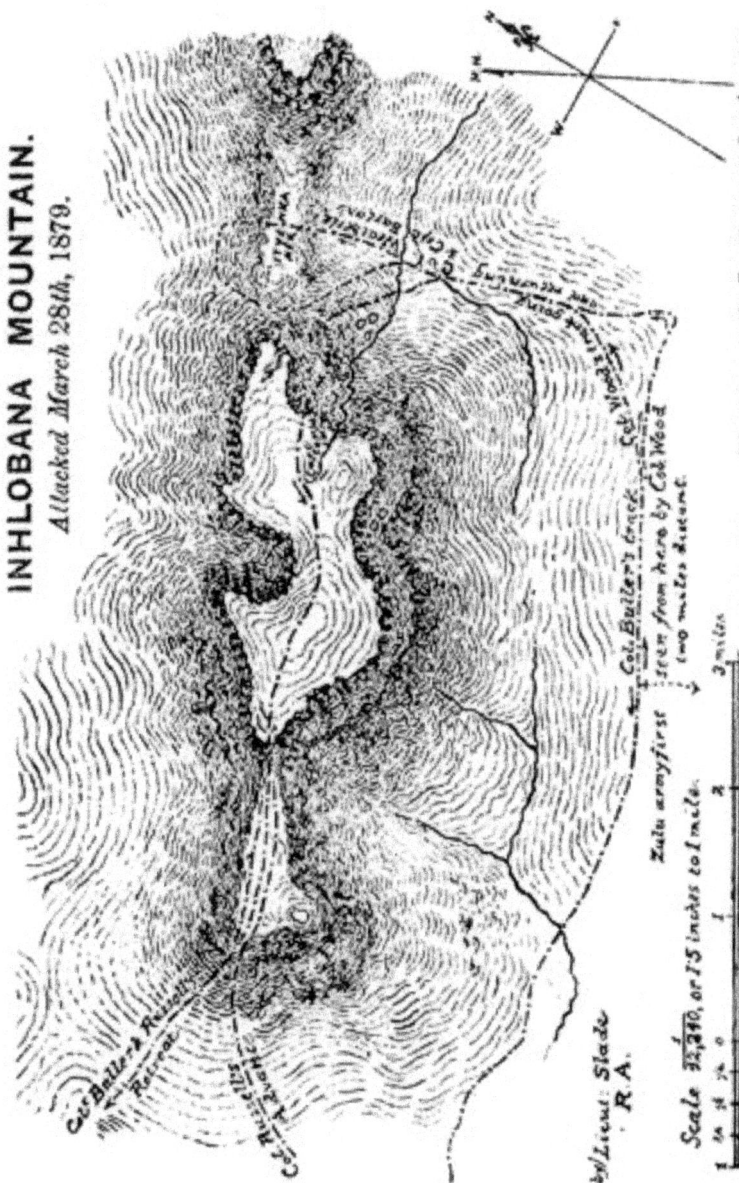

INHLOBANA MOUNTAIN.

Attacked March 28th, 1879.

by Lieut: Slade R.A.

Scale 15,840, or 15 inches to 1 mile.

3 miles

Copied from a Map done at the Intelligence Dep't, War Off.

was again struck, and fell upon him. The colonel was upon his feet in a moment, and assisted Captain Campbell and his orderly to carry Lloyd's body to a ledge more out of the way. The shot which killed poor Llewellen Lloyd tore Colonel Wood's sleeve underneath his arm before reaching its mark.

As Colonel Weatherly's men were engaged with several Zulus at close quarters, some little delay occurred in their advance upon the cave, whence the fire was most galling; and Ronald Campbell, calling on Lysons and some of the escort to follow him, dashed at the opening, having first cleared a sort of breastwork at the entrance. Poor Campbell fell, shot through the head; and Lysons and a brave fellow, Corporal Fowler, following closely upon the footsteps of the brave young guardsman, killed the two remaining Zulus within the cave, while another, severely wounded, managed to crawl away through a narrow crevice in the rock. Having ascertained that the enemy were retreating before Buller on the summit. Colonel Weatherly was sent to make a small circuit lower down the cliff, to endeavour to hit off the path by which the former had so successfully ascended, and which the others were unfortunate enough to miss.

Buller, in the meanwhile, was not only driving the Zulus' cattle before him, but was able to assist his comrades by his fire from his vantage-ground above. The enemy in front and flank retired, disputing every available spot, while Weatherly was most skilfully working round their left rear. His disposition of his men was most judicious, and he rendered very material help to Wood's portion of the force, intercepting and driving back a strong party which were coming up to assist the body they were engaging. These, however, eventually took up a formidable position in some caves in a deep *kloof*, from which they kept up a constant and dropping fire.

Amongst Wood's party they had up to this time but few casualties, though the loss of such splendid and noble-hearted soldiers as Campbell and Lloyd was a terrible blow to their chief, whose right hand men they were. Colonel Wood, in spite of the galling fire still maintained by the entrenched Zulus, assisted the party told off to carry the bodies of the dead to a place about half way down the first hill, where, in disregard of the bullets which kept rattling round, these noble young heroes were buried in a soldier's glorious grave, the funeral honours being discharged over them by the rifles of friend and foe.

Colonel Wood now made a flank movement with a portion of the column in a north-westerly direction, to see if a junction could be effected with that portion of the men which had been left in the charge of Colonel Russell. In effecting this change of position Wood had to pass under the steepest cliffs of the Zlobani Mountain. Umtongo, true to his Rob Roy and predatory instincts, had utilised his opportunity by a little cattle-lifting, and, in spite of the rather hot time he had been experiencing, was engaged in driving, with the aid of his people, a herd of sheep and goats abandoned by the foe.

As Wood's party were carrying their wounded men, and now and then halted to give them stimulants, their progress was necessarily slow, and this delay led to serious consequences, for the large reinforcements they knew might arrive from Ulundi later in the day had, without their knowledge, actually arrived, and were marching parallel to their right front, and concealed from sight. Umtongo was the first to discover the proximity of this hostile array, and, although without an interpreter. Colonel Wood understood enough of his language, aided by signs, to comprehend the gravity of the situation. The colonel, having obtained a fresh horse, cantered across some very broken ground to a high bluff just under the Zunguin's Neck, and, guided by some of Oham's people, managed, not without considerable difficulty, to reach a point upon a ledge of rock whence he could, without a glass, see the movements and exact formation of the enemy's force.

The column was evidently the reinforcements expected from Ulundi, and had a portion of the English column not missed its way on the night of the 27th, it is tolerably certain they would have effected the object of their raid and retreated to the shelter of the camp without much loss. Wood knew of the despatch of this army on the 24th, but did not calculate that it could have compassed the distance it marched in three days. As matters stood, however, the colonel and his staff could see from their coign of vantage that the Zulu Army from Ulundi were marching in a line of five contiguous columns, with a line of skirmishers thrown out in front and on flank, forming the usual horns and chest. From subsequent description given by Buller, it appears that the first part of his task was successfully carried out; that the track up the Zlobani was correctly hit off, the Zulu entrenched caves triumphantly carried by storm, and a large quantity of cattle taken and driven off.

Had Wood's portion of the attack and that commanded by Weatherly appeared on the scene of action in time to support Buller's splendid onslaught, all would have gone well, but the delay caused by their missing the track enabled the Zlobani followers of Umbelini and

Manyanyoba to hold their own ground until the arrival of the Ulundi army. Buller did all that a skilled general could effect to bring off his men with small loss, but from the nature of the ground it was in this instance almost impossible for cavalry to work with any degree of celerity. The mountain having been carried soon after daybreak, a long off-saddle to feed the horses and an unavoidable delay of four hours were made, to enable the main division to come up. Suddenly the immense force of Zulus, seen by Wood from the Zunguin's Neck, was observed by Colonel Buller and Oham's scouts.

An immediate but orderly retreat was commenced, but could not be effected without the most desperate fighting and severe loss. The enemy had massed themselves on three sides of the mountain, and only one terribly steep path was left to descend. This was thoroughly blocked by the Zulus, who, under cover, rained bullets and assegais upon these devoted men, and then, when the moment came for close fighting, dashed in dense masses upon their thinned and weakened files. Halfway down this fearful gorge the road was so narrow and so steep that it was nearly closed up by the proximity of the tall cliffs on either side. These hills seemed to be formed of smooth and slippery ledges, over which many wounded men and horses fell, coming down upon the points of the *assegais* waiting below to receive them. Caves, with natural breastworks, like casemated batteries, were on either side of the path, wet and slippery with blood.

Colonel Wood was of opinion that the Ulundi army did not follow up Buller's retreat for two reasons: first, because its wonderful three days' march had in a great measure exhausted the men, who came in such haste as to dispense with provisions and spare ammunition; and secondly, on account of the powerful demonstration the main or second division made on their flank even at the eleventh hour. To the cool valour and devoted courage of Colonel Buller the safety of those who came back to camp was due. He fought at the rear of the retiring column, assisting the wounded, charged desperately at the dense masses of fiery Zulus who were pressing on with the thirst of blood, and not until he saw the last of his band through this terrible *kloof* did he turn his horse to follow his men, or to think of his own safety.

Seeing that nothing more could be done to help Buller in his retreat, Colonel Wood despatched a messenger to Colonel Russell, who by this time had commenced the ascent of the extreme westerly point of the range, to retrace his steps eastward, and to cover the retreat of the native allies upon the camp. Russell lost no time in carrying out these instructions, but before he could arrive several natives had been overtaken and speared. The Kambula camp was reached by the column about 7.30. Buller, on learning that our gallant young friend Barton had not returned, and was away on foot with the survivors of the Border Horse, some ten miles off, at once obtained permission from Colonel Wood to go in search of the party. The evening had set in stormy, and torrents of rain were now coming down.

Buller had been in the saddle for forty-eight hours, was severely contused, and had escaped death by almost a miracle; but setting a noble example, he obtained a party of volunteers, and taking led horses, started on his expedition. Seven men, who would probably have never reached the camp, were brought in by this gallant act, and these were the sole survivors of Barton's Horse. It would seem that in attempting to follow Wood's track in retiring they were overtaken and cut off.

They then attempted to retreat by the north and the Hyntecha Kloof, where the majority died fighting gallantly to the last. Splendid, manly, honest, simple, and taciturn Piet Uys, whose father, uncles, and cousins fought and fell in the old wars with Dingaan! On the evening of the 17th, after the conference in Wood's tent, he spoke in the most feeling terms of his children, of whom, like all Cape Dutchmen, he was passionately fond, and Colonel Wood, with that thoughtful kindness for which he is so well known, at once said that, should anything happen to the father, he would interest himself with the government to provide for the orphans.

Piet Uys could have easily escaped, but, like Buller, he would see the last of his men clear before turning rein. He was last seen with his back to the cliff, standing across the body of his favourite "*mooi paard*" (grey horse), with six large Zulus lying dead in a circle round him, his empty revolver in his left hand and his body pierced by two *assegais!* Colonel Weatherly's Horse went into action about eighty strong, and of these brave fellows forty-five were dead, including the gallant colonel and his brave, intelligent, and handsome son, a lad of fifteen, who, at an age when many an English youth is celebrated only in the cricket-field or on the river, had seen more of real fighting than many a veteran in the regulars.

Nothing could be more sad than Weatherly's death. At the fatal hour when all save honour seemed lost, he placed his beloved boy upon his best horse, and kissing him on the forehead, commended him to another Father's care above, and implored him to overtake the nearest column of the English horse, which seemed at that time to be cutting its way out. The boy clung to his father, and begged to be allowed to stay by his side, and share his life or death. The contrast was characteristic. The man, a bearded, bronzed, and hardy *sabreur*, with a father's tears upon his cheek, while the blue-eyed and fair-haired lad, with much of the beauty of a girl in his appearance, was calmly and with a smile of fond delight loading his father's favourite carbine. When the two noble hearts were last seen, the father, wounded to death with cruel *assegais*, was clasping his boy's hand with his left, while the right cut down the brawny savages who came to despoil him of his charge.

★★★★★★

Though in all these operations of which mention has been lately made Lord Chelmsford never once appears, it must not therefore be supposed that he had rested from his labours. On the contrary they were more incessant and arduous than ever. When the news of Isandhlwana first reached the colonies, it caused the utmost excitement and wildest apprehensions. Nothing less, it was averred, was about to happen than an immediate and overwhelming invasion of Natal by the Zulus. The black men were on the point of sweeping the whites into the sea. Lord Chelmsford's first duty, after an urgent application to the home authorities for reinforcements, was to render these alarms groundless. To organise of a sudden the defence of so extended a frontier was no easy task. How thoroughly and conscientiously it was performed the result testifies.

Another duty scarcely less urgent was the rescue of Colonel Pearson. And in this project he received aid, as valuable as unexpected, from the governor of St. Helena. No sooner did that official hear of Lord Chelmsford's urgent need, than he at once assumed the responsibility of sending on the garrison of his island—in all 160 soldiers—to the rescue. Captain Bradshaw, of H.M.S. *Shah*, chanced to be lying in the harbour, homeward bound, after a period of foreign service, but he hesitated not one whit more than the governor. He embarked the garrison, and on February 19th had anchored at Durban. There a naval brigade of 400 men was furnished from his ship; and thus it came about that long before reinforcements from England could arrive, and on the day that Zlobani was fought, Lord Chelmsford was already well on the way to deliver Pearson from his captivity.

CHAPTER 4

Effects of Zlobani

Before Lord Chelmsford set out on his march, Colonel Pearson had sent messengers to warn him that not less than 35,000 Zulus were lying in ambush between the Tugela and Ekowe, in order to assail him as he advanced to the relief of that post. Orders were therefore sent to Colonel Wood to make an attack on the Zulu flank, and so to create a diversion in favour of the relieving column.

Accordingly, Wood advanced from his entrenched position at Kambula Kop to the Zlobani mountain, where Umbelini's chief stronghold and *kraal* was situated. This Wood assailed, and though after a sharp engagement, which has been previously described, his forces received a decided check, yet he may be said to have achieved a success, inasmuch as he undoubtedly drew away a large part of the force that was intended to operate against Lord Chelmsford. Another result of this battle was that it gave the enemy sufficient encouragement to induce them to attack the English troops on the following day in their position at Kambula, thus enabling Wood to obtain a solid and decisive victory.

From various incidents that came under his observation Colonel Wood formed an opinion, subsequently verified by the event, that an attack upon Kambula would not be long in following the check at Zlobani; a vigilant look-out was therefore maintained during the whole of the night of the 28th. The rain came down heavily during the early part of the night, and shortly before dawn Captain Raaf was sent out with twenty-five men to reconnoitre, and, if possible, pick up any wounded or straggling Zulus, who would give any information as to the movements of the strong *impi* known to be in the immediate neighbourhood.

About ten a.m. Raaf sent in one of Oham's people—a most intel-

111

ligent and witty fellow—who gave a graphic account how he was captured when left behind with the recovered cattle taken from Umbelini. Having taken off his distinctive head-badge, although he was recognised by a friend, the Zulus were not aware that he was one of Oham's people, or that he had joined the English cause. On this account, therefore, he was allowed to accompany the Zulu *impi* as far as Umsedosi. While with the enemy he obtained a tolerably correct notion of their strength, and was intelligent enough to remember the names and titles of the various corps sent from Ulundi, and, indeed, of those which were retained by the king. Cetywayo, he said, had divided his entire military available force into three formidable columns of four regiments each.

One of these, consisting of the Naxeane, the Undomandi, the Ucaridanburg, and the Macalsiene, was sent without commissariat, and by forced marches from Ulundi on the 24th March, and part of this column, but not all, was engaged with Umbelini against Wood at Zlobani on the 28th. This column numbered at the least 20,000 men, and was well supplied with arms of precision. Four regiments were retained at Ulundi as a bodyguard and garrison to the king, and the remaining four were told off to attack Lord Chelmsford at or near Ekowe. Very early on the morning of the 29th, Oham's friendly Zulu, feeling anxious about his own safety, persuaded some of the Zulu braves to accompany him some distance from their camp, under the pretence of obtaining them some drink.

Taking a favourable opportunity, however, he managed to elude their vigilance and give them the slip, when he made the best of his way to Raaf's party, who at once sent him on to the Kambula camp, with the information given above. This fellow gave an admirable account of the state of feeling in the Zulu armies, and his opinion was that great numbers of the men were now serving entirely against their will, as they found that, instead of getting plenty of booty in the shape of cattle, stores, arms, and ammunition, they were the losers, as during their absence with the army the English attacked their *kraals*, and carried off their oxen, sheep, and goats. This man, although quite a chief at Oham's *kraal*, would seem to be a sort of headman, and to be in the habit of conversing familiarly with those in authority; for, he added, that it was rumoured that Dabulamanzi would, if another reverse fell upon the Zulu arms, in all probability follow Oham's example, and proffer submission.

On receiving the intelligence of the Zulu advance, Colonel Wood

112

had few preparations to make, for in the camp at Kambula each corps, each company, each subdivision, each section, and each man had a place allotted, and had been taught to be in that place at one sound of the bugle. The little fort was in an exceptionally strong position, being laid out upon an elevated and narrow ridge of table-land. A complete precipice, perfectly inaccessible to a white man, even though a born cragsman, guarded the right flank. On the left a succession of steep terraces had been utilised, and carefully entrenched with lines *en crémaillere*, or outworks, each successive line defilading its neighbour.

In front there was a narrow slip of land, hemmed in by ledges of rock, and swept by two 7-pounders, while immediately in rear, upon an eminence about 120 feet above the fort was a small *lunette*, with open gorge, and armed with two guns. The camp at first consisted of one laager, but an outer defence with a hundred waggons, and an inner one with fifty, had been subsequently added. Deep and wide ditches flanked by *caponnières* protected the outer boundary, and were traced in the form of an irregular hexagon.

As soon as Oham's Zulu had made his report, the garrison were called to arms without the slightest fuss, excitement, or confusion, and messengers were at once despatched to order the return of a fatigue party which had been sent out in the early morning wood-cutting. These men reported on their return that they had seen Zulus scouting about five miles to the west, and had they not been recalled they would have stayed to get further intelligence.

As soon as the men of the various corps were at their posts, Colonel Wood rode round to give them a few final words of encouragement, saying in conclusion, that he knew they would hold the fort while a man was left to fire a shot. The tents were then struck, and the men lined the shelter-trenches. The horses stood to their bridles, and the ammunition was served out by fatigue parties told off for this duty. Most of the waggon-drivers had been taught to use the Martini, and a few were served out to each face of the laager.

It was now nearly eleven a.m., and shortly after that time the Zulu battalions were seen on the base of the hill. Here they halted for a considerable time, and apparently a council of war was held. Their movements were evidently not so decided as on former occasions, and it was more than an hour before any forward measure was taken. The cattle had been brought into camp, with the exception of about 220 which had strayed away towards the enemy, and it could be seen that the Zulu chief had detached a portion of his men to secure these animals. On this movement being noticed, Colonel Buller was ordered out to reconnoitre, and to see if any opening offered for a charge upon the detached body of the enemy, but no chance presenting itself, the cavalry retired, and took up an excellent position on the north front of the camp. A flanking movement was now made by a body of Zulus, numbering about 7000 men. These regiments broke from line into column, and ran at a tremendous pace along a ledge situated at the commencement of the cultivated land.

As the object of this manoeuvre was evidently to entice the cavalry to attack upon broken and difficult ground, Buller and Russell very wisely restrained their men from attempting any sortie. The Zulus were in range by this time, but it was thought desirable to reserve all fire until they were massed in closer order. It was nearly half-past one when the action actually commenced, and it was opened by a cloud of skirmishers, who, fed by supports and reserves, began to scale the north front of the English post. Here, behind the outermost line of entrenchments, Buller and Russell dismounted a portion of their men, and each trooper being cautioned to select his object and fire steadily, some excellent rifle-practice was made. No sooner did a head or a shield appear above a rock, a boulder, or a tuft of grass, than the *"ping"* of the deadly Martini-Henry rang out, and in nine cases out of ten there was an enemy the less to encounter.

Some portion of the band of the gallant but lost Piet Uys, had been sent to reinforce Buller's attenuated squadron, and these men particularly distinguished themselves as highly-skilled marksmen. Many of these Boers still retained their old national weapon, the long single-barrelled *roer*, carrying an enormous bullet, suited for the destruction of big game. There is no doubt that, in the hands of a South African Dutchman, this is a terrible weapon. The conical bullet, perhaps, has a greater power of penetration, but the larger ball of the old-fashioned fire-arm, which in appearance is not unlike a huge duck-gun, inflicts a wound which rarely fails to kill.

These splendid Dutchmen shot with all the skill that hatred of the savages and a desire for vengeance for their late leader could teach, and there could be noticed on the countenance of each a sterner expression and a more deadly resolve than usual. From the little fort a gun was now brought to bear upon the advancing line, but without much effect, as an intervening spur gave shelter to the foe.

The attack was now renewed on the north side with redoubled vigour; the lines of skirmishers fell back, and were replaced by a more solid line, supported by the usual dense column in its rear. Buller saw that it became necessary to remount his men, and this movement of course weakened the effect of his fire. He retired, however, slowly, halting now and then, and sending a volley into the masses which kept pouring up the slopes. Major Russell, at this juncture, executed a brilliant dash at a body of Zulus who were running in an easterly direction to gain possession of a ledge of rock, and, catching them on a favourable piece of ground, with about a score of his men managed to sabre a great many without the loss of one trooper. This, however, did not suffice to check the steady advance, and orders were sent for Buller and Russell to retire slowly within the *laager*, their retreat being splendidly covered by Colonel Gilbert and four companies of his fine regiment, the 13th, who were posted on the right rear of the laager.

One company of the 13th, under Captain Cox, an officer of former Cape experience, held the cattle *laager*, which gave a splendid flanking fire along the front, and these men waited until the Zulus were within 300 yards, and then commenced an independent file firing at the same time that Gilbert's men delivered a withering volley. As Cox and his men could not see the right rear, to which point the principal Zulu attack had now changed, a skilful counter-attack was ordered by Colonel Wood, who directed Major Hackett to take a couple of companies of the 90th Light Infantry to advance over the slope, and open a cross-fire upon the enemy.

This movement was magnificently carried out by Hackett, whose men moved out into the open as if on parade, and with a steady advance, such as British troops are proud of, marched on to the rear of the cattle *laager*, taking the Zulus completely by surprise. Nothing could be better than the calm and deliberate firing of these men. Every shot told with deadly effect, and dark bodies and shields soon began to dot the ground. Still, however, the living stream rolled on, and as one warrior went down in the death-struggle, another, with a shout of vengeance, sprang into his place.

It was now a little after two o'clock, and while this attack upon the left rear had been progressing, another strong body of the enemy had succeeded in gaining an eminence from which, although at a long range, they were enabled to keep up an effective fire and inflict considerable loss upon the British troops. Captain Woodgate, of Ashanti fame, who had been sent to support Major Hackett, together with his lieutenant (Strong), here behaved with conspicuous coolness and valour. These three officers advancing well in front of their men and waving their swords above their heads, showed such an example to their men that the Zulus were driven back on that side, the ground intervening being strewed with bodies of Zulus.

A difficult and brilliantly led flanking attack was now effected by the Zulu general, who, having retired a body of his best marksmen from his right along his rear, suddenly opened a galling fire upon the left flank of the 90th companies, who, having accomplished their task, were now ordered to retire.

In executing this difficult movement Major Hackett was badly hit, and had to be carried out of fire. Lieutenant Bright, also of the 90th Light Infantry, was here mortally wounded, and shortly afterwards died. Bright was a clever, cheery fellow, a capital artist, a good musician, and a most accomplished officer. It was in running forward to pick up Hackett that poor Bright received his death-wound. Meanwhile, from the lunette on the height, Nicholson's two 7-pounders did capital execution. The Zulu main body had now come within range, and grape and canister were poured into their masses until the slopes over which they were advancing became slippery with blood. Standing on the parapet, Nicholson was, field-glass in hand, directing the pointing of his guns, when a chance bullet struck him in the temple, and he fell upon the weapon he was directing.

The loss was observed from the *laager*, and Major Vaughan was at once sent to replace this gallant young fellow. Colonel Wood, not to expose unduly the horses of the artillery, had retained under the shelter of the *laager* four guns in reserve. These were under charge of Major Tremlett, R.A., who, with his subalterns, Lieuts. Bigge and Hughes, waited until the Zulus were within a thousand yards, and then making a dash to a small open space of rising ground outside the *laager*, worked his battery with immense effect. The guns did not return to the *laager*, but were shifted from time to time as the movements of the enemy warranted, and to their splendid service much of the victory was due.

The enemy had now varied his attack a second time, and nothing could exceed the bravery and skilful manoeuvring of his regiments. While the 13th and 90th vied with each other in noble rivalry, and beat back the hordes of the Zulus upon the two most exposed flanks, the mounted men under Buller and Russell were occasionally led forward at a gallop by Colonel Wood, who, whenever he saw an opening for a charge, swept down and drove the skirmishers on to the main body. These brilliant charges became more frequent as the day advanced, and their effect upon the savages, unaccustomed to cavalry, was beyond all expectation. At three o'clock a hot cross-fire was opened upon a company commanded by Captain Woodgate, who had been holding a point which was in a measure the key of the position, as it commanded the only practicable road to the upper lunette, which, as has been explained, was open at the gorge.

The enemy still held the range which they had occupied during the earlier portion of the day, and Woodgate was ordered to retire under cover of the fire from two of Tremlett's guns, which had now taken a favourable position for shelling the height. After one or two shots had been fired, a shell was dropped into the midst of the party holding this position, and this had a most useful effect, for the other gun coming into action at the same range, drove the enemy's skirmishers to ground much farther off. For another hour and a half the troops continued to be hotly engaged with the enemy, who, when dislodged from one flank, swept round in the most perfect order, and swarmed in masses upon another side.

A message now arrived from Colonel Gilbert, to the effect that he could spare Captain Cox and a company from his flank, as the enemy's fire was slackening, and they were gradually extending their line to the right rear. Cox had been hit early in the action, but refused to leave his men, and led them on gallantly till the day was won.

At half-past four the Zulu general seemed to concentrate his principal attention upon the northern side held by the 13th, and some desperate rushes were made almost up to the muzzles of the English rifles. Colonel Wood rode up, and complimented Colonel Gilbert upon the splendid firing of his men, and he was at once greeted with a ringing cheer, which was heard by the enemy. All sides of the *laager* had been in turn attacked, and soon after half-past four a simultaneous advance was made on the north and north-east face. An enfilade fire, however, was made by a couple of Tremlett's guns, and the 7-pounder directed by Bigge did great execution at 800 yards. Some of the bodies afterwards examined on the northeast face were found to be literally blown to pieces.

The Zulus at this time were working round from the right-hand hill, and here, unfortunately, a few large boulders gave them cover. The soldiers were here almost on a line with the enemy, who in other places were below and above them. They had therefore to keep a sharp look-out that the enemy did not break through the line and penetrate the *laager*. They therefore kept pouring in a heavy cross-fire upon them at 200 and 300 yards, while the guns were defilading them on the right. The enemy could not stand this treble fire, and, though disputing the ground step by step, began reluctantly to retire. Colonel Wood at once sent messengers to the *lunette*, to open upon them as they passed underneath.

At this period Lieutenants Smith and Lysons, seeing some Zulus advancing to *assegai* a wounded soldier of the 13th, who was lying under fire in the open, rushed out, and, led by Captain Woodgate, carried the man under shelter. In performing this gallant action Smith was badly wounded, and Woodgate's helmet was smashed by a bullet. Surgeons O'Reilly, Brown, and their staff, one and all exposed themselves freely in attending to the wounded who could not be moved out of fire. Soon after five o'clock it became evident that the Zulu fire was beginning to fail, and the English commander at once led a company of the 13th to the right rear of the cattle *laager*, where the cattle had been for some time exposed to the fire from the hill.

A little later on Captains Cox and Persse were taken by Colonel Wood to the edge of the *krantzes* on the right front of the cattle *laager*, where the discomfited and disheartened Zulus were retiring from the direct fire. Cox extended his men along the slopes, while Persse occupied a higher ridge, and thus a double-banked and deadly fire was opened upon the retiring enemy. Having driven the Zulus over the edge of the hill, the two companies followed them up in a splendid manner; Cox, although suffering greatly from his wound and loss of blood, leading on his men in the most gallant style to the best points for continuing the fire.

Word was now sent to Buller and Russell to mount their men and pursue; and the mule battery opened "action deft," and played upon the devoted Zulus, the regiment of Macalooroo, under Umlinoya, suffering most. Buller's gallant fellows nobly avenged their slaughtered comrades of the previous day, and for more than seven miles the broken Zulu Army was chased like a flock of sheep.

It was subsequently ascertained that the attacking Zulu force consisted of nine regiments sent from Ulundi—making a force of 23,000—and of Umbelini's mercenaries; together forming a total of not less than 25,000. Tyangwayo was in chief command, whilst Umbelini held the next rank. The latter having retreated in the direction of the Upper Pongolo Drift, was subsequently pursued and killed by a patrol under the command of Captain Prior, of the 80th Regiment.

A wounded prisoner of some importance, by name Waishlahla, who was brought into camp on the 2nd, pointed out to Colonel Wood the bodies of Mubalawa and Maheitjesa, sons of Mnyame, killed on the 29th; and this man said that he knew that Mabuna, son of Umbangasita, Makweli, son of Umlandela, Ummensododo, son of Umfoonsa, and Tyangwayo, his brother, were also killed on that day, together with, according to the Zulu estimate, above 3000 of the king's bravest and best men! There is little reason to suppose that these figures are exaggerated; for 1500 bodies lay about the vicinity of the camp on the night of the 29th, though in the morning many were gone.

The sad duty of burying their own dead and the bodies of the enemies occupied the troops nearly the whole of the week following upon the attack upon the Kambula camp. During the 1st, 2nd, and 3rd of April above 800 Zulus were buried, while others were subsequently found in the caves and *krantzes* near. There were also 326 firearms picked up, amongst which were recognised one Snider belonging to the artillery, and 16 Martini-Henrys belonging to the 24th and 80th Regiments. Lieut. Bright, 90th Light Infantry, Lieut. Nicholson, R.A., Mr. Ferreira, interpreter, seven privates 13th Light Infantry, ten privates 90th Light Infantry, and one colour-sergeant, two Frontier Light Horse, and one of Buller's Horse were interred on the day following the attack, the service being read in the most impressive manner by General Wood.

Wounded Zulus were for some days continually brought into the camp; and these men, as soon as they found that their wounds were attended to, and that the soldiers were kind to them, became most communicative. They said that Cetywayo had sent all his available men, with the exception of two of his favourite regiments, retained as a bodyguard. These prisoners also all agreed in setting down the Zulu losses on the 28th and 29th at 3000 men.

When such individual and numerous acts of bravery were exhibited, it seems superfluous to pick out any special cases; but it would be wrong not to particularly mention the name of Captain Woodgate, whose gallantry and *sang-froid* were the theme of the whole garrison. During the whole of the action, and while carrying orders from the camp to the fort, he was more exposed than any other officer, and on more than one occasion he deliberately risked his life to save wounded men from being *assegaied*. To Colonel Buller also the same praise must be accorded for his self-devotion at Zlobani and the heroic manner in which he exposed himself in carrying off wounded men from the very midst of the enemy.

The situation being in every way so admirably adapted to military requirements, it was now resolved to make a permanent station at the Kambula Kop; and new works were day by day added to those already completed. Four well-constructed magazines were built in hollow and sheltered spots, yet close to the guns. Each magazine was lined with wooden frames, with splinter-proof timbers to cover the top, while sheeting planks were placed round the sides and passages. These frames were all perpendicular to the length of the passage—that is to say, across its breadth and about two feet apart. Eight feet thickness of earth was placed over the roof of each magazine, while a stout tarpaulin was stretched over the splinter-proofs to guard against the wet. Gabions were sunk to act in the place of cesspools, and receive the drainage, while a small parapet guarded the entrance to the passage, with a small hole through which ammunition was handed out.

Twenty men, in relays, were detailed for this work—that is to say, for each magazine—and although they were to a certain extent unskilled labourers, the officers taught them in such an excellent manner that the four magazines were completed in twenty-four hours. The ditches round the fort were so deep that bridges had to be made, part of which was permanent and part movable. Four entrances into the fort were left, seven feet wide, so as to admit the guns and waggons when supplies arrived. These entrances were closed by rifle-proof doors and gates made of strong planks, strengthened by cross-beams, and lined inside with thin sheet iron and raw bullock hides. These hides formed an admirable substitute for sheet iron, as they were quite bullet-proof and not liable to be set on fire.

Two more ditch *caponnières* were also added, to give increased flanking fire. The *terreplein* of each of these works, was sunk, so that the loopholes were within one foot and a half of the level of the ditch. This method had many advantages, and provided for the trick adopted by the Zulus of lying down in the ditches and counterfeiting death, until an opportunity is afforded for rushing at the parapet. A large supply of brushwood was usefully employed to improve the drains under the parapets, which suffered severely from the continued wet weather.

During spare hours the men were never idle, and from the brigadier downwards every officer was encouraged to employ his leisure in instructing the men in every species of field-defence. Gabions for *revêtements*, fascines, hurdles, sandbags, sods, pickets, *chevaux-de-frise* palisades, and small shell *fougasses* occupied the surplus hours not devoted to drill, recreation, and rest, and the few engineers belonging to the garrison declared that as pupils the volunteers at this work were beyond compare.

As in the last action it was found that the enemy were enabled to considerably annoy the troops by occupying some neighbouring eminences, the interior works were strengthened with considerable skill. The parapets were raised, extra traverses erected, and the *terreplein* sunk. The faces of the work were also made more nearly perpendicular to the enemy's possible fire. Shelter-pits for skirmishers were dug in all directions. These trenches being only required upon sudden emergencies were not made large, being only two feet wide by a foot and a half deep, and with a parapet built so as to reach a height of a foot and a half. These gave room and partial shelter to a couple of men, and to each spot the best marksmen were told off.

Horse trenches were also constructed, so that these animals could be sheltered from musketry fire. These were twenty-four yards in rear of the line of the infantry trench, and were five feet long, three feet wide at top, and two feet wide at bottom, with ramps, with a slope of one-half at each end. The parapets of these trenches were three feet high, with a thickness of two feet at the top. Half a dozen men could make such a trench in half an hour. These shelter-trenches were not so neatly dressed as the models to be seen at Chatham or Portsmouth, but they were pre-eminently workmanlike. They followed the contour of the rather broken ground, and were so made that cavalry could easily advance over them. At the intervals for this advance each trench overlapped its neighbour.

In contemplation of the removal of the waggons as soon as the advance should be made, roughly-built block-houses, made of contiguous logs placed vertically and quite bullet-proof, were constructed to substitute the shelter afforded by the former. The logs were twelve feet long, and three feet of this were buried in the ground, the buried ends being spiked into transverse beams; roughly-hewn beams formed the roofs, and over these was placed brushwood covered with four feet of earth. Green timber, of which there was an undiminished supply, was used, and, when necessary, this was covered with raw hides to prevent danger from fire.

Now, as the enemy had no artillery, and was not likely to understand its employment, even if provided with the guns captured at Isandhlwana, no defence could be more suitable. An ordinary work could, it was found, be often defiladed from a neighbouring height, while a well-made blockhouse, with carefully prepared roof, was, in every case, impregnable to rifle-fire. The plan for the roofs was as follows:—The young trees or branches were placed with the roots and thick ends inwards, while the smaller ends, sharpened and shaved down thin, were allowed to project over the walls of the building till they reached to within three feet of the ground. These boughs, if thin and with smaller branches between them, would not allow the means for climbing on the roof, should the Zulus attempt it, as they would not bear the weight of a crowd of men. In positions where the block-house could not be commanded by any neighbouring height, the roof was made flat and surrounded with a parapet of earth, so as to afford a second tier of fire.

Whilst these works were in progression, and some few days after the Battles of Zlobani and Kambula, some officers sitting upon a coign of vantage at an elevated part of the fort, suddenly descried three dark figures with shields and *assegais* coming at a rapid trot towards their southern front, along the hunting-road which leads from the Blood River and the Buffalo. At first they seemed steadily progressing, as if wishing to make a quick journey, but under no apprehension of pursuit. As they moved quickly on they were lost sight of in the bush, and as the surrounding country was made up of wooded *krantzes* and dark ravines, in which an army might lie concealed, it was not likely that they would be seen again for some time.

Away, however, a little to the right of where these men had passed, was quickly seen a larger party, consisting of about a score of savages, evidently in pursuit of the first-named runners. Their shields were flourished aloft, and their *assegais* waved in triumph as they followed the spoor of the first party, who had evidently taken to the bush as the most effectual way of escaping the keen eyes of their pursuers. Finding no traceable spoor which they could with certainty follow, they became suspicious, and commenced retracing their steps; and while this was being accomplished the three runners were seen to emerge cautiously towards the crest of the left *krantz*, now holding a good start of the pursuing party. While they came steadily on in the direction of the camp, however, a keen-sighted scout, who had taken the precaution to climb a huge rock which jutted out above the gorge, saw the quarry, and announced his success by discharging his rifle, and waving the *assegai* in the direction of the fugitives, whom it was now believed were messengers bringing despatches.

The Zulu, it should be borne in mind, is a born athlete; usually until forty or fifty, and rich, he is a spare man, with scarcely an ounce of superfluous flesh about him, and kept in continual training by constant exertion and no excess of food. He can, as a rule, at a moment's notice take a letter or small packet and run his eight or ten miles, or even walk his seventy or eighty, without breaking down. The ground over which the pursued were running was grassy *veldt*, while that upon which were the pursuers was sprinkled with low thorn-bushes, mixed with rocks and gravel. The pursuing party, however, were evidently the fresher of the two, while the messengers looked like men who were at the tail of a long journey.

The foremost party came struggling on until they reached some clumps of thorn-trees, which, affording cover, were taken advantage of to recover breath and observe the enemy's proceedings. The chase was now getting most exciting. Both the chased and the chasers were plainly visible to those in the camp, while the former only could observe their enemies. Noting here and there a footprint, which served to show them that they were on the right track, the Zulus in pursuit dashed down the ravine and some distance beyond where the three had doubled. The whole party went nearly 300 yards before the leaders halted in consequence of finding no spoor, and they then spread out like hounds in a fox cover to find some signs of their quarry.

It was really wonderful, the rapid and dashing manner in which these human bloodhounds strove to hit off the trail, while, having regained their wind, the pursued trio moved on, not in great haste, but quietly and with a considerable amount of care, that they might not be seen by their enemies. For this purpose, they now moved with the utmost caution over a ridge, and entered the wooded valley which lay at the foot of the kop, whereon stood the fort, being there completely out of sight of the pursuers, who were still puzzling over the spoor. The messengers—aware that they were encountering a double risk, as they knew that the wood into which they had gone would probably contain Zulu scouts sent to watch the fort, and who might have seen and laid in ambuscade for them—therefore trotted quickly across till they came to a somewhat open plain, with a line of willow-like trees, evidently denoting the banks of a stream.

Knowing that the pursuers in rear would be only temporarily puzzled by the loss of spoor, they therefore decided that the least risk would be incurred by making a final rush across the open road. Waiting for a moment to decide for what part of the stream they should make, they took a rapid glance around, and then made a sudden bolt for the plain. Scarcely 200 yards had been crossed when a terrific yell broke out from the pursuers, denoting that the pursued had been discovered by the Zulus in rear, who immediately sent a couple of scouts to the heights, the better to watch which side of the plain the messengers would make for. These scouts at once shouted to the party below, and, joining them, the whole body was quickly in pursuit.

The messengers had, however, almost 500 yards' start, and had obtained their "second wind." They knew, therefore, that, if not lamed by a chance shot, they would probably get over the river and under the guns of the fort before they could be overtaken. How or where to cross the river they seemed not to know, as in some places it is deep and wide, and in others shallow, with marshy banks and long weed-like grasses. Here and there, also, the stream bubbles and boils through deep gorges where only a baboon could ascend or descend. Seeing the willow-looking trees, the stout runners fortunately concluded that the water would be deep where they grew, and they wisely chose another part where low bushes prevailed, and where there were indications of a rapid slope in the ground, which would give them shelter in crossing. The pursuers were about 350 yards behind when the runners reached the bank, which they found steep and rocky, the stream itself running rapidly over a stony bed.

Although, like most Zulus, these messengers could swim well, they could not swim safely encumbered with a heavy gun, a bunch of *assegais*, a shield, and a heavy leathern mailbag, nor could they calculate on reaching the opposite bank without being shot at while so encumbered. On examining the bed of the river, they decided that it could be waded, and that if not, drowning was a more preferable death than torture in the king's *kraal*, which, if found with letters upon them, was sure to be their fate. They instantly decided, therefore, to cross.

Meanwhile those in the camp had not been idle, for half a dozen of Buller's men, known marksmen, were despatched to a point where they could command the drift and catch the pursuing party *en flagrant délit* if they attempted to follow too closely.

A few minutes' interval and a smart canter brought eight rifles in all to a favourable spot, where, unseen by the enemy, they could watch the proceedings of both friend and foe, and materially assist the crossing and escape of the former. Quietly dismounting, and placing two men, both as vedettes and in charge of the horses, the remainder took up position and waited for the *dénouement* of this somewhat exciting little episode. Not long indeed had they to wait. As the quick-scented harrier changes from scent to view, and gives melodious tongue as the quarry is in sight, so dashed on the pursuing white shields right up to the banks of the stream, and looking for a moment at the troubled waters, seemed to hesitate what course to pursue, imagining perhaps that some ambush was intended.

Meanwhile the messengers had effected the crossing in safety, though not without difficulty. Taking up more tightly the straps that bound the mailbags to their naked bodies, and with their rifles in one hand and shields and *assegais* in the other, they scrambled like cats down the bank, selecting those points where most ripples appeared upon the water, and managed thus to wade to the opposite bank. The depth was in no part greater than to cover them above the waist, although the rush of the stream was so rapid as to render a foothold difficult. As soon as they found themselves all in the water, they linked arms in some peculiar manner and thus opposed a successful barrier to the current, which otherwise, and if taken singly, would have been too much for them. Half a dozen Zulus who had outstripped their comrades were the first to enter the stream in pursuit, which at the point where they took it was not so favourable, and about fifty yards in width.

Though magnificent specimens of their race, burly and brawny, of immense chest depth and breadth of shoulder, the men in the stream could only advance at a slow pace in consequence of the slippery nature of the rocks and stones on which they had to tread, and on account of the rapid nature of the stream. So entirely were they absorbed in the excitement of the chase that they seemed to have no idea of encountering any risks .as they ventured into the river.

The main body of the pursuers meantime lined the banks, lustily cheering on their more adventurous comrades. Suddenly there rang out the simultaneous reports of half a dozen rifles, and as the smoke cleared away two or three arms raised above the blood-dyed waters of the torrent, which whirled the bodies of the baffled Zulus down and away from view, testified to the skill of the marksmen. As the surviving savages regained the opposite bank they gave a yell of defiance, which was answered by a volley which rendered several others *hors de combat*.

The horsemen then mounted, and rode down to meet the rescued runners, who turned out to be messengers from headquarters, and the bearers of most welcome despatches from the commander-in-chief to General Wood, in which his lordship, in the most cordial, kind, and flattering manner, sent his congratulations and thanks to the latter, and those under his command, for the manner in which his camp had been defended in the last attack.

A general parade was at once ordered, and the commander having formed up the entire force—horse, foot, artillery, and native contingent—read out in firm and ringing tones the welcome and honourable terms in which his lordship had expressed himself. By permission of the commandant three ringing cheers for the queen were then given, followed by three as hearty for the commander-in-chief.

CHAPTER 5

Organisation of Column for Relief of Ekowe

We must now turn attention to Lord Chelmsford and his plan for the relief of Ekowe. Tenedos was the base from which he purposed starting; the distance between this and Ekowe, even by the short route discovered and improved by Pearson, is a good thirty-three miles. To accomplish this distance in wet weather and with almost insuperable difficulties in the way of transport was no light task. However, by the 27th of March all was ready for a start, and the relieving column set out in the following order. The vanguard was composed of the Naval Brigade, formed of the seamen and marines of Her Majesty's ships *Shah* and *Tenedos*—640 men and two Gatlings; the 91st Regiment (ten companies), 900 men; 99th Regiment (five companies), 400 men; 3rd Buffs (two companies), 180 men; Mounted Infantry, 150 men; Mounted Native Contingent, 200 men; Native Infantry Contingent, 1600 men—making a total of 3720 infantry and 350 cavalry.

This leading division was commanded by Colonel Law, R.A. The second or rearward division, under the command of Colonel Pemberton, was composed of the bluejackets and sailors of the *Boadicea*, 200 menandone Gatling; 37th Regiment, 900 men; 3rd battalion 60th Rifles, 900 men; and two troops of mounted natives—thus giving a total of 2060 infantry and 190 cavalry—the two divisions making a grand aggregate of 6320 men, with 9-pounders and rocket-tubes. The convoy was made as small and compact as was compatible with the necessary carriage of supplies for the Ekowe garrison, and no tents were taken, each man being allowed only a blanket and a waterproof sheet. Still the waggons numbered 113, and there were also fifty Scotch carts on two wheels, and fifty-six pack-mules.

Each waggon was strongly spanned, having twenty oxen instead of the usual eighteen. Two hundred rounds of ball cartridge per man were issued, each soldier carrying seventy rounds in his pouches, and the remaining 130 being carried in reserve by the pack-mules. These waggons and pack-animals marched in the closest possible order, and were capitally flanked and guarded by Nettleton's Native Contingent on the right, and that commanded by Barton on the left. In spite of the comparative smallness of the convoy, Lord Chelmsford managed to bring with him not only full supplies for the fort, but twelve days' complete rations for his own column. Most of the baggage was brought across the Tugela on the 28th, and, in spite of the flooded state of the river; no casualty occurred.

The rain did not cease till daybreak on the 29th, when the passage was completed. It must be borne in mind that the Tugela at Fort Pearson, where the column crossed, is more than 600 yards wide, and it is then possible to estimate the difficulties encountered at the outset and before the journey could be fairly said to commence. But there were willing hands and zealous hearts to carry out Lord Chelmsford's minute and ever thoughtful instructions. No detail, even of the smallest, was omitted or forgotten by him, and with such men as Commissary-General Strickland, Surgeon-Major Tarrant, and his dozen assistant-surgeons, as well as Commissary Walton and Transport Officers Lawrence and Findlay, things were bound to go well.

The first plan was to force a passage through to Ekowe with all possible despatch consistent with the safety of the column and its convoy, and then, having exchanged the garrison and having provisioned the brave little fortress for a month, to form another and corresponding post on the Inyezani hills, leaving the latter munitioned for a similar period.

But this plan was afterwards considerably modified. On the first day's march no difficulties as to enemy or transport were experienced, the weather had cleared, and the road from the Tugela to Amatikula was far better than expected. Giving up all idea of the road by which Pearson had originally advanced when he first marched inland. Lord Chelmsford, following Colonel Pearson's advice, determined to move by the coast road, which crossed much more open country, was far more adapted for wheeled transport, and, indeed, for the march of all three arms, while it afforded fewer opportunities for the Zulus to attempt surprise. So satisfactory was the road on the first day's march that the only wonder was that it had not been previously destroyed by the Zulus.

In fact, the column had made good more than half the distance before any serious difficulties began. It will be seen in the map that at the villages of Inyoni and Amatikula their respective rivers cross the old road. Now, these rivers cross the coast road as well as the main road, flowing from west to east, and several halts at these two places are mentioned; it is not intended to refer to these villages, but simply to the encampments on the banks of the rivers of the same name.

On the arrival of the column at the Inyoni and Amatikula rivers the waggons were carefully packed in laager, and a well-made ditch and parapet formed around the camp. Sentries were posted at the various angles, and outlying piquets thrown well forward. No noise, or even loud talking was allowed, and the bivouac, for it could scarcely be called a camp, was each night as silent as a graveyard. Two miles beyond the Zulu bank of the Tugela good camping-ground was passed, but the troops pushed on without any difficulty to the Inyoni River, finding the road very good, although a little heavy for the waggons, from the rains. They were so lightly laden, however, that the drivers managed to get the oxen along at a fair pace, the waggons marching four, and sometimes six abreast.

Scarcely any water was met with, but numerous Zulu *kraals* were passed, so streams or wells must have been in the neighbourhood. The country through which the column passed was very open, affording no cover, except between three miles south of Inyoni and the banks of the river, where there is a gully with thick bush, which scouts carefully explored before the main body came up. The water of the Inyoni was found so brackish that the horses would scarcely drink of it. The Umsundusi and Amatikula Rivers are very sweet, the latter particularly so.

Leaving the Inyoni, the next river passed is the Umsundusi, which runs into the Amatikula, northwest of which lies the thorn country. The road thence to Ingesani is good, but there is a mud gully to the south of that place almost impassable after heavy rain. The column now marched more to their right, where the country was still open, although there was considerable cover in places, and *kraals* were seen around. Near the Umkukusi is a hill, which was occupied for a time, but from which nothing could be seen in the shape of an enemy. Keeping in a north-easterly direction they now reached a lower portion of the Inyesani, and then bore westerly for Ginghilovo, where on the afternoon of the 1st they encamped. Here a *parley* was held with the besieged, from Pearson's lofty signal-tower at Ekowe, and signals were made warning Lord Chelmsford of the impending Zulu attack.

A few words of digression may here be allowed to the system of signals which proved of such use to both Pearson and Chelmsford at this juncture. When Lord Chelmsford came first to Tenedos and Fort Pearson, it became evident to him that Pearson was so completely blockaded that runners could rarely get through. It was at the same time most essential to his plans that the general should know exactly how the colonel's resources were lasting, and the exact time to which his garrison could hold out. In this emergency Haynes, of the Engineers, was sent for, and asked if he could not do something with the heliograph, and bring the rays of the sun into requisition for the transmission of messages.

The general was at once seen, and although by no means sanguine, he gave every facility for the attempt. The difficulties were by no means light. In the first place there were no proper mirrors, and a most diminutive chamber looking-glass had to be employed. Then again there were no skilled or mechanically-trained workers for the improvised apparatus, and all appliances were of the most primitive nature. Another and, as was feared, the most fatal difficulty was that there was no way of attracting the notice of the Ekowe garrison, which from the nearest vantage-point, was fully thirty miles as the crow flies. Nothing daunted, however, by these obstacles Haynes persevered, and knowing that the lives of many gallant soldiers were dependent on success or failure, redoubled his exertions, which after long anxiety and delay were crowned with success.

The most sanguine hopes lay in the fact that the Naval Brigade were with Pearson, and that some of them would undoubtedly be trained to mirror signalling. After much delay in getting everything ready, Haynes chose a bright sunshiny morning and went to the top of a hill about five miles from the fort and commenced his flashing, but without the smallest success. The church tower at Ekowe could be plainly seen, but there was no response, and it was evident that the attempts at communication were not noticed, or, if noticed, not understood. Nothing discouraged, although a little chaffed by his comrades, the young Engineer continued day by day, whenever there was a gleam of sunshine, to attend the hill and work his mirror.

At length, after a whole week had passed before any indication from the garrison at Ekowe had been made, another thought struck Haynes, and this was to flash occasional whiffs of gunpowder to attract notice. To his intense delight, after a few attempts, this plan succeeded, and when a gleam was once flashed from the beleaguered fort in return the rest was all plain sailing. Another week, however, elapsed before a perfectly intelligible answer was received, and then it was found that Haynes's messages had been read from the beginning, but that they could not get the Ekowe answers at first to work. It is hardly necessary to mention how pleased Lord Chelmsford was, and that Haynes was sent for and thanked in the most flattering manner for his ingenuity and perseverance.

As has been said, Pearson informed Lord Chelmsford of the imminent Zulu attack; he also added that his last raid had been successful and that some cattle had been captured; and that the road he had cut under fire through the bush southwards would shorten the advance or his sortie by at least five miles, and that his people were under no apprehensions of famine or assault for some days. He had improved his defences, his parapet having a command of six feet, flanked by a couple of well-made *caponnières* on the northern and southern faces, with a loopholed building on the north-west and a sunken stockade in the south-west angle.

His four guns—two Gatlings and two rocket-tubes, in addition to his Martini-Henrys—he considered sufficient to render his fort impregnable to everything except hunger, and should the latter come on through Lord Chelmsford's inability or delay in coming, he purposed making a final and desperate sortie for life and liberty. This message was committed to writing, and read out to the men, who answered it with cheers of delight and enthusiasm.

At four a.m. on the 31st *ult.*, in the early dawn the troops paraded outside the laager on the Inyoni. For the first day the march had been without impediment or opposition; progress here and there, it is true, was slightly impeded by portions of swampy ground; but so eager were the men to get forward that the waggons were pushed vigorously through the mud by willing hands. The 57th Regiment, which had only lately arrived from Ceylon, were a little out of condition, and the fatigue and wet had told upon them in a greater degree than the regiments arrived from England. After a pleasant march, the Amatikula River was reached, where the camp was formed with the waggons as usual in laager, and shelter-trenches formed at fifteen paces beyond. The night passed without any alarm, and at six the column marched for Ginghilovo.

The drift on the Amatikula was so swollen that a long time was occupied in getting the waggons across it, and the result was that on

Monday very few miles were made. Soon after the troops had crossed, outlying bands of Zulus were seen by the scouts hovering on the flanks, but no attack was attempted. The largest body of these Zulus kept moving in a line parallel with the English march. Towards the afternoon of this day Barrow's Horse was directed by Lord Chelmsford to make a reconnaissance in the direction of the *kraal* of Makuendo, another of Cetywayo's innumerable brothers, and they returned with the news that they had surprised and fired it.

On the previous day Barrow had made a reconnaissance away to the north-east, at least seven or eight miles off, without falling in with any Zulus, whose power of concealment is certainly marvellous. At three o'clock on the 1st of April it became dark overhead, and a severe thunderstorm broke over the *laager*, wetting nearly every one to the skin. The night of the 1st of April will long be remembered by those who were with Lord Chelmsford on that occasion. Not a sound was heard in the camp, but outside the howls of the wandering jackal and the pariah dog were occasionally echoed by the hoarse scream of the foul birds which hover near a probable battle. At intervals were to be heard the patrols going their rounds in the fitful gleams of the moonlight, which were succeeded by black and rolling masses of cloud chasing each other in the sky, still thunder laden and lurid. The whispered "Who goes there?" and the almost inaudible countersign, told, however, that the utmost vigilance was awake, and that all felt that England's honour was at stake.

At two a.m. Lord Chelmsford, with two of his personal staff, went quietly round. This tour of inspection lasted till three o'clock, as here and there trifling details had to be changed and plans to be explained to the various officers who held the most important points of defence and danger. In front of the camp, but sheltered behind trenches and abattis, were that glorious and time-honoured corps, the 60th, who have no colours on which to record their proud deeds, but whose escutcheon is emblazoned with some of England's hardest-won fields. The general warmly eulogized the neat and workmanlike trenches made by his favourite greenjackets, and passed on next to Brackenbury, of the *Shah*, who, with his "little bulldogs," as the bluejackets term the Gatlings, held the right angle of the entrenchment.

Next to Brackenbury and his stout fellows came Clarke with his detachment of the 57th, and at the second corner were two 9-pounders excellently placed and guarded by their watchful gunners, eager as greyhounds held back in the leash. Round to the rear, but by no means a post of less honour, came the gallant old 91st, whose former Cape services have long been their pride and distinction. Four companies of this fine corps were here, and although the ranks were made up by drafts from many other corps, the men had wonderfully soon assumed the peculiarly smart bearing of their new corps. At the next angle were two more Gatlings, and prolonging the faces were posted two companies of the 91st, then three companies of the Buffs, and the 99th. As nearly as possible in the left rear face Lieutenant Cane, of the *Shah*, had charge of the ship's rocket-battery.

Lord Chelmsford expressed himself extremely satisfied at the manner in which all his arrangements had been worked out, and the low murmur of gratification, which even discipline could not repress, showed how much his men were devoted to their chief.

It was as nearly as possible a quarter past four when the welcome news was passed from man to man that the Zulus were seen in skirmishing order, supported by dense masses, away some miles off on the right front. It was nearly six o'clock, however, when the enemy's plan of attack appeared to be decided, and this delay, it has since been ascertained, arose from the fact that they had heard that the troops were about to inspan and march in the early morning, and the Zulu general anticipated catching them in all the confusion of starting.

At six a.m., then, somewhat favoured by the long grass and weeds which want of time had not permitted the soldiers to cut down, the Zulu array was hurled upon the laager. The regiments which came on in front were the Unembomanaba and Unemsilya. These were in extended order, but much closer than skirmishing order; in fact, somewhat akin to the Prussian infantry first attack. These corps were flanked by the usual horns or wings, composed of the Nokene and Nodwen regiments, formed in respective columns right and left. In the rear, as the body or heart of the formation, were the Monamonosi and a favourite corps of the king's called Zwawani. Somapo was in chief command, while his lieutenant was Dabulamanzi.

The British front enticed the Zulu force, as easy of attack, as the green-coated rifles were lying down in their shallow trenches, and their strength could not well be seen by the enemy. Nothing could have fallen out more fortunately, as the fire from those deadly tubes was doubly fatal in consequence of each man being enabled to have a firm rest for his weapon. There could not be a grander sight to a soldier's eye than to watch these magnificent specimens of savage pride coming on in their mighty strength to sweep the sturdy little riflemen from off the earth. Their white and coloured shields, the crests of leopard skin and feathers, and the wild oxtails dangling from their necks, gave them a terribly unearthly appearance.

Every ten or fifteen yards their first line would halt, and a shot would be fired, and then, with an unearthly yell, they would again rush on with a sort of measured dance, while a humming and buzzing sound in time to their movement was kept up. When the first line of skirmishers came to within 300 yards, a terrible and deadly sheet of flame flashed from the shelter-pits, and a great number of the Zulu warriors reeled howling to the earth. This only seemed to incite the main body to renewed exertion, for they came up hurling themselves through the skirmishers, and not even allowing them to get out of their path, but dashing them to the ground in their rage to close with the main array. A perfect *feu d'enfer* was now rained upon the denser masses of the Zulu main body, and this was maintained for at least twenty minutes, the savages coming on, still fed by columns from their rear, which deployed in excellent order as they reinforced the first line, and alternately halted, fired, and advanced, beaten back some scores of times, and returning as desperately as ever to the front.

About half-past six this front attack and onward rush was checked by the gallant 60th. Lord Chelmsford on several occasions rode along their line, giving an occasional kind and complimentary word when a particularly good shot was made or an especial coolness was observed. A sudden and wonderfully well-executed change of front was now made, without the smallest confusion or delay, and the masses of Zulus in front faced to their right and ran round in column to the face held by the 57th and 91st. Here their courage was, if possible, more pronounced, and their welcome was as hot. The 91st had not so many good marksmen in their regiment as the colonel could have wished, as many of his best shots were taken to supply Indian reliefs; but even the youngest soldiers seemed to gain skill and inspiration from what they had seen performed by the 60th.

The 57th ably fulfilled their share of the duty, and the torrent of lead poured upon the enemy from the murderous tubes of these seemed to literally plough through the hostile ranks. Notwithstanding this deadly hail, the Zulus came on with what was now the mute valour of despair. They had ceased to shout and only seemed anxious to dash upon the British bayonets. Twice, three times, a fourth, they literally swarmed up to the entrenchments, and if one break in the ranks had taken place the English loss must have been terrible.

At one moment, about a quarter before seven, it seemed as though they would have forced their way in, and upon several occasions wounded Zulus were noticed taking aim from behind the cover of the bodies of their dead comrades as they lay in pools of blood in the open. Now that they were within easy range from the tops of the waggons, an effective and galling fire was opened upon the Zulus by the native contingents, who were not allowed in the first line.

This double tier of fire was of great help, and so far thinned the assailant ranks that the second attack was after a time renounced as hopeless. Once more, however, a shorter, more desperate, but, as it proved, final rush was made by Cetywayo's doomed and devoted troops. This time it was upon the left of the laager that they delivered their last and supreme effort. They came up on this occasion to within ten or fifteen feet of the muzzles of the men's rifles, and, indeed, one or two of their chiefs seized the hot barrels with one hand, while they stabbed at the men with their shortened or broken *assegais*.

It was curious to remark the three separate lines of Zulu corpses which marked the respective ranges at which the death-dealing Martini-Henrys had swept their ranks. At 300 yards a thin boundary of black bodies and white shields might be traced; at 200 and 100 yards from our lines their walls of dead were more thick, and even up to the trenches wounded men had staggered to receive their *coup de grace*. In spite of all their efforts, the Zulus, however, never succeeded in bringing matters to a hand-to-hand struggle, though, if they had done so, Lord Chelmsford's admirable formation would have doubtless saved the camp, although no doubt with more than treble loss.

The last attack, and perhaps the boldest—for it was evidently the most desperate—was led most heroically by Dabulamanzi in person, who, with voice and gesture, came on a dozen yards in front of the leading files, as Ney led on his Guard at Waterloo. As on that occasion the French horsemen, so now these stalwart warriors could not stand against the calm, steady, and unflurried *mitraille* of English infantry fire, and at seven o'clock the flower of Cetywayo's warriors were scattered and broken on the plain they had so magnificently fought and drenched with their blood. Lord Chelmsford saw the moment had come; Barrow, who had already mounted his men in anticipation, scarcely waited for the orderly to repeat the permission to dash forth. Away charged the little band of sabres, and the mounted infantry came at the flying groups like a whirlwind, their sabres flashing bright in the morning sun, but soon dyed crimson with the best of the Zulu blood.

During the attack 1200 rounds were fired from the splendidly served Gatlings, and about 40 rounds of case and shrapnel from the 9-pounders, which subsequently shelled the bush as the Zulus fled for cover. Colonel Crealock, military secretary, and Captain Molyneux, of Lord Chelmsford's staff, had their chargers shot under them. Poor young Johnstone, of the 99th, was killed at nearly the commencement of the fight; and Colonel Northey was badly hit early in the action. He at first could not be induced to leave his men, but at last was reluctantly compelled to do so, as he fainted from loss of blood.

At the close of the action, however, and when he was aroused from his state of insensibility by the ringing echoes of the British cheers which proclaimed the flight of the enemy, he suddenly raised himself on one hand from under the waggon where he was lying, and joined in the shouts of the men, thus bursting the bandaged wound and causing violent haemorrhage to recommence. This gallant and valued officer subsequently died, on the afternoon of the 6th, having lingered in considerable pain for four days.

The entire English loss was wonderfully small, being but 2 officers and 4 privates killed, and 3 officers and 34 privates wounded! The Zulu loss, on the contrary, cannot altogether be set down at less than 1000; for the English troops buried between 700 and 800 Zulu corpses; and about 300 rifles, which they discarded in their flight, were subsequently picked up. Zulu prisoners stated that there were 180 companies present with Somapo and Dabulamanzi on the 2nd, and allowing each company to be composed of 60 warriors, the actual fighting array must have been about 11,000.

Information was also shortly afterwards received that another *impi* of about the same strength was despatched the day after Dabulamanzi marched from the king's *kraal* at Ulundi, and this latter force, misled by erroneous information, was unable to effect the intended junction with the force defeated. These prisoners also maintain that neither Somapo nor Dabulamanzi was aware of Lord Chelmsford's march for Ekowe till the day before he was assailed. Barrow's admirably planned and executed reconnaissances and raids on the 30th, 31st, and 1st undoubtedly had much to do with hoodwinking the Zulus, and it is tolerably certain that the military promenade made by him on the 31st towards the Ingoya led them to believe that the whole force was likely to operate in that direction.

On the following day, the 57th, 60th, and 91st were formed into a flying column, taking with them nothing but some light Scotch carts and three days' rations, together with the mounted men and some of the Naval Brigade, and started *en route* by way of the coast road for Ekowe. The portions of the Buffs, 99th, and a detachment of the *Shah's* men were left behind to garrison Ginghilovo, under the command of Major Walker. The heliograph was set to work, and Pearson replied that he should certainly come out to meet Lord Chelmsford and his party. At daybreak, therefore, Barrow went on with his horsemen to reconnoitre, and to see if any remnant or fresh portion of the Zulu Army lay between Ekowe and its relievers.

The line of country to be traversed was known to be more difficult than that passed, and it was thought that the Zulus might have had sufficient tenacity of purpose to make one more effort to stay the general's purpose. The first part of the journey was anything but pleasant; swamps, morasses, bogs, watercourses, *nullahs*, *spruits*, boulders, and all the disagreeable features of South Africa were in abundance; progress, consequently, was very much impeded, and at one time it was thought the troops would have to encamp on the way, and make a two days' march of the journey. Several small but awkward streams had to be crossed, and the General very wisely served out an extra ration of grog after the passage of these places.

After travelling about five miles, a halt for breakfast was called, and here Barrow rode back to report that all was clear in front, and that not a single Zulu could be seen, although the plains and bush had been most diligently scoured. Barrow reported that in the direction he had been, assegais, shields, feathers, ear and head ornaments, skins, furs, blankets, and even guns were lying about in profusion, evidently cast away in the hurried and headlong flight of the Zulus to their *kraals*, but that no bodies, however, had as yet been seen by the scouts.

The shrill notes of the bugles sounded the halt, and soon after the "Prepare to dismount," and "Offsaddle." Although no precaution was neglected to guard against surprise, a certain amount of latitude was now allowed, which on the previous three days' marches had not been sanctioned. Piquets, as usual, were thrown out on the neighbouring heights, and a chain of vedettes posted, which commanded ten miles of country in every direction. This being effected, the infantry formed up and piled arms, the cavalry off-saddled, and the horses, having first been allowed their usual roll in the dusty *veldt*, were turned out, under the protection of a guard, to enjoy a short graze, having, of course, been previously knee-haltered.

This knee-haltering process is universal throughout all the Cape

Colonies, and is effected in the following manner: by simply taking a couple of half-hitches round the horse's fore-leg with a strong rein or reim attached to the neck-strap, which brings the animal's head towards the ground, and effectually prevents his running away. This is the simple precaution adopted by all travellers in South Africa. The men now were told off in sections to draw water and collect wood to make fires for their morning or midday coffee. The officers collected in groups, and compared notes and exchanged anecdote and repartee.

After an hour's rest, which men and horses required after their severe four days' work, the bugles again summoned all to the ranks, and they started anew to complete the journey.

From this halting-place the road had a rather dangerous appearance, and every precaution was taken, lest Dabulamanzi should have received any reinforcements, which would enable him to attack the somewhat weak column at a disadvantage. The road over which they were passing was in itself open and fairly easy of transit, but not far to the left, and running parallel to the waggon-track, there were patches of bush so dense that horsemen could not enter, and they had to be examined with the aid of an infantry contingent, a few of whom had fortunately been brought in case of an emergency of this sort. Not far from the foot of one of the ascents to Ekowe on the left of the column lay the spot where Pearson was attacked on the 22nd January, and which, although called the Battle of Inyazani, is some distance from the banks of that river.

Some cavalry were taken over by Barrow to explore, but nothing marked the locality of the action except a large mound and a roughly carved cross where the dead were laid. On this cross were roughly cut the names of those who lay at rest below. Leaving at length the bushy country, the column now came to some steep and broken ground, and here were seen the remains of some of the waggons which had to be abandoned from Ely's convoy. Strange to say, some of the contents, tins of provisions and other stores, were still intact; but no arms nor ammunition had been left behind. Seven miles from Ekowe the troops came to a plain from which they were divided by a broad and well-worn watercourse. Here they faced the steep and scarped sides of a mountain, and in the distance could see a long unbroken range over which the sun was beginning to set.

At this spot the Zulus had evidently attempted to impede the advance, as part of the road had been cut away. Engineers, however, soon remedied the damage, and they were enabled to push on; although it

138

was fortunate that they had no waggons, as it was not without considerable effort they managed to get the two-wheeled carts across. As soon as this spot had been passed, the whole character of the landscape changed as if by magic; and as the wind freshened and carried away some misty clouds, the remnants of the late rains, a splendid prospect was seen, as the column wound its slow trail along a steep and rugged *kloof* leading into a fair and fertile valley beyond. Here, however, was a position that might have been held for some considerable time had the enemy chosen this spot to oppose the march.

A sheer precipitous rock frowned on the right, and the only possible track lay exactly under its base, where with a few resolute savages above, huge boulders and masses of rock could have been hurled upon the column as it passed. On the left was a spongy swamp perfectly impassable to wheels, and not particularly easy to troops or human feet. Here a short way up the mountain farther on were seen the remains of a ruined *kraal*, and of some huts apparently not long vacated. These dwellings were formed, as usual, of rudely twined canes wattled and filled in with clay, and they had somewhat the appearance of a cluster of huge beehives.

As the leading files quitted the low ground, signals were made by the advanced patrols that cavalry were in sight, and the General and several of his staff at once galloped past the column to the front. All anxieties were briefly at an end, for, mounted upon an exceedingly handsome charger, and attended by a numerous cavalcade, coming towards the column at a smart canter was the gallant soldier who had held his inhospitable guard at Ekowe for more than seventy days.

Lord Chelmsford at once spurred forward, and warmly grasped Colonel Pearson by the hand, whilst discipline for once gave way, and the respectful silence of the general's escort was broken by a cheer such as only English throats can give, waking up every echo of the Zulu caves and valleys.

Colonel Pearson brought with him, according to his promise, about 500 men, and his staff, consisting of Colonel Walker and Captains McGregor and Knight. A long conversation at once took place, and the general informed Colonel Pearson that, anticipating the evacuation of the fort, he had left part of his force to entrench Ginghilovo, and make it a permanent station. The reasons for this were manifold. In the first place the approaches to Ekowe were easy to the Zulus, unencumbered with baggage or other *impedimenta*, but most difficult and trying to a European force. Ginghilovo or its neighbourhood answered every purpose as a link in the line of communications, while a site could be chosen equally as formidable in a defensive point of view. The column did not reach Ekowe fort till nearly eleven p.m. Here the welcome of comrades, fellow-messmates, and men of the same ships and corps, was a happy and fitting sequel to the *rencontre* of the reliever and the relieved.

It was a pleasant surprise to the general on arriving at Ekowe to find that matters had been made much worse by report than they were in reality. No gaunt and famine-stricken faces greeted him, but, on the contrary, there was a look of plumpness about most of the privates that savoured more of want of exercise than want of beef. In fact, the medical officer stated that the meat ration had never been diminished, as it was considered just as advisable to kill and consume the trek oxen as to see them die for want of forage. Now a trek ox in the best condition is not particularly tender, or even when fed upon the best of food, but when kept short of fodder, and without proper shelter from the sun and rain, he cuts up anything but well for beef Tobacco was the article most wanted by both soldiers and sailors, and the most agreeable gift that could be made by the relievers to their lately besieged comrades was this luxury in any form or shape.

The health of the garrison at first was good, but gradually the want of vegetables and useful medicines filled the hospitals, and made the cemetery more full. Anxiety, doubtless, had much to do with the sick-roll, and until communications with St. Andrew's Mission had been established a certain amount of uneasiness was felt as to how the war was going. Thirty deaths occurred during the seventy days the garrison were shut up, but several of these, it must be remembered, were cases of wounded men from the fighting at the Inyezani. At Fort Ekowe the hero of the scouting parties was undoubtedly young Rowden, of the 99th, who was detailed by Colonel Pearson to form a mounted infantry corps similar to Barrow's, from volunteers from the Buffs and his own corps. It is no secret that one of the great advantages we possess in our service is that we are never at a loss, when we can get horses, to find riders.

Most of our youngsters in the service would rather have a stigma on their morals than on their knowledge of horseflesh and of horsemanship, and herein lies the secret of our bearing up against our first reverses in Zululand. Every officer, serving in South Africa, whether cavalry, infantry, artillery, engineers, medical staff, or commissariat, gets rations of allowances for horse or horses, according to his rank. This is one of the secrets, combined with the sport and shooting, why South African service is so popular. Now both the 99th and the Buffs vied with the 13th and 90th in their equestrian proclivities, and, in default of regular cavalry, a large body of mounted infantry was raised, and in a great measure mounted from the horses belonging to the officers of their respective regiments, lent or sold to government for the purpose. Rowden's patrols were literally the "eyes and ears" of the garrison, and ably fulfilled all the onerous duties of light cavalry. In short the great value of their services may be gathered from the frequently and openly stated opinions of Colonel Wood and of Colonel Pearson, that all infantry regiments serving at the Cape should have at least one Gatling and one mounted company.

The great event of the camp life in Ekowe was the discovery of certain queer flashes of light on the white walls of the church tower. These, after puzzling many of the officers and soldiers, were at length brought under the notice of an officer of the naval brigade, whose education in the use of the heliograph enabled him at once to explain the apparent mystery. Three days of unpleasant suspense, however, elapsed before the first message could be clearly made out, and then three more before an apparatus could be rendered workable to reply. Fortunately, an old mirror was found, and this, with an empty wooden cartridge case, sufficed. Within the week, therefore, conversation was opened, and its effect on the imprisoned garrison was seen by all to be more beneficial than all the tonics the hospital could afford.

The next great event was, perhaps, the construction of the road from the fort to the lower coast trek, and the consequent excitement of having to work with the chance of feeling an *assegai* or Zulu bullet whizzing into the party. But the long days and longer nights were not at all devoid of recreation. Lawn tennis, bowls, ninepins, and quoits were devised. Concerts were organised, and dramatic recitals on a modest scale were improvised.

A cavalry raid had been, it will be remembered, made some time back upon Dabulamanzi's *kraal*, which was shelled and burned by Pearson. Some cattle and sheep were captured, and a desultory and running fight was kept up between the discomfited chief and the English patrols, which resulted in no casualty to the troops, while several Zulus were killed. This attack did not, however, extend to Dabulamanzi's private habitation, as its approaches were considered too far off and too difficult of access. No sooner, however, had Lord Chelmsford arrived at Ekowe than he determined to complete the blow already commenced. It was decided to effect this raid with Barrow's horsemen. The whole affair was promptly and admirably organised, and at eight o'clock on the morning after Lord Chelmsford's arrival a group of officers might have been seen on foot conversing, while their horses were led up and down by the attendant orderlies.

First of all, there was the commander-in-chief, and with him his military secretary. Colonel Crealock, whose recent wound did not even place him for one day upon the sick report. Major Barrow was there in his workmanlike dress, a Norfolk shirt patched with leather, high untanned boots, and a stout sabre at his side. With him were John Dunn, Lieutenants Sugden, Rawlins, and Courtenay, Captains Addison, McLean, and Ganz.

The entire force consisted of 50 mounted infantry under Barrow, 55 volunteers under Addison, and 120 volunteers under Ganz and McLean. At a quarter to nine the cavalcade had been inspected by their respective commanders, and in sections of fours moved off, amid the smiles and congratulations of the garrison. The road was as usual over that sweet-smelling and springy turf which makes walking an impossibility, and any pace but a canter impossible to man and beast. A little more than half an hour, or about a four-mile spurt over the elastic *veldt*, brought them in sight of Dabulamanzi's "great place." A rolling grassy plain, leading to some easy and gentle slopes, was presented to view, and evidently to the astonishment of most of the party, who had been accustomed to the rude and rooky fastnesses in which these *kraals* are usually built.

Beyond these smiling and inviting hills the *kraal* itself could scarcely be seen, but its locality was indicated by half a dozen Zulus running away with some cattle at full speed. Their measures were quickly taken, as their information forbade them to imagine that any trap could be laid, and they knew that the chances were ten to one against the chief having any force near enough to make a stand against them. Lord Chelmsford paid Major Barrow the high compliment of allowing him to take an independent command of the whole party, and remained more as a spectator than as an active official on the scene. Barrow at once detached mounted portions of his men right and left, while he led the way direct at a smart canter at the *kraal*.

The combined movement answered admirably, and the place was surrounded as if by magic, without any resistance or a shot being fired. Rawlins, and a few of Barrow's men, were now ordered to dash into the *kraal*, and as soon as they had assured themselves that there were no women of children or sick people there, to fire it in various places. They had scarcely galloped off to carry out this order when the silence was broken by the well-known "*ping*" of a rifle, sounding from the near vicinity of the *kraal*; and on looking in the direction from which the sound came the general and his staff could see a small group of Zulus taking deliberate aim at them. The distance was about 1200 yards. But the general still moved on, although the bullet had been well aimed, for it whizzed just over the head of one of his *aides-de-camp;* and John Dunn, putting up his glass, declared that he recognised Dabulamanzi by his head-dress and peculiar method of walking. With the utmost nonchalance John began to load his weapon, and remarked to the general, "See what will happen!"

One of the Zulus at this moment was coolly making a rest for his rifle upon a ledge of rock behind which his chief had retired, and Dunn, taking a long and careful aim, fired, and evidently wounded his man, who slipped back into the arms of a comrade. As the party sent to fire the *kraal* emerged from its outer enclosure, a heavy cloud of smoke betokened that their mission was accomplished. This white column hid the horsemen from the natives, who finding themselves in danger of being surrounded and captured by Sugden and his detached party, made a hasty and somewhat undignified retreat.

The general now moved round to the right, and found that the detached party under Nettleton were coming back with a fine young Zulu, whom they had overtaken and captured on the left of the *kraal*. They had secured him with some buffalo-hide girths, and he readily—too readily for belief—answered John Dunn's questions, informing him that the cattle, women, and children had time to escape from the *kraal*, as the horsemen were discovered cantering across the open. He added that had they advanced a little faster they would have captured them. But this was not their object, and they were rather glad not to have the encumbrance of prisoners, remembering the trouble Oham's wives and relations gave at Kambula.

The return to Ekowe was accomplished without further incident. On the following day, having destroyed as much of the fortifications at Ekowe as time would permit, they started upon the return journey to the camp at Ginghilovo. They overtook Pearson in laager after having marched about six miles; and while he and his column moved on later in the day to his destination on the Lower Tugela, Lord Chelmsford and his division halted and laagered camp at about two miles north of Inyezani, and about five from Ginghilovo. Here an unfortunate disaster occurred. A young sentry of the 91st fancied he saw Zulus in the bush. He at once, without challenging, as he should have done, fired. The picket to which he belonged at once retired, and as Dunn's scouts were out reconnoitring, they ran in upon the next picket to the camp, composed also of young soldiers of the 60th, who, mistaking them for Zulus charging upon the *laager*, recklessly opened fire, by which four of their own men were wounded and one killed, while nine of the unfortunate scouts were badly wounded.

The officer commanding the picket did all he could to steady his men, and did not even retire with them, so he was quite blameless. On the 24th April they reached the entrenchments at Ginghilovo, which were about two miles from the former *laager*, and Lord Chelmsford, having given the fullest instructions in regard to strengthening and guarding the camp, started on the following day for Fort Tenedos, *en route* for Durban, to reorganise an immediate advance.

CHAPTER 6

End of First Period of the Zulu War

The relief of Ekowe, and the Zulu defeats at Ginghilovo and Kambula, mark in a most unmistakable manner the conclusion of the first period of the Zulu War. All fear of an invasion of Natal was now completely dissipated, and the only task that remained to be accomplished was to organise a force to carry an offensive war into the heart of Cetywayo's kingdom. Kambula and Ginghilovo had neutralised the disastrous results of Isandhlwana—the winning blow was still to be struck. It will be remembered that after the fatal field of Isandhlwana no time had been lost in applying to England for large reinforcements, and the home authorities were in no way slack in acceding to this urgent appeal. Lord Chelmsford on his part was no less active in preparing and getting these forces to the front, and though to the ordinary observer there might seem to be a period of inaction and sloth, since there was indeed a necessary lull in active operations, yet in reality no cessation of labour really occurred in any of the military departments.

Within one month seventeen transports brought from England and landed on the shores of South Africa more than 9000 troops and 2000 horses, and all the munitions and stores, not only for the maintenance of such a force, but also for other regiments at the front. As each ship arrived at the outer anchorage, she was discharged without difficulty, and in no case were the troops kept on board an unnecessary hour, while in no instance was any damage, accident, or loss sustained during the process of disembarkation. To the enterprise, energy, and forethought of the contractors was due this satisfactory result; and the timely engagement of all the available steam-tugs by these authorities enabled them to carry out their undertaking in a manner beyond the most sanguine anticipations.

In addition to the employment of the tugs *Union*, *Somtsen*, *Adonis*,

and others, the hulls of two fine schooners were prepared and specially adapted for the accommodation of horses, and these being lashed
alongside the transports, with the aid of steam-cranes and excellent
wharves, the rest was not a matter of difficulty. The weather, most
fortunately, was generally favourable, while the equinoctial gales were
so slight that the dreaded bar was never quite impassable. There were
at this time no less than sixteen magnificent steam-transports, some
of them the largest afloat, lying at the outer anchorage. Twenty-three
vessels were in the inner harbour, and there were, irrespective of local
tenders and tugs, at least thirty vessels in the roads. Such a sight had
never been seen in the colony, and Durban will never again exhibit
such a martial aspect.

While from time to time returns were issued of the reinforcements as they arrived, no complete field state was made out till April
16th. It will be well here to give a brief resume. In the *Egypt* and
Spain were embarked at Southampton the King's Dragoon Guards,
whose muster-roll gave 31 officers, 622 men, 91 officers' chargers, and
480 troop-horses. In the *France* and *England* were the 17th Lancers,
numbering 31 officers, 622 men, 91 officer's chargers, and 480 troop-
horses. These embarked at Blackwall and Southampton.

The *Manora* and *Olympus*, from Southampton, brought M and N
Batteries, 6th Brigade Royal Artillery, with 10 officers, 536 men, and
161 troop-horses. The *Palmyra*, from Chatham, came with the 30th
company Royal Engineers, composed of 6 officers, 196 men, 2 officers' chargers, and 44 troop-horses. The *City of Paris*, from Queenstown,
brought the 21st Royal North British Fusiliers, with 30 officers, 906
men, and 7 officers' chargers. The *Russia*, from Portsmouth, embarked
the 58th Foot, consisting of 30 officers, 906 men, and 7 officers' chargers; while the same vessel brought the 3rd battalion 60th Rifles, with
30 officers, 906 men, and 7 officers' chargers. From Ceylon came the
67th Foot, which, with drafts from England, made up 30 officers, 906
men, and 7 chargers. The *China*, from Southampton, brought these
drafts, calling at Ceylon for the 57th.

The same fine and roomy ship brought also from Southampton
the 94th Foot, with 30 officers, 906 men, and 7 chargers. The *City
of Venice*, from Queenstown, brought the 3rd and 4th companies of
the Army Service Corps (transport branch); while the *Queen Margaret*, from Woolwich, brought No. 5 company of the same, the whole
making up 19 officers, 550 men, and 480 horses. The *Palmyra*, as well
as the Engineers from Chatham, brought 4 officers and 140 men of

the Army Hospital Corps from Portsmouth. The numerical strength of these reinforcements was therefore, according to return, exactly as follows:—Cavalry, two regiments, making 1250 sabres; artillery, two batteries, 12 guns, and 540 men; engineers, one company, 190 men; infantry, six regiments, 5320 bayonets; Army Service Corps and drafts, 1200; total, 8500 men and 1871 horses. The two batteries of artillery were not armed alike, the one being equipped with the usual 9-pounder field-gun, and the other having the six new 7-pounders similar to those employed in Abyssinia, but mounted, owing to the advice of General Sir John Bissett, K.C.B., upon the tall and special Kaffrarian carriages recently introduced into the service.

These carriages are totally diflFerent from the small 7pounder carriages with which the Abyssinian guns were fitted, as they are raised upon wheels five feet in height, the carriage, although lighter, being exactly the same as to size as that used for the 9-pounder of eight cwt. These little guns, however, weigh only 200 lb., and have rather a queer dwarfed appearance mounted on their long axles, between their tall wheels; but the plan was found in many cases successful in this and late Kaffir campaigns, owing to the obstacles presented to the dwarfed carriage by the long grass so abundant in all parts of the colony. Mules had also arrived for these guns from Malta and Gibraltar.

Most of the regiments brought out their own equipment complete and ready for the field—tents, waterproof sheets, cooking utensils, barrack and camp stores—which enabled them to be ready at once for the forward movement. This arrangement was not fully carried out by the Royal Artillery and Army Service Corps, as they had a long train of carriages to take to the front; but the company of the Army Service Corps which came in the *Queen Margaret* from Woolwich brought 100 splendid waggons, light yet of great strength, and others came from Queenstown in the *City of Venice*.

As the transports engaged for the infantry regiments had a considerable quantity of spare room for cargo, all the available space was utilized for stores, munitions, and supplies. Preserved meats, preserved vegetables, and other victualling stores were landed in quantities of an almost alarming nature, while about twenty tons of 7-pounder shells had arrived by the *Donald Currie*, *Duart Castle*, and other hired transports.

Undoubtedly the most interesting event to both civil as well as military circles in Durban was the arrival of the two cavalry regiments destined for the front. The absence of cavalry was indeed one of the great defects in our army, and had there been previously a couple of regiments of real light cavalry the progress of the campaign would doubtless have taken a far more favourable turn, while some of our misfortunes or disasters would never have happened. The value of cavalry was so abundantly manifested by the services of Piet Uys, Colonels Russell and Buller, Major Barrow, and Captain Rowden, that it would be idle to dwell upon the subject.

In the expedition, again, to Ekowe, how completely was the value of this force shown by Major Barrow's horsemen. This officer had not more than 200 sabres with him, while at least half of these were natives; but the completeness of the success achieved by General Chelmsford was attributed in a great measure by his lordship to the services of this contingent, who were literally the eyes and ears of the main column. They were, during the march, effectually scouting the country around, ahead, and in rear, and so constantly did they perform this work that the Zulu spies, who swarmed around, could not by any possibility get close enough to learn the real strength of the column. Again, until Zlobani, all or nearly all Wood's most brilliant successes were gained by his mounted men, and he himself never ceased deploring the absence of a stronger body of horsemen.

The *Spain* and *Egypt*, which brought out the King's Dragoon Guards to their first South African service, two as fine-looking vessels as ever floated in African seas, both arrived and anchored in the outer roadstead on Sunday morning, the 13th. The *Spain* made a most successful voyage, having left Southampton on the 27th of February, touched at St. Vincent on 16th March, and arrived at Capetown on 5th April. She had on board 312 troops and 286 horses. There was scarcely any sickness at all on board during the voyage, and all the horses, both officers' chargers and troopers, were landed in a very fair condition.

The horses submitted to the slinging, almost without an exception, with the greatest docility, and the whole of them were landed in a wonderfully short space of time, considering the distance and the state of the weather. The whole of the left wing of the regiment was on shore by half-past five, and was at once marched to the 17th Lancers' encampment at the foot of the Berea. The *Egypt* was a trifle less in tonnage than the *Spain*, but the difference would not be noticed by an unprofessional eye. She had on board 20 officers, 300 troops, and 300 horses. Her horses were also in excellent condition, and were all landed on the 14th. By the 16th the men had quite settled down in their new quarters at the cavalry camp at the Berea, and everything was in the most admirable order.

The ground was admirably chosen for the 1250 horsemen who were there under canvas, and the considerations of water, wood, health, and position were all carefully thought of and provided. Each regiment was formed in column of troops, occupying 172 yards of front and 130 yards of depth. From the centre to centre of tents was ten yards, and each horse picketed was allowed four feet by twenty feet. In front of the camp was a fine open space of level parade, which was employed as a parade-ground for duty, and an agreeable lounge and sort of out-door club after stable-hours. The hours for reveille and tattoo, the time for the promulgation of orders, the arrangements for rations and forage, the position of the brigade office, commanding officer's tent, head-quarters, commissariat depot, hospital and guards, the postal arrangements for letters and telegrams, the arrangements for water for men and horses, the police arrangements, the detail for guards and pickets, the detail of other duties, and the statement of returns required, were all noted in daily orders, and printed for circulation amongst men and officers.

By this means a system of discipline was established as strict and regular as if in presence of an enemy, and every officer and non-commissioned officer was made acquainted with the usual system of encampment in his branch of the service, and the principles which govern such arrangements, in regard particularly to quickness of change and means of transport, compactness, and safety from an enemy's attack by day or surprise by night. On April 12th General Lord Chelmsford and staff arrived back at Durban by special train from the Lower Tugela, *via* Saccharine, at 6.15. With him were Colonel Crealock, military secretary. Commodore Richards, and Lieutenant Milne. A very large crowd was at the station to greet the General.

Not the least notable figure among the brilliant group who waited to receive the commander-in-chief was that of the Prince Imperial of France, whose bright, intelligent face, as he conversed with Sir John Bissett, was lit up with the anticipation of a possible campaign.

Besides General Sir John Bissett and the Prince Imperial, there were present at the railway station Major-General Newdigate, Major-General Marshall, Major-General Clifford, V.C., Colonel Bellairs, D.A.G., Colonel Riley, Major Huskisson, Captain Somerset, Hon. W. Drummond, Captain Granville, and many others.

The 19th of April was a day that will long be remembered in

Durban; for then was seen a sight such as had never before been beheld in that town, and probably will never be repeated. On that day Lord Chelmsford inspected the two lately arrived regiments of cavalry, the 17th Lancers and the King's Dragoon Guards. As each regiment passed before the General, it was noticed that its rear squadron had attached to it half a company, and its usual complement of store and supply waggons. These consisted of four waggons, carrying three days' supplies of food, and one day's oats for the horses, four waggons for squadron equipments, such as tents, blankets, and cooking utensils, together with one head-quarter waggon and one quartermaster's stores waggon, making ten vehicles in all.

Each of these waggons was drawn by four horses, while the armourers' forge waggon was drawn by six horses, and the ambulance waggon by six fine mules. Both regiments were in full dress, but in the lightest possible marching order, but even in this, the men's average weight was not less than 18 stone. The regiments were both encamped at Cato Manor, which is admirably suited to cavalry purposes, having good grass and plenty of wood and water. The column extended a long distance, and wound its way along West Street, Abnel Street, Smith Street, past the Royal Hotel and the new club, and *via* Field Street back to the Manor, where the inspection and march past were held in the presence of the general-in-chief. The top of West Street was reached at half-past seven, and here the largest crowd was assembled.

At the corner of Gardner Street, the column was joined by Lord Chelmsford, who was loudly cheered, while handkerchiefs were waved from every carriage and window. Outside the town gardens a number of private carriages were drawn up, and each of these was fully occupied by ladies in full toilette, who seemed delighted at the novelty of the spectacle. Such a sight as six hundred British cavalry seemed to raise the enthusiasm of the townspeople to a great pitch, and on all sides expressions of delight and gratification at the fine and imposing appearance of the two corps were freely vented. The entrance to the picturesque grounds of the manor is situated within easy walking distance of the town, but in Natal few people ever think of pedestrian exercise, so that the cavalcade was supplemented by almost an equal number of mounted spectators of both sexes.

The cavalry brigade was, as soon as it entered the manor, wheeled into line, and after receiving Lord Chelmsford with a general salute, was minutely inspected by his lordship, who expressed himself in the most flattering terms to both Colonels Lowe and Alexander, remarking particularly the excellent condition of the 17th's horses. The Dragoons and Lancers quitted Durban for Helpmakaar on April 24th, and every precaution was taken by easy marching at first to avoid sore backs and girth galls. Lord Chelmsford also left Durban, and proceeded to Maritzburg: thence he travelled on to Dundee and Utrecht, and then on to Wood's camp at Kambula, where he arrived on May 3rd.

The main features of the plans for the fresh campaign were, roughly speaking, as follows.

Two principal forces, operating from separate bases, the one at Utrecht, and the other at Durban, were to be held in communication by Wood, with a flying column, and by Marshall's cavalry. The common objective of these four columns was to be Ulundi, the king's chief *kraal*. To keep up communications with these two flanks, to make occasional raids and dashes forward into the enemy's country, and at any favourable moment to convert a feigned into a real rush upon Ulundi, Wood was to retain his separate and independent command. His force, however, was to be largely reinforced, and more troops, if possible cavalry, sent to him. The first column, as it was called, under Major-General Hope Crealock, C.B., was to advance rapidly by the coast road, having as its respective bases of operations Durban, Fort Pearson, and Ginghilovo.

The other column, under the personal command of Lord Chelmsford, with Utrecht as its principal base on the extreme north, was to move also upon Ulundi. Meanwhile Wood, who had been strongly reinforced, while nominally forming part of Lord Chelmsford's headquarter division, practically retained his independent command, and formed a sort of flying column connecting the two flanks with each other. No. 1 division, then preparing for advance from the Lower Tugela, consisted of three fine brigades.

The First Brigade, commanded by Colonel Pearson of Ekowe fame, consisted of the 3rd Buffs, the 88th Connaught Rangers, and the 99th Foot, each of these corps averaging 800 bayonets. The Second Brigade, under the command of Colonel Pemberton, had in it the 57th, the 3rd battalion 60th Rifles, and the 91st Highlanders; while the Third Brigade, under Colonel Law, had a battery of Royal Artillery, the Naval Brigade from the *Shah* and *Boadicea*, at least 800 strong, with four guns and two Gatlings, Barrow's Horse, and a Native Contingent.

Before the final advance was made, it was determined that posts of communication should be established at the Amatikula and the Inyezani Rivers, over which pontoon bridges were to be constructed. Meanwhile for temporary purposes there was constructed over the Amatikula stream a cask bridge, by laying two slings, with eye splices at one end, parallel to each other, at a distance in proportion to the length of the casks. On these ropes were placed as many casks as required, bungs uppermost, and side by side. Across the upper surface of the barrels balks were laid parallel to each other, and the ends of the slings at each end of the row of casks were brought up and fastened to the ends of the balks. A small rope with an eye at each end was fastened to each sling between each pair of casks.

These "braces," as they are technically called, were then carried once round the nearest balk, and afterwards passed over to the other side, carried round the opposite braces, returned to its own side, and finally made fast to the standing part of the brace close below the balk by the assistance of two half -hitches. Each pier of casks made in this fashion can be completed in a marvellously short time by skilled engineers, and in a reasonable period by infantry who have been exercised at such work under the supervision of their scientific comrades. Transoms or beams connect each pier with its neighbour, while chesses and outriggers can be laid down as in a regular pontoon bridge.

When crossing these cask bridges great care, of course, has to be taken by officers in charge of waggons and supplies to see that no undue weight is carried beyond what must be theoretically allowed by the practical methods of calculating the relative buoyancy of the casks. In addition to the redoubts thrown up to protect the laagers at Amatikula and Inyezani, *têtes-de-pont,* or bridge-heads, were also constructed to form a safeguard for pontoons. The position on the Amatikula was admirable. It was not too steep, having a hill which formed as it were, a sort of natural glacis, with a slope of not more than 10 deg., which is about the most favourable for infantry. The post could not be overlooked at any point by the enemy, while the ground in front, being duly cleared, gave no cover.

The flanks rested upon natural obstacles easily strengthened. The post on the Inyezani was situated upon an eminence which fell away to the rear, so that its second line and reserves could be placed almost entirely under cover. A lake on one side and a ravine on the other, both perpendicular to the position, gave additional security to the fort, and these were strengthened by every means at disposal. In the armament of these works the guns were placed *en barbette,* as being more suitable to distant fire, and as our antagonists had no artillery with which they could reply, no anxiety was entertained as to their being dismounted. Guns, of course, which are fired over a parapet instead of through an embrasure have a far greater lateral range, and as the Zulu mode of attack invariably includes rapid changes of front and frequent flank movements, this mode of armament was calculated to prove the most effective, as fire could be brought to bear in all directions.

A further advantage is not to be lost sight of, and this is, that guns fired over a parapet, or *en barbette*, are higher, and could therefore plunge into such hollows as the Zulus invariably made for when exposed to the rifle fire. Gabions and screens of sand-bags, to save the men from undue exposure, were placed on each side of the guns.

While No. 1. column was thus employed in fort-building, Lord Chelmsford was moving from Utrecht to Kambula and Dornberg, where the following corps were being concentrated, to form his column:—General Newdigate's division, a formidable body, consisting of the 2nd battalion 21st Fusiliers, the 2nd battalion 24th, the 58th and 94th Regiments, with M and N batteries 6th Brigade Royal Artillery: Brigadier-General Evelyn Wood, V.C., who had now with him the 13th and 90th Light Infantry Regiments, Tremlett's battery of Royal Artillery, and Buller's Light Horse, strongly augmented. Major-General Marshall's cavalry brigade was also attached to Lord Chelmsford's command, and was composed of the King's Dragoon Guards, the 17th Lancers, and Russell's Horse, lately augmented.

Finally, Major-General the Hon. Hugh Clifford, V.C, C.B., whose former South African services go back to 1846, remained in command of the base, depot, and reserves at Durban, with Major T. Butler, C.B., of Red River and Ashanti fame, as chief of his staff.

It has been stated that one of the points at which Crealock was to concentrate his forces was Ginghilovo; but by the advice of high medical authorities, Lord Chelmsford ordered the camp at Ginghilovo to be broken up and shifted to a more favourable site near the Inyezani. The Ginghilovo camp, as far as strategical position was concerned, was all that the most fastidious engineer could desire, but upon sanitary grounds it was decidedly defective. It was favourably sheltered in a sort of hollow having defensive heights, which were to have been entrenched on either side, but want of good water and other reasons made it desirable to abandon the idea of converting it into a permanent post. Two strong laagers were now, therefore, constructed, the first about seven miles beyond Tenedos, and the other on the Inyezani river, a few miles from where Pearson's first battle took place.

The former of these was called Fort Crealock, the latter Fort Chelmsford. As far as position, and indeed construction, Fort Chelmsford had many advantages not possessed by Fort Crealock. The nature of the soil upon which the latter had been built had much to do with this; but there was but little choice in the matter, as it was absolutely necessary that a strong post should be built in this particular neighbourhood. The soil from which most of the works had been thrown up was unfortunately of a light, sandy nature, and of that particular unbinding description so disliked by engineers. The high winds and rain which prevailed also quickly found out the weak points in the armour of the fort, and working parties were constantly employed in restoring what had been blown down or washed away.

Fort Chelmsford, on the contrary, had the advantage of a fine firm soil, neither too heavy nor too light, while some quarries which had been found within easy distance were of great assistance in supplying the *revêtements*, galleries, and platforms. The fort itself was situated in a most picturesque part of the country. The pass leading into the valley through which the river runs was most romantic, winding through a delightful parklike country, crossed by rapid streams of clear, ice-cold water, and, as it narrowed became quite precipitous the road dwindling to a mere footpath, so narrow that mounted men could not ride more than two abreast.

The *kloof* was flanked on the precipice side by loose masses of rock, intermingled with trees and bush, and tangled with monkey-ropes and creepers of all kinds. The lower side sloped suddenly with a fall of about sixty feet to the bottom of the valley, where a rapid mountain stream, gurgling as it rushes over its rocky bed, fell soothingly upon the ear with a most dreamy yet refreshing sound. The other road to the fort passed through a still more beautiful valley, leading to the Inyezani *kloof* by a path cut in the precipitous face of the hill, whose sides were clothed with "*spekboem*" (elephant bush) and all kinds of flowering shrubs. The road looked down a declivity of some 200 feet, and was worn in places into a perfect staircase of boulders by successive torrents of tropical rain, and would be quite impracticable for any other species of vehicle than a Cape waggon.

The edge facing the precipice had no kind of parapet, and the dangerous nature of the pass was brought into still greater prominence by the debris of an ox waggon still lying broken up in minute particles at the bottom of the valley, where it had evidently gone down bodily with its span of oxen. The pass was, however, in spite of its danger, very beautiful. Convolvuli ran over the bushes in rich clusters, the star-shaped jessamine, with its pink undersides, and the magnificent specimens of mesembryanthemums, or fig-marigolds, of which there are hundreds of different species, having little transparent pellicles, containing pure liquid, scattered over the leaves, giving them the appearance of being sprinkled over with ice, and scarlet geraniums, attaining a height of ten or twelve feet amidst the thick bush, glowed on every side.

Meanwhile General Wood had been no less busy in and around his camp at Kambula. On April 17th he made a reconnaissance, at Lord Chelmsford's suggestion, to the Blood River, where a site had been chosen for a permanently entrenched camp, to serve as a large depot for the main body of the army. The ride was about fifteen miles, and the General and his party passed through some beautiful valleys, and through a path cut in the precipitous face of a pass whose sides were clothed with "*spekboem*" (elephant bush) and various other flowering shrubs. After four miles' cantering, they came to a part of the road which looked down a declivity of some 200 feet. The scene was, however, most picturesque. *Convolvuli*, the star-shaped jessamine, and the magnificent Strellitzea Regina flourished around, while scarlet geraniums attained to a height unthought of in England.

Two excellent sites for outposts were selected, by which communication could be kept up with the large depot and Kambula. These had commanding positions, and subsequently stone buildings were solidly constructed, square in form, but loopholed and flanked by ditch *caponnières*, while each fort contained accommodation for mounted men and a detachment of infantry. The Blood River, like most South African streams, is subject to great fluctuations. At that period, owing to recent rains, it was in flood, and in many places twenty and thirty feet deep, running with a powerful current that rendered it most dangerous to cross. The banks in most places are dangerously high, and the sides are steeply scarped by the force of the stream. Fording-places only occur at long intervals, so that when crossing in a flood, it is not at all easy to hit them off, while if once carried down by the force of the current the traveller has very little chance of escaping an accident.

The best way of crossing a flooded river, and that which was adopted by regulation in Wood's column, is the Kaffir plan of taking off some way up the stream, and so making a good allowance for driftage. Old settlers and Boers often undress themselves completely before mounting their horses, and carry their clothes and arms in a bundle on top of their heads, in case of a capsize. The stirrups should, of course, be crossed over the pommel of the saddle, and the horse allowed to have his head, the rider guiding him by the snaffle, while in difficult cases it is better for him to relieve his animal of weight altogether by floating alongside and guiding his head in the proper direction.

The Blood River flows through some fine scenery, bordered, however, at times by impenetrable bush and tangled vegetation of all descriptions, again winding under lofty mountains of basaltic rock, beautifully variegated with foliage, the thickets affording shelter to swarms of animal and insect life, giving rise on a still evening to a perfect babel of sound, amidst which the plaintive coo of the ringdove, the incessant chirp of the cicala, the twittering of many-plumaged birds, and the hoarse challenge of the bull-frogs are pre-eminent.

Conspicuous among the birds are to be noticed especially the little crested kingfisher, showing a perfect gem of colour, several varieties of sugarbird—a species somewhat allied to the humming-birds, or "hoverers," which are constantly to be seen flying restlessly over the aloe blossom—the orange-throated lark, the blue jay, and the Zulu finch, whose black and white plumage and red throat are set off by his long, streaming tail, the feathers of which are so prolonged that when flying they nearly overbalance him. The sandy plain on which the first fort was built was covered with stunted karoo bush, and was full of Duyker gries-buck and bush-buck, while two kinds of hares frequented the plain, the larger kind grey-furred like the English rabbit, and a small red mountain species, much better eating than the former, but which is scarcely considered fit for the European table, on account of its scavenging propensities.

Colonel Buller's Frontier Light Horse was also largely reinforced, its last augmentation being Captain Marshall's new troop of eighty well-armed and well-mounted men. A corps of Natal Mounted Kaffirs, principally recruited from the Edendal Mission-station, had also been added to this command, and they were found most trustworthy and intelligent. They were armed with the short Martini-Henry carbine, and drilled with equal steadiness to the European troopers.

Buller's Light Horse were destined to play so important a part in the final advance on Ulundi, that a short description of their appearance and equipment will not here be out of place. The first requisite was a well-built, sober, and intelligent horseman, who in addition to being able to shoot with the Martini-Henry, knew also how to groom, saddle, and nurse his horse. This was required to be an animal neither leggy, long-tailed, nor showy, but a clever, cobby sort of quadruped, who could climb like a cat, and obey its master like a well-broken spaniel, endued with a sound constitution, stout and wiry, and with a good turn of speed. The saddlery was, as far as possible, of a uniform pattern, and selected with considerable judgment and care.

The great points were that the tree should be wide enough in the fork not to pinch the shoulders, but yet not so wide as to let the saddle right down on the withers, with the seat long enough to sit in comfortably and to spread the weight to some extent over the horse's back. As many of the Cape horses are buck-jumpers, slightly-padded flaps were in vogue, although not insisted upon. They are a great protection to the knees in riding through bush. The saddle, of course, was provided with wallets in front, which contained a couple of pairs of socks, one flannel shirt, a tooth-brush, towel, and piece of yellow soap. Saddle-bags were worn only when going on distant expeditions, but a tin mug, knife, fork, and spoon, revolver, and flint and steel formed the invariable equipment of these troopers, and with a cloak or blanket à *discrétion* made up the weight carried by the horse.

Although the mounted infantry were volunteers drawn from various line regiments, there was sufficient leaven of the cavalry element to insure efficiency in the mounted duties. When the corps was first raised any kind of dress was worn, but fashion subsequently exerted its sway, and a rather picturesque "get-up" became almost universally adopted. Broad-leaved felt hats, with coloured *puggarees*, brown cord breeches, "baggy" to the last degree, and so patched with untanned leather that the original material had almost disappeared; a sort of patrol jacket, all over pockets, dyed mimosa colour, and also patched with leather of any colour on the shoulders and wherever the gun was accustomed to rest, brown laced gaiters, coming high up the leg, and even thighs, and a rough coloured flannel shirt, entirely open at the neck; such was the most usual costume.

The rifles were of various patterns—long Martinis, Martini-Henry carbines, some of Sharpens old-pattern Sniders, and Snider carbines. No bucket, however, was ever used, as it was considered better that a man unencumbered with a long sabre should have his weapon slung to his body, and not to his horse.

Another business that had also engaged Wood's time and attention was the shifting of his camp. In point of fact, in spite of every precaution taken, it was impossible to disguise the unpleasant fact that the very air around the Kambula camp was tainted with blood and putridity, while in the crevices and amidst the long, dank grasses which concealed the bodies of those who after the battle crawled away to die unseen, lurked the unmistakable odour of human decay and putrefaction. These were the principal reasons which induced our chief to consult with the medical authorities upon the advisability of moving away to fresh ground, and this determination arrived at, its execution was not delayed for an hour. In point of position, the site of our present *laager* was preferable to the one quitted.

The move was commenced and finished on the same day, the 14th, and there was every reason to be satisfied with the change. For beauty of site, as well as strategical considerations, the position could scarcely be surpassed. It was as nearly as possible a mile and a quarter west from the old camp, and towards the north-west the view was indeed splendid. In front, and across the river, lay a grassy plain, dotted pleasantly here and there with mimosa and camel-thorn. This plain is hemmed in by the Zlobani Mountains, on the right by the spurs of the Inhlomiga, and away to the left by the towering heights of the Makamba, rising to 4000 feet above the sea level. The plain narrows backwards between the ranges into a *"poort"* or valley, which, as it recedes away from the fort, presents a gloomy and terrific aspect of solitude.

Through it, and winding in and out amongst tall boulders of rock, and under dangerous precipices, past wild and gorgeous hollows, rank with the semi-tropical vegetation so peculiar to this part of the country, runs a small footpath, by which, through heavy clumps of thorny bush and over naked rock-bound ridges, the explorer reaches the fertile valley, over which till lately frowned the stronghold of Umbelini. To the north, and trending northwards ten or twelve miles, spread the Elandsberg mountains, the lower portion of whose sides are clothed with bush, presenting a sombre aspect, but the upper portions of which, formed of huge crags and scarped walls of granite and porphyry, glitter grandly in the sun, affording a glorious and ever-changing panorama, stretching out for miles to where the range terminates near the Pongolo River.

The new fort was not so elaborate in its design as the last, though, perhaps, as a defensive work more formidable. It was a six-angled enclosure, about sixty yards wide, having a wide and deep ditch, drawbridge, and platform. From its eastern angles projected two long curtain walls, which enclosed a roomy and well-guarded "*kraal*" for cattle and horses. These curtain walls were protected by the fire of the angles from which they sprung, and the cattle enclosure did not in the least interfere with the *enceinte*, as it had its own gateway and drawbridge.

At the end of the *kraal* furthest from the fort was a sort of irregular redoubt, with a deep ditch and earthen walls riveted with gabions, and defended by a formidable lot of cactus and thorns laid along the parapet. This constituted the fort, which was situated on a flat plateau overhanging a sharp bend of the river, which, being commanded by the guns, afforded a fine supply of water and an excellent bathing-place for the officers and men. This change caused a great improvement in the health of the division generally, and especially amongst the invalids in hospital. The deaths reported up to this period were the following: The Hon. Rudolph Gough, from dysentery; Lieut. Alderton, drowned; Captain Sandham, of the 90th, and Assistant-Commissary Phillimore, of fever; Privates Achmuty and Moone, 13th Light Infantry, of wounds received at Kambula.

On the 16th April there occurred an event that caused a great sensation in the camp, the history of which throws into the shade so many tales of romance and fictions of adventures in savage lands, and narrow escapes by flood and field, that it deserves to be recorded at length.

Among the fifty horsemen who rode under the command of poor Weatherly there were no better soldiers nor more popular comrades in their corps than two young Frenchmen, named respectively Ernest Grandier, a well-made, athletic, and powerful trooper, and Cramazan Baudoin, a stout and equally stalwart fellow. Both these men were natives of Bordeaux, and had come out to the colony together about five years before with the intention of trying their fortunes in the wine trade. They had both served their time in the French Army, and when the present war commenced could not resist the temptation of seeing service under such a gallant commander as Weatherly, whose knowledge of France and the Continent generally obtained him many excellent French and German recruits.

On the day of the Zlobani attack, owing to a thick fog which suddenly came on, Colonel Weatherly's troops missed their road and were unable to effect the junction with Buller ordered by Colonel Wood. The Zlobani mountain was successfully carried by Colonel Buller and his horsemen at daylight on the 28th March, and Colonel

Wood, who was with Russell's horsemen a few miles to the west, pushed forward on the same morning with his usual small escort of the 90th mounted men and overtook Weatherly, who had been all night trying to find the path. After the summit of the mountain had been gained, under a heavy fire, during which Captain Ronald Campbell and Mr. Lloyd were killed, Colonel Weatherly was ordered to move round to the other flank, and make good his retreat by the eastern side of the mountain.

In endeavouring to effect this movement they became surrounded and cut off by Zulus in front and rear. Weatherly was killed in the endeavour to save his son; a few of the troopers managed to cut their way, under the most terrible difficulties, through the bloodthirsty hordes hemming them in on the far east of the mountain; and Grandier and his friend, who had promised to keep together, found themselves, with a couple more of their comrades, in the midst of about a hundred yelling Zulus, while the bodies of their slaughtered friends were being hurled over the rocks on every side. Grandier, although slightly wounded in the side and wrist, was still mounted, but Baudoin's horse had been shot early in the day, and he was, bruised and blown, about to fall into the hands of the pursuers, when his gallant comrade sprang off his stout little horse and placed the fugitive upon the saddle, intending to mount also as soon as more favourable ground could be reached.

He saw, besides, that two of his comrades were not far in front, and twice called upon them to turn and make a stand. Unfortunately, the shouts of the Zulus and the clang of the conflict drowned his voice, and they rode on, while Baudoin in the meanwhile was compelled by a fresh rush of Zulus to turn up another path. Grandier now endeavoured to follow the two horsemen on foot, and being tolerably fresh he managed for some little time to keep on his legs. Passing some large rocks, however, which jutted out half across the pathway, a large piece of stone was hurled at him from above, and felled him to the ground, and while half-stunned and insensible, he was overtaken by half-a-dozen savages, and after receiving several severe blows from knobkerries, was seized and pinioned with thongs.

Even as they lifted him, he could see in the distance that Baudoin had managed to gain the troopers in advance, and the three seemed to have some chance of escape. Umbelini's "big place," or *kraal*, is on the south side of the Zlobani, and rather more than half way up from the valley. To this place, with a considerable amount of abuse, Grandier was led. Wounded as he was, beaten, bruised, and footsore, the prisoner was dragged round the slopes of the mountain, and forced by assegais to keep up with his escort, who, like all their countrymen, went at a sort of double stride or trot until the outskirts of the *kraal* were reached.

The sun was still high over the mountain when they reached Umbelini's stronghold, and he was at once placed under an escort in one of the Zulu huts, which formed part of the outer circle of the defences. It was constructed of strong wicker-work, and thatched with reeds and long grass, the door being merely a small matted hurdle, which did not so entirely block the doorway as to prevent those outside from looking in—an advantage of which the crowd of men, women, and children did not fail to avail themselves to the fullest extent. The walls were so thin that voices and conversation, even though carried on in a moderate tone, could be distinctly heard from hut to hut.

After having been kept without food or water for some hours, Grandier was brought the same evening before the chief, Umbelini, whose appearance he described as at the same time villainous and ferocious in the extreme. The interview was certainly an interesting one. The name and power of the ex-Swazi chief were known and renowned all over Zululand. The recent favour shown to him by Cetywayo, and his position being now considered as more that of an ally than a vassal, gave to his authority and prestige an influence they had never before possessed. So blindly did his people believe in him, that it is more than probable had further success crowned his efforts, he would have been found a dangerous rival for the Zulu throne. Umbelini sat in front of the principal hut, surrounded by about fifty of his favourite warriors, while large numbers of savages appeared to be leaving the *kraal* in different directions.

Masses of natives, evidently belonging to outlying tribes, were continually arriving, and reports were brought from time to time to the chief, who gave his orders rapidly and without hesitation. Upwards of a hundred principal men appeared to be in conference with Umbelini, and the number seemed rapidly increasing. Many of these men, Grandier had reason to believe, were ambassadors from Cetywayo, and officers belonging to the force he sent to assist in Wood's destruction. A covering of skins was fastened round the waist of each, and broad rings of copper were worn round the ankles and arms of those of the highest rank. Plumes of feathers adorned the heads of others who were more scantily clad, and who were evidently dressed for battle; while others again wore, something after the fashion of a Hungarian *pelisse*, skins of panthers or other striped animals.

The array of dusky savages was certainly imposing, and it was doubtless arranged with a view to effect. Each left hand supported a shield of tanned buffalo hide, surmounted with plumes of ostrich feathers. The same hand grasped a long bunch of *assegais*, while the right held the short stabbing-spear. Round the necks of those of high rank was usually a necklace, made of some wild animal's or possibly human teeth, from which hung a long knife or dagger.

About half of these warriors carried fire-arms, which were, however, of every conceivable make and pattern. The enclosure into which the prisoner was conducted, or rather hurled, was formed of the branches of the mimosa, strongly and tightly interlaced, and from the height at which it stood a splendid view could be obtained. All round were situated the huts of the tribe, looking like large-sized beehives, while close to each was a little walled space, in which the family wealth, consisting of oxen and other cattle, was kept. Umbelini, in spite of the sinister and ferocious aspect he wore, was not without a certain savage dignity which evidently impressed not only his own people, but also the *indunas* from Cetywayo. Perhaps the consciousness of their presence, and the knowledge that this scene would be reported to headquarters, gave an increase of grave majesty to his manner, and rendered him less repulsive in his action and speech.

There was a certain air of thought, and even command in his face, which was in striking contrast to those around him. His hair was plastered with the usual circlet of red clay, but his forehead was encircled with a fillet of young ostrich feathers, terminating in a single plume hanging behind. Heavy rings of polished metal spanned the thick part of his arms, and lighter ones of the same material were round his waist. The neck, thick, massive, and bull-like, was adorned with a necklace formed of human teeth, from which hung the usual knife, while over the broad black and hairy breast swept a splendid ostrich feather. In the right hand he held his only weapon, a kind of short but deadly knobkerrie, while his left hand rested upon his naked knee. But for the low forehead, the large mouth, and the enormous under-hanging animal lip, Umbelini might be described as a fine, indeed splendid specimen of the South African warrior.

A chief named Nyamba, who had spoken a few words of English to Grandier, now explained to Umbelini who the prisoner was, and under what circumstances he had been taken, and at his suggestion a Zulu named Nicohlomba, who was known to have once lived in Natal, was brought into the enclosure as an interpreter. "What have your English dogs done with the traitor Oham?" was the first question asked by the chief. "I hear the English are going to make him king in our land." Grandier, with composure, replied he knew nothing of Oham or the intentions of government. "What has become of Somtsen (Shepstone)?" was the next query, and then, when the prisoner said he was equally ignorant on that point, a whispered conversation took place between the two chiefs, who ordered Grandier to be taken back out of earshot, while the indunas were called up to confer.

After five minutes' anxious deliberation, the prisoner was again called up, and severely and minutely questioned as to the numerical force at Kambula camp, and as to who was in command. Through the Zulu interpreter, whose English was not much better than that of the younger chief, Grandier explained that he was but a simple trooper fighting for his daily pay, and knew little or nothing of the questions demanded. Umbelini, who had been hitherto seated, rose up, looked round the circle, and all at once poured forth a torrent of words, which seemed to have a wonderful effect upon the crowd. He seemed, as far as Grandier could glean, from the few Zulu sentences he knew, to be a sort of welcome to some honoured arrivals (probably the indunas from Ulundi), and when the Swazi chief had finished, a young Zulu chief named Umlambongwenya (the Great Alligator) stepped forward and warmly congratulated Umbelini on the battle of the previous day, and, pointing to the prisoner, added some request.

The circle of warriors loudly applauded, striking their shields, and this brought a large increase of numbers to the enclosure, where the applause became almost deafening. Grandier now fancied that his hour was come, and prepared to meet his death like a brave man; but to his astonishment, he was taken out of the enclosure, and once more bound to a heavy log or stump outside the hut, where he was allowed a little milk and a few husks of maize. When the next day came, at daybreak, he was again brought forth to be examined.

A circle was now formed round the unfortunate prisoner, who was firmly bound with thongs of raw hide to a stout tree in the centre, while round and round the youngest of the warriors danced, chanting a melancholy dirge, and keeping time upon his naked body with the butt ends of their stabbing *assegais*. Suddenly these proceedings were disturbed by the arrival of a new actor upon the scene. A tall and elderly savage, almost a skeleton in attenuation, bounded into the inner circle.

This creature, who was a sort of witch doctor, prophet, and sorcerer, commenced to execute a species of weird dance, spinning round the circle like a *teetotum*, and uttering all the time hideous and guttural sounds. All the warriors now remained silent, and crouched down, still keeping the circle intact, and kept time to the old savage's dance by monotonously beating the hard ground with their *knobkerries*. Again did the wretched prisoner, now almost worn out by cold, hunger, and thirst, believe that the torture was about to commence, and once more was he agreeably disappointed, for, stopping suddenly in the midst of his mad antics, the sorcerer flung himself violently at the feet of Umbelini, and breaking as he did so a necklace of human bones which he wore, pointed over his head towards the east, where the sun was now lighting up the hills and valleys towards Ulundi, in which direction, coming across one of the mountains some ten miles off, could be seen, so clear was the pure atmosphere, a huge and dusky column, marching with a cloud of skirmishers running along the terraces of the rocks lower down.

These were evidently the advanced guard of the *impi* promised by Cetywayo to Umbelini for the destruction of Wood's *kraal*; and as the troops came nearer and more into the sunlight, the principal warriors round Umbelini executed a war-dance round the sorcerer and Grandier, who had now given up all hope. The savages yelled, leaped, threw themselves bodily into the air, and went through all the motions of savage conflict, gesticulating, threatening, pursuing, stabbing the fallen, and rehearsing, in fact, the performance they soon expected to go through at the expense of the British soldiers.

The advent of the coming reinforcements caused the wildest excitement in the camp of Umbelini, and the horror of Grandier's impending death was infinitely aggravated by the helplessness he felt in not being able to give any warning to his gallant chief and comrades. Still lie was in some degree consoled by the subsequent reflection that his commander at Kambula was a most unlikely man to be caught unawares, and he therefore resigned himself calmly to his fate. He was not left long in doubt as to his destination, for the chief, Umbelini, considered that it would be a compliment to Cetywayo to send him a white prisoner.

While waiting, however, to be taken to Ulundi, he could not avoid seeing the preparations for the forthcoming attack, and, before his departure he witnessed the march of Cetywayo's *impi* towards Kambula. Before commencing the journey, his guards carefully stripped him of all his clothes, which they divided amongst themselves and wore, and likewise compelled him to carry their food. For four days, quite naked, with the exception of his hat and a pocket handkerchief, which he had tied round his waist, he was compelled by his escort to keep up with their rapid pace.

Barefooted, black and blue with bruises, and still suffering from exposure and want of nourishment, this brave and devoted soldier bore up against his torture. Each night he received a small handful of green mealies, and was bound tightly with sharp and cutting thongs to a thorn bush; and while he reposed, taking it in turns, one of his guards always kept watch over him. Now and then a *kraal* was passed on the road, and here old women and children, the only creatures who seemed left, came out and reviled and scratched him. On the fourth day, towards sundown, Grandier could tell, from what he overheard, that they were drawing near to the king's *kraal*.

When close to the king's *kraal*, on the afternoon of the fourth day's journey, one of Grandier's escort went forward to announce his arrival; and after suffering the usual torment of being tied all night to a tree (this time his clothes, now torn to rags, being given to him), on the next day at noon he was brought before the king, whom he described as a stout, medium-sized man, not so fat, however, or so tall as his brother Oham. Almost the same questions were now put to the prisoner as he had previously declined to answer at Zlobani, and this time the conversation was carried on by means of a man who had the appearance of a mongrel Dutchman, who was known to belong to Cetywayo's staff.

In speaking of his brother Oham the king seemed greatly enraged, and he vowed with many emphases that he would mete out a terrible punishment to him and the dogs who had dared to invade his country. Grandier, on being pressed, saw no reason to deny the strength of General Wood's force or the name of its commander, and he set it down at 4000 men, at which the king seemed astonished.

Grandier described the king as having frequent interviews with him, during which time he would have colonial newspapers, of which there were a quantity, translated to him. This fact will probably be taken as the means by which he had been able to learn Lord Chelmsford's movements; and if he read the contemptuous tone in which our soldiers were spoken of by these journals, it would, in a great measure, account for the poor opinion he seemed, till Ginghilovo and Kambula, to entertain of our commanders.

The king made frequent overtures to his prisoner, to induce him to join his army, and offered him wives, cattle, and land if he could assist his half-caste Portuguese armourer in unspiking the two guns taken at Isandula. These interviews continued for several days, and finally, when nothing could be obtained by the offered bribes, he was relegated to a hut, where, bound each night with painfully tight thongs, he was watched by relays of old women—hideous hags, whose amusement was to tear out his hair and stick pins into him whenever he endeavoured to sleep.

In the daytime, during eight days, he was regularly tied to a tree, and beaten by *assegais* by every warrior whose fancy it was to pass that way, the offers, however, being daily repeated. At last came a messenger with the news of the Kambula battle, the Zulu defeat, and the deaths of Umbelini and his brother; and the king's grief first, and rage afterwards, exceeded all bounds. Grandier was then ordered to be reconducted to Umbelini's *kraal*, and there to be tortured and put to death as a sacrifice to the spirit of Umbelini, and on the following morning, at daybreak, he was sent off, fortunately with an escort of only two men, each armed with *assegais*, and one with a muzzle-loading rifle. After ten miles' journey, the chief Inyaneme was met returning to Ulundi, and he was informed by Grandier's escort of the fate awarded to him.

About midday on the 13th Grandier, worn out with heat and thirst, bleeding and swollen feet, and nearly starved, sank upon the veldt, and said he could go no further. He was then severely beaten, so severely that he fainted; and his guards, fearing he would die in their hands, gave him some water, and took him to a ripe mealy field to eat. Being a man of iron constitution, he was soon revived; while, having his wits about him, he thought that now or never was his hope of liberty. When he had eaten a few mealies he returned to his escort, and found them reclining—the most dangerous antagonist, the man with the rifle, being in a sort of half-doze, while his comrade, who had just finished his midday meal, was employed in packing away the remnants.

Pretending to totter, Grandier sank upon the ground, as near as possible to the man with the gun, and while affecting to sleep, saw that no suspicion was aroused. The gun could not be reached, but the *assegais* were not far, and better, he thought, would be a bold struggle for life, even if he failed and was killed in the encounter, than the agony of slow torture he would otherwise endure. Watching his opportunity, and while the least drowsy Zulu was turning his head to take some snuff from the little horn usually worn in the ear, Grandier leant silently over, and noiselessly removing the stabbing *assegai* from under the arm of the man with the gun, with both his hands, for they were still tied, he nerved himself with the courage of despair, and throwing his whole weight into the blow, pinned the sleeping Zulu to the ground, while at the same instant he seized the gun. The shock was fortunately so great that the thongs were burst, and he had time to face the other savage with the loaded weapon, and both wrists free.

This spectacle so astonished the Zulu, that, giving one glance at his impaled comrade, he darted away without attempting to fight. Grandier, of course, saw the imprudence of risking a shot, so first despoiling the dead man of his ammunition, he crept away, and took refuge in the nearest bush. After the excitement of the last hour he was not sorry to obtain some rest; accordingly, he lay down for twenty minutes or half an hour, and then thought he might venture to reconnoitre as far as the top of the hill. He saw nothing; so, making his way back to the bush, he remained till dark, when he made up his mind to travel all night, finding his way luckily by his knowledge of the position of the constellations. The next day from a high cliff he watched a large body of Zulus quite close to him underneath, driving cattle in the direction from which he had come, and he consequently did not venture to move out of a cave he had found till they were well out of sight.

For two nights, and while subsisting on the small store of mealies he had taken from the dead Zulu, he travelled, fortunately in the right direction, but with more than one narrow escape on nearing Zulu *kraals*. On Wednesday, the 16th of April, just three days after his escape from his guards, this brave and resolute man espied, away in the distance, what to his practised eye was a European scout. Fortunately, he was seen. As the remainder of the patrol came up to him he fell, bleeding and exhausted, but undaunted, at the feet of some of Ralf's Horse, who were exploring, and was by them carried back to Wood's camp, where after some days in hospital he was able to resume duty and share in the final attack on Ulundi.

A very few days after the Battle of Kambula sufficed to clear the neighbourhood of Zulus, though occasionally skirmishes kept occurring farther off; and the latest news received was that Captain Prior, of the 80th Foot, proceeding with a mounted patrol from Luneberg in the direction of the Upper Pongolo Drift, had fallen in with Umbelini's force. Having trotted about ten miles from Luneberg he came up with about twenty friendly natives, who informed him that a band of Zulus were sweeping horses and cattle from the valley. Guided by these people, he made such good use of his time that he soon came within 800 yards of the marauders, who were driving away a large quantity of horses and cattle.

Captain Prior charged into and dispersed them, recapturing eighteen horses and a number of cattle, and, leaving these in charge of Lieutenant Ussher, he continued the pursuit, killing several of the enemy, amongst whom was a younger son of Usyrayo. It has since been ascertained that Umbelini was of the party, and was so badly wounded in the skirmish, that he subsequently died in a cave where he took refuge. This Zulu party was subsequently ascertained to be a portion of the force that fought at Zlobani, and one of the recaptured horses was recognised as belonging to a mounted private of the 80th, attached to Russell's Mounted Infantry.

CHAPTER 7

Lord Chelmsford with Wood at Kambula

On the morning of May 3rd, Lord Chelmsford, with Prince Louis Napoleon, Colonel Crealock, and Captain Molyneux, arrived at Wood's camp at Kambula. His lordship went round the camp soon after his arrival, and expressed himself uncommonly pleased with all the arrangements for the discipline and internal economy of the laager, being particularly struck with the quiet and easy way in which all the duties were carried on, without noise, excitement, or delay of any kind. The whole force was paraded in the afternoon for the general's inspection, and his lordship took the opportunity of saying a few well-chosen and appropriate words to each corps.

On the following morning (Sunday), after divine service was over, Lord Chelmsford suggested to General Wood that it would be advisable to make a reconnaissance in the direction of the White Umvolosi valley in view of choosing a suitable position for an entrenched camp within easy communication of Durnberg and Conference Hill. The day was fine and pleasant, and Buller, who had proceeded in advance with a number of his scouts, soon signalled back that the patrol were watched by a number of Zulus, who now and then exchanged shots with his men from the neighbouring hills.

After riding about three miles towards the southeast in the direction of the Zinguin Neck and Tonguin mountain, the party entered a rugged part of the country near where the White Umvelosi takes its rise, passing along by a winding road, flanked on either side by the usual mimosa thorns, when suddenly was heard the "*whirr! Whirr!*" of a couple of leaden messengers, though as yet nothing in the shape of an enemy could be seen. In a short time, however, Wood, who had cantered on in front, saw with his practised eye sundry copper-coloured bodies creeping along in the bushes below about half a mile off.

They were so intent upon watching Wood and his group of horsemen that they did not at first see that about a score of Buller's men had gained their flank, and almost cut them off. It was a most exciting scene as the mounted scouts were observed looking about for something in the shape of a path by which to descend the cliff which formed at this part almost a sheer precipice of some 300 feet.

They, however, managed the descent by a rough cattle-path, sending down showers of loose stones and debris before them as their horses half slid, half scrambled to the base. All this time the main body were crossing a wide plateau dominating the White Umvolosi valley and the river, which wound away at the base of the cliff. Looking over the precipitous sides, they could perceive a small herd of cattle penned up in a *kraal* in the centre of a little bush-covered flat adjoining the stream. As it was thought just possible that they might capture some prisoners, and obtain information of what Zulu forces were in the neighbourhood, and as cattle-hunting is one of the great ends of Zulu warfare, half a dozen of the general's escort were detached to see what they could effect. Getting down the cliff as well as they could, and then winding through the dense thorns in the valley, they soon found the *kraal*, and, having collected the cattle, began to return.

But this was certainly a puzzle upon which they had not calculated. To ascend the cliff by the way they had come was impossible, whilst on the other side ran the river, wide, and apparently very deep. Undoubtedly the only way out of the difficulty was to find a ford. They were, therefore, busily occupied in searching for one, when they perceived a mounted scout, sent by Buller, on the other side of the stream, who was gesticulating very excitedly, and trying to warn them of some danger. As it was impossible at the distance to hear what he said, one of the mounted men was sent down to the bank, and he came back with the news that the bush behind was full of Zulus. The warning did not come a moment too soon, for within fifty yards of them came a crowd of naked savages, yelling and flourishing their assegais and rifles, in evident triumph at the success of their stratagem.

Shouting, therefore, to the men who were staying behind with the cattle, the rest put spurs to their horses and galloped along the banks of the river, looking out all the time for any sign of a ford by which they might cross. Fortunately, this situation was seen by that portion of the party who had gone round by the opposite bank, and they had

170

come down to meet their comrades, having hit upon a ford higher up the stream. It was, however, a close shave, so close indeed that by the time they had reached the other side of the river by the ford, which was up to the horses' girths, and which they splashed through at a gallop, the Zulus had actually reached the bank, and were only prevented from capturing the two men left behind with the cattle by some well-directed shots. The yells of baffled rage from the disappointed Zulus were answered by a ringing cheer of triumph from the little party as they rode up the steep which led to the column.

The enemy, however, still continued to appear at various points along the sides of the hills, and in some places appeared to be dropping like monkeys from crag to crag, and it was easy to see that had not these scouts been mounted they would have been greatly at a disadvantage on such difficult ground. In fact, part of the line of scouts was in a valley surrounded by mountains, and from which egress, in case of a struggle setting in, would be difficult. They, therefore, hurried to get upon ground more favourable for cavalry movements. As they did so the rear sections had twice to turn and drive off the enemy, who began to come closer to their rear. Facing about, one of the sergeants charged right at them with half a dozen men, and silenced their fire on the right.

Several more galloped to the left rear, where the fire was as close as fifty and sixty yards, and on this occasion all had some narrow escapes. However, in about a quarter of an hour they rejoined the main body, having driven off the Zulus. Their horses' heads, however, had hardly cleared the bushes when shriller yells than before arose along the mountains in front, and they had only commenced riding into the plain when another sharp rifle fire began crackling along the ridges of the Zinguin Neck. As they steadily advanced this firing ceased, and the scene along the hills, which seemed to terminate to the west in a stupendous cliff, became more varied and interesting. Signal fire after signal fire of grass was lighted, and broad columns of smoke rolled into the air, and these being repeated from summit to summit, evidently showed that their movements were carefully watched.

A party of horsemen was now despatched to scour the valley on the left front, and all along the woods, which fringed the sides of the steep hills in front, jets of smoke marked their downward progress. As the crackling and flashing approached the bush where the hills met the plain, individual forms of Zulus could be seen, and then coming swiftly towards the main body there broke out from the dust and smoke a small mob of cattle, quickly followed by the skirmishers galloping in. Three small *kraals* were found to be in flames, fired by the Zulus as they retired with their cattle before the advance of the English horsemen. Two mobs of oxen could be seen, numbering some hundreds, which were being hurried away to inaccessible places. The ground in front of the English force was of a loose and calcareous nature, and, occupying as it did the space between mountain and river, was torn and cut up in every direction by deep white gullies, by which the Zulus were retiring sheltered from attack. The ridges between these gullies afforded the enemy additional shelter, being grown over with scrubby brush. Half the cavalry were now sent on to secure the approaches to the river, and guard against any surprise in that direction, and in a quarter of an hour, protected by the horsemen in rear, the whole body had passed over in safety.

The general, with his escort, had during the morning's march passed two of his old camps on the Kambula, and about twelve miles further on came to a piece of elevated rock or hillock, whence they had a capital view of White Umvelosi valley, while to the south-west they looked down upon the Blood River, Conference hill, and the dark shadow of the Durnberg range beyond. The Zinguin Neck, where the White Umvolosi has its source, stretched away at their feet, and farther behind they looked upon the southern slopes of Zlobani, rising in ledges or bastions in the distance. Just underneath the shoulder of Conference hill could be seen, in the bright sunlight, the white tents of Newdigate's division, and in the opposite direction was a magnificent view of the precipitous terraced ledges of the Zlobani, down which our brave fellows had been driven on the fatal 28th of March.

As soon as they reached the top of the Zinguin they were met by Buller, whose people were actively engaged in harassing a number of Zulus who were keeping up a desultory and harmless fire from the *krantz* in front. The breeze now cleared away the mists which hung over the valley, and away to the west could be made out what seemed to be a village perched upon a terrace half way up the berg. The face of this terrace presented a wild and singular appearance.

What at a distance had appeared level and almost unbroken was in reality a sort of amphitheatre not less than 1000 feet high, crescent shaped, and with a terrace fortified by low stone walls springing from rock to rock, and intersected by enormous fissures or caves connected with each other, and from which cover a dropping fire was kept up.

Leaving their horses in charge of some few of the men, some twenty riflemen dashed into these rocks, where the cover would equally shelter them with the enemy.

From this moment the ringing of shots was incessant, and it soon became evident that the Zulus were in force in a favourable position to annoy the column until they were expelled. The face of the crescent seemed as if some powerful eruption had flung from the top of the hill on to its sides tons of black and jagged rocks and stones, which, piled in wild confusion and irregularity on top of each other up the face of the position, presented innumerable caves and crannies, from which, as well as from stone walls, jets of smoke and bullets were continually issuing. The dismounted men, meanwhile, began to swarm up the right and left hand ridges, potting away as they advanced, while a few moved up the centre, firing when necessary and taking advantage of what cover was afforded. Several exciting incidents now occurred.

As these sharpshooters gained a better and more commanding position for their concerted attack, the Zulus, finding the situation rather too hot, one by one began to escape, and the moment a dusky form was seen gliding through the thorns half a dozen rifles rang out, sometimes succeeded by the crashing sound of the body of a huge savage rolling from a high rock to the stones below. It was simply wonderful to see in what small crevices these big Zulus had squeezed themselves. Sometimes three or four would get together in one spot, generally a small cave almost inaccessible from above or below, and which could only be approached by working along the sides, under the fire of dozens of other caves and loopholes, every one of which seemed scooped out for the purpose of creating a cross-fire.

As, therefore, to force home an attack on such positions was not the present object of Lord Chelmsford, whose purpose and that of General Wood had already been achieved in the survey they had made, the further retreat of the savages was not molested, and the order was given to remount and prepare to return to camp. As the mounted men extended to cover the rear of the column they were greeted by yells from the few Zulus they had not dislodged, and a few parting shots were sent after them as they descended the slope.

On the following morning Wood's entire force paraded at daybreak, tents were struck, waggons packed, and they bade farewell to Kambula range, upon which they had been so long encamped in various positions, and set out for Mayegwhana, where a fresh camp was pitched. Mayegwhana, or Queen's Kraal, is as nearly as possible three miles north of Bembas Kop, on which some months ago, and before he went on to Kambula, General Wood was encamped. In this new camp Wood had with him the following troops:—The 13th Light Infantry, under Major England (their colonel, Gilbert, having gone into Utrecht on a few days' well-earned sick-leave. Of this fine corps Captains Cox and Persse, both rather badly wounded at Kambula, were rapidly progressing towards convalescence. Poor Leet, the other major, still suffered from his crushed foot, which was caused as far back as February, but which accident did not prevent his saving a comrade during Zlobani's fatal day, and for which General Wood recommended him for the honour of a Victoria cross); the 90th Light Infantry, under their own commanding officer, Colonel Cherry; the two corps making up a compact and admirably homogeneous brigade of 1200.

One thousand men of Buller's and Russell's Horse, now in better condition than ever, and excellently mounted, with a body of Royal Engineers and Major Tremlett's battery of mounted guns; a total of 2000 Europeans, and about 1200 Native Contingent, or in all about 3200 men. With this force, and supported actively from its base, there could be no difficulty or danger in pushing on, and it was no secret that the inactivity they were forced to endure did not lie at General Wood's door, for he on more than one occasion suggested substitutes for waggon transport—the cause of the prevailing inaction.

Drivers and foreloopers were what could not be obtained. One of such is required for each span of oxen, the driver, who stands on the front seat of the waggon and wields an enormously long whip, and the *voorloper*, who leads in front. Ever since the day of Isandhlwana, and on account of the panic which prevailed from that date, due to the massacre of the natives then employed, it was found impossible to obtain their services in adequate numbers; and even of those still in employ numbers were continually deserting, for the purpose of returning to their respective homes within the border.

Meanwhile Wood was not idle, but, day by day, was making the best use of the scanty material at his disposal. The few drivers and foreloopers he had been able to retain were sent for and paraded before the general, who briefly explained to them that in future they should be armed, fully organised, receive regular rates of daily and liberal pay, while their personal safety should be looked after by the employment of strong guards and convoys wherever they had to march.

This, it must be allowed, was much wanted, and gave some grounds for complaint, as in the earlier stages of the campaign the waggons on too many occasions were not only allowed to straggle, but were left to shift for themselves. Behind General Wood's new camp, about ten miles off, and at right angles to Bempas Kop, was Conference hill, at which place General Newdigate was concentrating the bulk of his command. He had with him at this time the King's Dragoon Guards, the left wing of the 17th Lancers, part of the 21st Fusiliers and 58th Regiments, with N Battery 6th Brigade Royal Artillery.

Seven miles away from Conference hill was Doornkop, and here were the 94th Regiment, three companies of the 21st, and four of the 80th. Conference hill was within a very short time rendered practically impregnable by works constructed by the 94th Regiment, who, under Colonel Malthus, encamped at this spot; it also became one of the chief depots for the supplies of Newdigate's division. This depot was formed upon a *kop*, or rising ground, to the east of the larger hill, and was protected by three exceedingly well-built forts, constructed *en echelon*, so as to afford a mutual and most effectively-planned flanking defence.

The largest of these forts was a regularly traced bastion of polygonal form, with the length of its lines of defence in due proportion to the range of the weapons likely to be employed. The exterior sides of this work were 150 yards in length, and the parapet was sufficiently thick to resist anything but artillery fire. The flanks were drawn at right angles to the faces, so as to give a fire which could sweep the ditches and ground in front of the bastions. A couple of ramps were cut in the prolongation of the ditch of the face, whose surface passed through the crests of the flanks and lines drawn parallel to the bottom of the counterscarp of the opposite flank, and about two feet and a half above them.

This fort was garrisoned by the headquarters of the 94th, and the other two, of somewhat smaller dimensions, by a company each of the Royal Engineers and the 94th. Considerable pains were expended in the construction of these works, which did the Engineers and the 94th the greatest credit for the workmanlike line and scientific character of their tracing and position. The plan of these works somewhat resembled that adopted by General Newdigate at Landsman's Drift. The cattle *laager* was composed of waggons formed into square, while at each salient angle were small forts—one of which had artillery— and the whole were joined corner to corner, so that a straight line drawn between their extreme points would pass through the centre of each square.

By this means a perfect flanking defence was obtained, as each fort commanded two faces of the *laager*. Meanwhile the First Division had been by no means idle, in spite of their difficulties as to transport and the attacks of camp fever, which had been so much more frequent with them than with No. 2 column. From their base at Fort Tenedos a convoy was started every eight days to Fort Chelmsford, on the Inyezani, and its regular departure did much to expedite the forward movement of that force. On the 5th May, however, a somewhat more exciting episode took place. A convoy of the usual description was paraded on that day for the conveyance of stores and ammunition to the Inyezani. Fifty waggons, not too heavily laden, with 3000 barrels on each, were detailed under the protection of a convoy, composed of C Troop of Lonsdale's Horse, commanded by Captain Hampden Whalley.

From the foot of the fort whence the convoy started stretches a sandy plain, dotted with trees, and containing about 3000 acres. This, as it gets narrowed into a gorge between the river and the mountains, becomes broken, being intruded upon in every direction by foot-hills and watercourses. The fort cattle were grazing upon this plain under the charge of some of De Burgh's horsemen, when, as the convoy was passing across the first drift over the river, about two miles from the fort, but out of sight of the sentries, suddenly there sprang out from gully and *kloof* hundreds of swarthy warriors, who set to work, some shouting and firing, to try and drive the cattle away through the pass, whilst others, by far the larger portion, made a combined onslaught upon the leading and rear waggons of the train.

The convoy had, therefore, a double duty to perform—to assist De Burgh's men in recovering the grazing cattle, and also to beat off the Zulus who were attacking the waggons. Their object was to intercept the cattle now being run off at a rapid pace, and to secure the waggons in front and rear, which had been partly surrounded by the enemy. Whalley at once despatched a messenger to the fort for assistance, and remaining himself, as in duty bound, to repulse the waggon attack, detached about twenty of his best men, under his subaltern, to overtake and bring back the absconding oxen. The waggons were soon out of danger; for the men dashed at the Zulus in such a determined manner that the attacking party, not very numerous, soon bolted into the bush, but the other portion of the skirmishes deserves description.

After a gallop of a mile the leading troopers in pursuit came up with the enemy and the cattle, which were now all in confusion and involved in the broken waterworn hills at the foot of the pass, and, on looking back, they were astonished and considerably mortified to find that they did not appear to be followed by the rest of their party! Undauntedly, however, the sergeant in command pushed on, firing steadily and with fatal effect from the saddle, and, with his gaze fixed firmly upon the leading cattle, worked his way through the frightened oxen to the front. He was well and gallantly followed by half a dozen men, who had managed to keep up with him in his rapid ride in pursuit, and these fine fellows, nothing daunted by the numbers of the enemy, kept potting away at every Zulu that showed his head from behind the rocks, to which most of them had now retreated.

Suddenly the low banks of the ravine, up which they were now rushing, swarmed on both sides with the enemy, and it was evident that the driving of cattle into this position was one of the usual Zulu artifices by which they were so often successful. The Zulus kept up a feeble and ill-directed fire from the crevices of rock where they had taken cover, and all this time the troopers were employed in heading and turning back the cattle, a task which would have been far beyond their best energies had not an episode occurred which materially changed the aspect of affairs. Alone, in the midst of a score of enemies, the sergeant fought steadily on, loading, firing, advancing, and driving back the cattle as if he bore a charmed life.

The Zulus seemed paralyzed, and shunned his vicinity, for when he trotted to where a shield or *assegai* was seen, it immediately disappeared. He had, however, great need of help, for he had come to his last cartridge; but at that moment he felt a chance of life, as he heard the welcome shout of an English cheer, and, looking in the direction whence the sound seemed to come, he saw rapidly descending the steep *krantz* above the remaining horsemen of his party, who had chosen another and easier path up the ravine, which enabled them to take the Zulus in flank. The affair was now over; and although no prisoners were taken, the bloodstains on the rocks and boulders around proved that there must have been many wounded. The cattle were all recovered, and Whalley's convoy reached its destination without further molestation.

Great changes for the better had also been made in the distribution of the First Division. The 88th had been shifted from their former position on the extreme left front of Fort Tenedos to the commanding hill in its immediate front. In like manner they had been advanced *en échelon* to the extreme left front, and the Buffs had been moved in laager to the right rear of the 88th; while Lonsdale's Horse held the hill formerly occupied by the 99th.

The Naval Brigade were in camp behind the fort, with Cook's Horse posted in their immediate vicinity, and the Mounted Infantry upon a hill immediately below Lonsdale's Horse, and a portion of the artillery were on the old ground of the Engineers, with the Native Contingent in their front. The forts also belonging to this division on the Tugela, Inyezani, and at Ginghilovo were by this time completed, and admirably manned. To guard against any surprise pickets were posted in advance and on the flanks of these works, to watch every line of approach, and especially those where the country afforded cover and concealment. Sentries were placed at the salients of all entrenched works, and double sentries at the entrances, while whenever a drawbridge had been made it was carefully drawn up at sunset.

Occasional patrols during the day, and frequent patrols during the night and in thick weather were not relaxed, and the result was that the Zulus, seeing such activity, scarcely ever molested the working parties. In the ditches of the four coast-line forts were placed at intervals quantities of dry straw and brushwood, with oil and tar poured on in profusion, to fire in case of attack, and trustworthy soldiers were told off to fire these on the approach of the enemy. Sandbag loopholes were constructed on the tops of each parapet, while large beams, supported at intervals by sods of earth, were used for the same purpose. Fire-shells were placed in readiness to be rolled into the ditch. The distances from each parapet of all conspicuous objects was carefully measured and communicated to the garrison, and rods with whitewashed tops, so as to be visible at night, were erected, to mark the various ranges.

Port Durnford also had been reported practicable, and a fort and depot was being established there.

It was now the end of the third week in May, and all was ready for an advance, with the exception of the dearth of transport beasts and vehicles. It will be well, therefore, to briefly recapitulate the military situation. Crealock, now at Fort Chelmsford, was to connect himself with Port Durnford, and then to move along the coast with 10,000 men, supported and supplied by the Naval Brigade from Port Durnford. This was called No. 1, or the First Column. The second division in the north under Lord Chelmsford, his immediate subordinates being Generals Wood, Newdigate, and Marshall, was to move from Dundee, their advanced posts being already Doornkop, Landsman's

Drift, Ladismith, Conference hill, and Mayegwhana.

General Newdigate was now at Dundee, and had with him the King's Dragoon Guards, under Colonel Alexander; the left wing of the 17th Lancers, under Major Boulderson; the headquarters 21st Fusiliers, the 58th Regiment, with N battery, 6th Brigade, Royal Artillery. At Doornkop, about seven miles from Dundee, were three companies of the 21st, and four companies of the 80th. Wood occupied the most advanced point at the front, at a place called Mayegwhana, or the Wolf's Kraal, and had with him the 13th and 90th Light Infantry, 1000 of Bailer's and Russell's Horse, a strong native contingent, and a battery of six 7-pounder mountain guns. Again at Conference Hill were a company of Royal Engineers and the 94th Regiment, under their commanding officer Colonel Malthus.

In addition to Colonel Malthus's regulars there were at Conference Hill about 150 Basutos, some volunteers, and a few Natal natives, all under Captain Birkett. Dundee and Conference hill were the two most important bases of General Newdigate, and convoys of supplies were daily arriving at each. At Landsman's Drift there were three strong forts, with an intervening space for cattle. These had been designed by General Newdigate himself, and were constructed *en échelon*. They were occupied by the 21st, 58th, and five companies of the 2nd battalion Natal Native Contingent. These three entrenched fieldworks were admirably constructed, so as to afford each other mutual defence.

In tracing these works great care had been taken that the angles should be directed upon inaccessible ground, such as a *krantz*, a marsh, or a pond. None of the faces were exposed to enfilade, and the longest were so traced that they looked towards the ground over which an enemy would most likely advance, and which could be swept by the fire of the garrisons. These works were all somewhat in the shape of demi-bastions, and were constructed on a square or polygon, whose exterior sides were about 150 yards. The parapets were only breast high, but unusually thick, and, allowing for the penetration of rifle-fire at ten yards being twenty-one inches, the parapets had been constructed six feet, having a base 3.1, while the interior slopes are maintained by strong *revêtements*.

Works of this character have certain advantages, which are, that they require less length of parapet than a bastioned fort; although, on the other hand, there are these disadvantages, namely, that there is on each side one dead re-entering angle, *i. e.*, an angle perfectly screened from fire, and that the ditches are not so perfectly defended as they should be.

Each of the battalions above named built one of these demi-bastioned forts, and the tents of the respective corps were pitched outside two of the faces, with advanced pickets thrown out well to the front. In the interval between the right rear angle of the most advanced fort and the left front of the second demi-bastion was the cattle *laager*—a most important matter in Cape warfare. This arrangement enabled the fire from the first fort to rake the ground in its front and left faces, while the fire from the supporting work could do the same duty for the rear and right faces. From this description it will be understood that the works spoken of effectually covered the cattle *laager*, as well as afforded perfect cover for their garrisons. These three entrenched positions at Landsman's Drift were the delight and the pride of the regiments who built them; for although the Royal Engineers had been employed in general superintendence, it was well known that the actual designs were made by General Newdigate, and the labour carried out by the 21st and 58th.

The arrangements for the garrisoning of the posts in the rear of the advance were as follows:—Forts Pearson and Tenedos had each assigned to them two companies, while a reserve upon which they could draw was placed at Stanger. Upon the Lower Drift, down as far as Kranzkop, the river was to be guarded by 2000 of the border natives, under Captain Lucas, supported by 130 Natal Volunteers stationed at Thring's Post. Thirteen hundred men of the Native Contingent garrisoned Fort Cherry, in rear of the abandoned post which formerly covered the ferry drift, while the border for seven miles was watched by 2000 natives, under the superintendence of Mr. Wheelwright, at Hermanberg. Greytown was held by a garrison of two companies.

Three thousand natives lined the Umzinga border, and Helpmakaar was held by the Natal police and Carabineers. The defence of the new entrenchment at Rorke's Drift, now called Fort Melville, was entrusted to three companies of the 2-24th, which regiment was anything but pleased at the preference which had been given to the first battalion, newly arrived from England, by allowing it to participate in the active operations, while the second battalion was detained in the rear. There were to be four other companies of the 2-24th, and of these one was to hold Landsman's Drift, while two were to be left at Conference hill. At Balter's Spruit two companies, and at Burgher's Laager, Utrecht, and Luneberg each one company, formed the respec-

180

tive garrisons. It will be observed, therefore, that the line of the Tugela was but thinly defended, but, on the other hand, there was a strong chain of posts on the advance along the coast.

The force at this period in the Lower Tugela command may be summarized as follows:—The 2-3rd Foot, the 57th, the 3-60th Rifles, the 88th, the 91st, the 99th, or six battalions of infantry, mustering some 5400 bayonets, with M battery, 6th Brigade, battery 6th Brigade, 8th battery 7th Brigade, and the 30th company Royal Engineers. To these may be added the Naval Contingent, and with the native force the total amounted to quite 10,000 men.

But before the general advance was commenced there remained one sad duty to be performed—the burial of those who were still lying on the fatal field of Isandhlwana. It will be asked why this had not been done long since? The answer is simple: want of cavalry, want of transport, and want of opportunity. Since the day upon which the fatal surprise took place, there had rarely been an hour to spare from the trying ordeal of official duty, while the task of providing for the living and feeding the daily reinforcements had left no time to attend to the dead.

The moment, however, Marshall's troopers were upon the frontier, it was felt that something could be done, and every measure and precaution were taken to bring about a satisfactory result. To avoid any chance of a mishap or failure. Lord Chelmsford personally consulted General Wood when at Kambula, and subsequently at Utrecht, and it was decided that, previous to any formidable cavalry patrol being undertaken in force, a series of short reconnaissances should be carried out by the indefatigable Buller and his ubiquitous horsemen.

The purpose of this plan was twofold. In the first place, these perpetual scoutings so harassed the natives, that the majority, and certainly the wealthier majority, heartily wished the war was over; secondly, it was of great importance to learn the whereabouts of the two *impis* which it was well known had been for months waiting for the return of English troops to Isandhlwana, and this information was effectually obtained by Buller's zeal and activity. The first and most important reconnaissance was made by General Wood in person, who ordered a night-parade of a selected body of horsemen on the 9th May. The force on this occasion consisted of sixty Frontier Light Horse, under Captain D'Arcy; thirty Mounted Infantry, tinder Captain Brown; and forty Natal Native Infantry, under Captain Woodgate, 4th Regiment, General Wood's staff officer.

Their road at first was an easy descent into the fertile plain that was spread out like a map at their feet; it then wound up in a somewhat zigzag manner by the sides of a steep hill, flanked on the one side by a ravine, and on the other by a dense bush. Presently a black body was seen by the advanced scouts, whom Buller always sent out as "feelers," creeping through the bushes on the left, and in our rear came a second. No shot, however, was fired, but a Zulu perched high above, and sheltered in the bush, hails the passing troops in a jeering manner, and asks them to come and see his *kraal*. Orders had been given to the soldiers not to fire unless fired upon, and this act of forbearance seemed to wondrously puzzle the native followers, who were with difficulty prevented from "potting" the interlocutor. They had made about ten miles, when the sun began to shine over the edge of the horizon in all the splendour of an African morning.

The dew had fallen heavily during the night, and consequently the first rays of the sun produced a mist, which hung like steam over the valleys. This, however, soon cleared away and left the atmosphere clear and transparent, so that the far-off ranges seemed within a short distance of the column, whereas they were distant at least thirty or forty miles. This clearness of course was now a great advantage and aid to the English party, as it enabled the scouts to observe far ahead, and rendered surprise less possible than if the mist and fog had prevailed. Pushing on now at a canter, they soon came to a trek, which led them between two tall hills called Nkandi and Mhundla. Here in the *kloof* were two deep *spruits* or streams, which, however, were avoided by hugging the sides of Mount Mhundla, and it was noticed that waggons could be dragged without any considerable difficulty along this path.

The sun was now well above the horizon, and General Wood decided to halt, off-saddle, and let the men have their breakfasts. The place selected for the "off-saddle" was a slightly wooded ravine, amidst the rocks of which ran a clear stream over a grassy and pebbly bed, while behind was a range of rocky hills, the summit of which was crowned by huge masses of rock, looking from the distance like vast Titanic slabs placed by giant strength in their present position. Before was an undulating plain, bounded on the right by a river, and on the far left by a dense bush.

After one hour's rest the order was given to mount, and away they went, men and horses thoroughly refreshed and eager for the road. The bush was gradually getting thicker, and the road wound by a deep descent into a thickly-wooded valley. Every one of the party instinctively felt that Zulus must be near, and bracing up the body and nerves each man prepared for attack. The leader, too, thought the place suspicious, and made his dispositions accordingly. Two bodies of horsemen, each a dozen strong, were sent out to make a wide detour on either flank, while flankers were also sent out on either side of the column. The mounted men who formed the advanced guard closed to their centre, while those who had been extended in skirmishing order in the rear had orders to close up to the column when the defile was approached, ready to dismount, should it be found impracticable for horses. It is pretty well known that the most frequent point of attack in Zulu warfare is the rear of an enemy's column, particularly when the attack can be made in a defile.

The head of the column is often allowed to pass unmolested by the Zulu general, who waits patiently until the main body has gone by, and then commences a furious onslaught upon the rear, which will perhaps be followed up for miles. So these precautions were not superfluous. Where the column now was could be seen the traces of burnt *kraals* and partly destroyed mealie gardens, showing unmistakably that a skirmish had taken place not long ago, and Colonel Buller at once recognised the locality as the spot where, some ten days before, his scouts had had a skirmish with Zulus, on the occasion when an *impi* was reported as being in the neighbourhood of Balte Spruit. The anticipations of attack were soon verified, as a couple of shots rang out from the right wall of the defile, and this was at once followed by a tremendous shout coming from the rear.

The leading files of the little party had meanwhile reached the mouth of the gorge without any casualty, and General Wood and his escort on hearing the firing at once galloped back to the rear, from whence it came, and saw in a moment that Zulus were swarming on the sides of the cliff as if to attack in rear. The bugle at once sounded the halt, and the word was suddenly given for twenty men to wheel about and charge back in full force upon the unsuspecting foe, who imagined no doubt that he was going to be allowed all the fun of peppering the rear without receiving any punishment in return. With a hearty English shout these fellows, led by Buller, went straight at the enemy, and bursting over rough ground and through the high and tall grass drove the flying Zulus in panic before them. Buller's appearance at this moment combined an element of the heroic and the terrible with a strong infusion of the ludicrous and burlesque.

183

Leading his men on at a swinging canter, with his reins in his teeth, a revolver in one hand and a *knobkerrie* he had snatched from a Zulu in the other, his hat blown off in the *mêlée* and a large streak of blood across his face, caused by a splinter of rock from above, this gallant horseman seemed a demon incarnate to the flying savages, who slunk out of his path as if he had been—as indeed they believed him—an evil spirit, whose very look was death. The tables were now completely turned; the whole of the column is safely through the *poort*; one or two Zulus are seen limping away, assisted into the bush by their comrades, while the rest stand not upon the order of their going, but rush pell-mell to gain the shelter of the neighbouring caves. One large Zulu is seen to be badly hit, yet he manages to crawl away out of sight, and doubtless is assisted to escape by his fellows.

The fun is becoming fast and furious. Buller's men are in their glory. They have dashed into the *kloof*, and are driving the Zulus out of it in parties of six or eight at a time. Everybody who an hour ago was as silent and sombre as the grave thinks it now necessary to yell with excitement. The sun is now at the meridian, and the day fearfully hot. The pursuit has been carried through valley and over ridge; by *kloof* and through *bosch*, by *bron* (spring) and drift (ford), and the whole column is scattered in every direction. It is, in fact, a regular scramble, and all ranks and uniforms are mixed up together. But the chase begins to slacken; the pace is too good to last. The recall sounds, and the firing dies away to a few desultory shots, while the troopers canter back, dishevelled and puffing like schoolboys after a hard-won goal at football.

As soon as the skirmish was over, and the column clear of the *kloof*, the journey was continued, and they soon reached the southern termination of the high valley two or three miles farther on, where the mountains and table-land descend to the more level and open country beyond, and by a slope which was noted as too steep for waggons. The general was the first to set the example of dismounting and leading his horse straight down most of the way, while the main body of the little column diverged to the crest of the hill to the west, where the trek wound gradually away in a spiral manner to the plain. This path offered no obstacle whatever to the transit of waggons, and, moreover, avoided a deep *donga* which lies right across the straight course.

Here General Wood, having an engagement in camp, left Buller and his men with his orderly officers and escort, while they continued their investigations in a direction almost due south, over a series of rolling plains upon the table-land. The mist now most unfortunately came on again just as they had prepared their glasses for a good inspection of Ibabanango and the Alarm hill, but they could distinctly see on the right the high ground before the Khandi and Iheensi hills, and thence onwards to the Ingutu mountain, where they were not surprised to see that a signal-fire of considerable magnitude had been made by the Zulus as soon as they had fairly been discerned in the open and on lower ground.

About five o'clock they reached the banks of the Unyunyebea River, one of the tributaries of the Ityotyosi, which in its turn flows eastward into the White Umvolosi. Here, as the locality seemed favourable, they off-saddled, and the men cooked their dinners, or rather evening meal. Captain Woodgate, with a Zulu who had returned lately from Ulundi, and half-a-dozen mounted natives as escort, rode away to a *kop* some three miles on, to reconnoitre. A few Zulus were seen on the opposite ridge, evidently watching the party's movements; and as they reached the top of the eminence, a messenger was despatched by them across the valley at speed to the next mountain, where soon after smoke was seen, showing evidently that their advent had been signalled to the next post.

The remaining Zulus incontinently disappeared up some rocky ground to the left, and although one of them was chased by four Natal natives, he as well as his comrades escaped without injury. Colonel Buller and Captain Woodgate, not having been able to see anything of the range of mountains for which they were looking, went back to explore the river, but they had scarcely disappeared down the slope when the mist cleared off, and there could be distinctly seen the clearly defined outlines of a high isolated mountain towards the south-east, and this Zulu scouts declared to be Ibabanango, the principal object of their search. A number of deserted *kraals* belonging to Malafchey and his tribe were close at hand, and it was found that there was plenty of mealies and firewood, and a very comfortable meal was obtained for men and horses. As soon as it was sufficiently dark to hide his movements.

Colonel Buller, who always adopted the plan of never bivouacking where he had halted during the day, quietly shifted the column across the stream to a spot where a deep *donga*, sheltered on all sides but one, gave protection from any night-surprise. The Natal native cavalry did not bivouac with the remainder of the patrol, but were allowed to post themselves and lie down without off-saddling at a point indicated to their commander. Captain Cochrane, by Colonel Buller. Sentries were posted, patrols sent out, and the night passed without incident or alarm. The next morning, soon after daybreak, they were again in motion, and were far more successful in their observations.

Colonel Buller, assisted by Captain Woodgate, obtained excellent data referring to the position of the two mountains. From the observations and sketches they were enabled to make, they came to the conclusion that there would be no difficulty in the transport of waggons on either side of the road as far as Ibabanango, or in their getting on to the Rorke's Drift road to Ulundi. Another, and not the least important, point was noted, namely, that although the district they surveyed was not nearly so well-watered as the Kambula country, the grass improved and became of a better quality the more one went into Zululand. It was so thick, and at the same time so green, that it would be practically impossible to get it to burn for at least another month, so that up to the end of June oxen would be tolerably sure of grazing. After carefully reconnoitring for some distance further, without being at all molested, although a few Zulu scouts were seen here and there, the column returned to camp, which they reached about 7.40 p.m., after a most exciting ride of some fifty miles and two days' experience of Zulu skirmishing.

Another reconnaissance was organised for the 12th instant. Colonel Buller's patrol on this occasion was composed exclusively of picked and seasoned men, and consisted of 60 of the Frontier Light Horse, under Captain D'Arcy and Lieutenant Blaine; 40 Basutos, under Captain Cockerell and Lieutenants Henderson and Rane; and 80 of Baker's Horse, together with a few mounted scouts and orderlies, making altogether a well-mounted, well-armed, and well-trained band of 200 horsemen. Colonel Buller's guests, on this occasion, included the Prince Imperial, whom he was to meet at Conference hill, Mr. Drummond, several officers from headquarters, and Lord William Beresford, who had earned the soubriquet of "The Ubiquitous."

Having received full instructions, and been supplied with the usual three days' rations, with the best wishes for luck from their comrades, and a cheer from the men and officers, they filed out of the camp in the highest of spirits and eager for the road. Their first halt was to be Conference hill, where the Prince Imperial was to join them. This post was at that time the most advanced point of General Newdigate's division, and from Doornkop the distance is about fifteen miles. From Wood's camp at Wolfs Kraal the distance would be about seven miles, and this was soon accomplished. They found His Imperial Highness waiting for them, with Colonel Malthus, commanding the 94th, and some other officers, showing the prince round the defences. After duly inspecting all the defences shown to them by Colonel Malthus, they made the best of their way to a spot selected for their bivouac, about six miles farther on, and where they remained the night, while their horses grazed contented in some mealie fields.

Half an hour before dawn on the following morning Colonel Buller was to be seen scanning the horizon in all directions, and by sunrise his party were all in the saddle, and *en route*. They soon reached the ford at the Blood River, which had gone down considerably since Buller had last seen it. The country over which they rode was fairly open. They crossed the ford without difficulty, and gaining the opposite bank, reached a plain, from which they were, however, divided by a broad and well-worn watercourse. Here they faced the mountain, a long unbroken range, varying in height from 1000 to 1500 feet, which ran down the left of the valley.

A portion of the mounted men were now sent away to the right, with instructions to ride up the *kloof*, then dismount, scale the rocks, and await the result of the advance of the main body. Should natives oppose the latter in force, the flanking party were then to drive them down the mountain, where it was expected they would fall into the hands of the Basutos under Henderson and Rane, who were placed in ambush on the left. After half an hour's careful scouting, not a sign of a Zulu could be seen, and Colonel Buller then gave the not unwelcome order to off-saddle at, or rather close to, a *kraal* which bore unmistakable evidences of recent native occupation.

The troopers had no sooner off-saddled, however, than the wily savages emerged from the caves and crevices where they had been hid, and could be distinctly seen making the best of their way with considerable speed up Sirayo's *krantz* exactly opposite to where Buller's men were. They evidently were in some force, and two or three men on horseback were observed directing their movements as their reinforcements came rapidly in. The force, however, they were able to collect was extremely small, and certainly would not have numbered more than half Colonel Buller's command. The Prince Imperial was excellently mounted upon a handsome and powerful horse, who seemed, however a little fidgety under fire. Lieut. Rane was now sent on with a few Basutos, to see whether any stand would be made by the enemy; and the Prince Imperial immediately galloped after him, to see what he could of the fun.

187

When these men arrived at the foot of the mountain, they found a much easier ascent than they had expected. A footpath, which, however, was quite practicable for horses, was seen winding in a devious manner in and out of the tall mimosa-trees which fringed the belt of the wood, and along this path dashed Rane and his Basutos, closely followed by the prince, whose impatience to get to the front was noticed by all. On reaching the summit, however, not a Zulu or an enemy of any kind was to be seen. This was soon accounted for by the fact that halfway up the *krantz* on the right were posted a number of Zulus—perhaps about 100.

While the main body were watching these people, to see if they would attempt to cut off from the column the prince and the Basutos, who were surrounding the plateau above, about 100 savages now suddenly showed themselves, as if to invite combat, on the opposite side of the ravine. The object of all these manoeuvres was now obvious enough. The Zulus who were running away on the plateau above were so doing to lure the English force on to follow, when the party halfway up the *krantz* would probably be joined by a number of men from the *kraals*, and endeavour to block them in from the rear. It was now noticed that they were about to send messengers away for assistance, and this they could not do without running the gauntlet of fire of Buller's column.

Crouching down, so as to be concealed as much as possible from the fire of the English rifles, two of the men belonging to the Zulu party ran rapidly away from the native column until they were within fifty yards of Buller's position. As they passed, a man raised his gun, and made an excellent shot at the leader, who never moved after he touched the ground, upon which he fell headlong. The remaining man, seeing the fate of his comrade, ran back to his people with wonderful activity, sharpened no doubt by the *ping* and *whiz* of half a dozen rifle-bullets sent after him at about 200 yards. Baker's Horse were now sent on to the table-land above, to look after the Prince Imperial, Rane, and the Basutos, whom they found in high glee, chasing some flying Zulus, who seemed too scared to notice that their assailants only numbered eight men.

They now surveyed the surrounding country without further molestation. In front lay a broad valley, in the midst of which ran the Blood River, now shrunk to a thin silver thread; on the left at some distance off could be seen the table-shaped mountain of Mhlatze; and on the right was that spot of fatal memories, Isandhlwana, with its huge crag in the rear, raising its lion-like crest over the veldt below. After descending the mountain and burning the *kraals* on its south-east slopes, Buller and his party returned to camp without any event happening on their homeward route.

It was now determined at headquarters that a reconnaissance in force should be made under the command of General Marshall, for the double purpose of still further pursuing the investigations begun and of burying the dead at Isandhlwana. For this purpose, a force of no less than 2490 men was detailed, and consisted of the 17th Lancers, the King's Dragoon Guards, four companies of the second battalion 24th, and a number of native auxiliaries. Major Black's experience and knowledge of the road were found of great use, and the two cavalry regiments were capitally handled by Colonels Drury-Lowe and Alexander. Major Bengough had charge of the native battalion.

The Natal mounted police were under Major Dartnell, and one hundred and fifty Army Service horses were led, in order to bring back the waggons. The entire force was gathered together at Rorke's Drift one hour before daylight, and carefully inspected by the light of the camp lanterns. They marched down to the river at daylight, and commenced to ford the stream, which was finally crossed by six o'clock. Colonel Drury-Lowe commanded the First Brigade, consisting of two squadrons of his own corps and two of the King's, and made a detour round the head and crest of the Bashee valley behind Sirayo's celebrated mountain, and, without any mishap or molestation, effected a junction with the remainder of the column at Isandhlwana.

Colonel Alexander, with a brigade similarly constituted, marched by the direct waggon road straight upon his objective, while he threw out strong flanking parties right and left as he advanced. A squadron was sent at Colonel Black's suggestion to hold the gorge of the Bashee on the right, and a number of vedettes were occupied in patrolling the left of the same valley. Bengough's natives, meanwhile, came on at a rapid pace, and were thrown out into skirmishing order along the slopes of the Ingutu range, where the English troops once had such a tussle with Sirayo and his men. In fact, here, it may be said, the first blood in the campaign was shed, when they destroyed this cruel chief's stronghold.

The manner in which Bengough's well-trained men scoured and scouted was most gratifying to observe. Every nook and comer, every crevice and cave, were carefully explored, and as the men advanced slowly along the valley and slopes of the mountain, every *kraal* was

189

fired that came in their way. These men gradually worked their way round until they came along the range to the eastern limit of the valley, where the hunting-path trends towards the great *kraal* of Cetywayo. Meanwhile the cavalry were not idle. Crowds of vedettes swarmed along the sides of the valley ready to outflank any enemy or take him in reverse should he appear.

While this was undertaken, the main force moved steadily along the front of the valley, and over the brow of the opposite ridge Bengough's men swarmed, chanting their war-song in native fashion. Down the hillside, to hold the head of the valley, came the four companies of the 24th, marching steadily in column of fours. The sun streamed in splendour upon the glittering files of cavalry as they wound like a brilliant chain along the greensward. Nothing could exceed the picturesque ensemble that greeted the eye on all sides; nothing could be sadder than the mission upon which they came.

As soon as the entire force was concentrated on the neck, their solemn but ghastly duty commenced. Rider and horse, officer and private, boy and man, their grim and parchment-looking skins half eaten by the carrion birds and half covering the bleaching bones, gave to the scene a terrible and weird significance, which can never be forgotten. Many of the bodies were easily recognised. Captain Shepstone at once pointed out that of Colonel Durnford, which was interred with deep respect in a donga near the spot where he fell. Forty-five waggons were brought away by the horses and mules, and a quantity of stores still intact was carried in them. The staff of the 24th's colours was also recovered; and the troops, having fully carried out their sad devoir in the most effective manner, returned home with the same precaution with which they had moved on to the field.

CHAPTER 8

Advance of the 2nd Column

The force thus gathered at Landsman's Drift was now quite ready for an immediate advance. It was therefore determined to push on this column (2nd) at once. Accordingly, on the 27th May the troops were formed up in line of contiguous quarter-columns by eight a.m., and after the General and his staff had ridden down the ranks, making a minute and detailed inspection, the various columns moved off by fours in succession from the right precisely at nine a.m. Newdigate's Division, which led the way, consisted of the 21st Fusiliers, the 94th Foot, the 58th Foot, and the 2nd battalion 24th Regiment, together with a wing of the King's Dragoon Guards, a wing of the 17th Lancers, a battalion of Native Contingent, two batteries of Royal Artillery, and a company of Engineers.

The crossing of the Buffalo at Landsman's Drift was commenced at half-past nine, and the rear had crossed by two o'clock. The exact distance to Kopje Allein as the crow flies is said to be ten miles, but the route taken was somewhat circuitous, so as, for the sake of the waggons, to avoid many bad places, swamps, morasses, and mud-holes, which abound in this part of the country. The country between the Blood River and the Buffalo is tolerably well supplied with water, comparatively open, but singularly treeless in its character, though there were patches here and there along the road, and the district seemed well adapted for cattle posts and grazing purposes.

Indeed, there could be seen a number of large deserted *kraals* and homesteads, which had once evidently been the depots of pastoral wealth and prosperity. These sites of industry had suffered a hard and rough usage in the terrible necessities of war. These depredations were largely caused by the foraging parties in search of fuel, the great want in all our camps. Supplies, indeed, on more than one occasion, were brought even as far as from the northern slopes of the Durnberg, a distance of twenty miles. Most of the best information in regard to the topographical features of this portion of the campaign was furnished by the very excellent reports drawn up by Colonel Buller, Lord William Beresford, and, above all, the Prince Imperial, whose pen and pencil gave a vivid and life-like idea of the physical characteristics of this line of advance.

On the 16th instant Colonel Buller's second patrol returned at noon to General Wood's camp at the Wolfs *kraal*, and had been so successful in its reconnoitring operations that its officers were able to report that no large bodies of Zulus were within twenty miles of the Blood River, or, indeed, anywhere between the White Umvolosi and the Buffalo River. The same evening on which the patrol started it bivouacked at Kopje Allein, and, indeed, it was owing to the excellent reports made by Buller and his staff that the place was chosen as one of the links in the line of advance, A few Zulus there were, it is true, hovering about in the distance, and attempts were made by feigned attacks and feigned retreats to lure the troops into ambush, but Buller was far too old a soldier to be taken in by such wiles.

When the men had got steadily on the summit of the hill they were exploring, the Zulu skirmishers disappeared into some of the caves surrounding Sirayo's old *kraal*, and nothing but some huts full of mealies could be found. The patrol that night slept on the slopes of the Ingutu mountains, and the following morning scouted in a southerly direction in rear of the Ingwe range, as far as the White Umvolosi, showing in a tolerably plain manner that the country about there was quite denuded of its population, at least between the Buffalo River and the White Umvolosi, while to the eastward and the northward of the latter river there were plenty of Zulus and cattle, but no large or important bodies were assembled north of the Isandaka range.

The Prince Imperial had won all hearts during these three days in the saddle and night bivouac, and was seen to have considerably improved in health since his last visit to the camp.

From the notes and sketches made by the officers above named the following data may be adduced:—The key of the road from the Utrecht to the Ulundi country is undoubtedly the Inhlazatye mountain, and, although this road runs along a narrow ledge with a precipice on the one side and with huge boulders on the other, interspersed with thorns and bush, yet still it is actually the most direct line of advance upon Ulundi. This Inhlazatye mountain covers a vast extent of country, has an immense quantity of thorn-bush over it, is very broken and steep, but undoubtedly can be turned by an invading force from the north either to the east or to the west, probably the latter, where little bush worth mentioning would have to be passed through.

The most commanding and open positions are upon the highlands to the south of the White Umvolosi and Umtatoosi Rivers, girdling the new capital, Ulundi. These are the Emtonjaneni hills (which are called Magnibonium on most maps), near the White Umvolosi, and the Tyoe and Entumeni heights in rear of the Umtatoosi, all healthy positions, well-watered, and with abundant grass and wood. From the Emtonjaneni hills, explored by Colonel Buller, who estimates them at 200 feet high, the circle of royal *kraals* on the farther side of the White Umvolosi can be seen; three roads lead to the rear into the colony, the upper, central, and lower. The Ekowe, Entumeni, and Ungoga ranges, from 1500 to 2000 feet above the sea level, dominate the valley of the Umtatoosi.

Healthy positions suitable for cavalry encampments may be found on these heights, well wooded and watered, with excellent grass and roads leading to the rear into the colony; and here Marshall's cavalry kept open our communications and effectually severed connexion between the Zulu's right and left *impis*. These central and coast lines, which are joined by a cross-road, both follow the course of the Umtatoosi. During the march, and whenever the country would admit of such formation, the leading corps halted, and the extended line of march was curtailed by the succeeding regiment forming upon its left; waggons came up in a sort of deployment into line, and certain simple movements were practised which would be carried out in case of sudden attack. Lord Chelmsford invariably made a great point of concentrating his waggons whenever the slightest opportunity offered.

General Newdigate and General Wood between them had 900 waggons, and it may easily be imagined what a column 450 of these would make. Allowing 30 yards to each—and that is not much, there being 16 or 18 oxen to each load—each column of baggage alone is 15 miles long, but to this distance must be added 5 yards' interval, and this gives 18 miles to defend. Of course, the forage for the large cavalry force made one of the greatest strains upon the commissariat, and all had to be sacrificed to this necessity. This column and Crealock's were in this respect not upon a par, as it had to provide for not less than 2000 horses, each receiving 12 lb. of corn daily; which gave a total of 24,000 lb. daily, or 3000 lb. per waggon load, or 6 waggons daily to supply them. At this rate, therefore, it required 120 waggons to carry the oats for the cavalry alone. All Lord Chelmsford's and the staff horses were, however, placed upon half rations.

Ibabanango, which Lord Chelmsford had selected as an advanced depot for the united forces of his column and that of Wood, is again situated about midway between this place (Kopje Allein) and the king's *kraal* at Ulundi. The troops in this camp consisted of a company of Engineers, the cavalry brigade, two batteries of Royal Artillery, four line battalions, and 800 natives. The encampment was rather extensive, but this upon sanitary grounds and the best medical advice. The battalions were encamped as at open order, front as in line, with a depth of 116 yards, which is unusual, for half the above frontage is the usual encampment, and 30 yards were left between each of the four battalions. Each regiment of cavalry usually occupies 172 yards of front and 130 yards of depth, but its camp can be condensed to 120 yards of front by crossing heel-ropes, and this, for defensive reasons, was the plan adopted by General Marshall.

This could not be done with Cape or Indian remounts; as entire horses would fight if so close to each other; but English horses are so accustomed to this proximity that it was found they throve better when allowed companionship. To each battery of artillery was allowed a frontage of 133 yards, with a depth of 114 yards, or 70 yards front at close order, while from centre to centre of the tents 10 paces were allotted. The kitchens were simple enough, being nothing more than a trench to catch the wind and hold the usual pattern of Flanders or Torrens kettle—the former, weighing 8½ lbs., holding twelve quarts, and cooking for eight men, while the latter weighs 3½ lbs., holds six quarts, and cooks for five men. Whenever the ground was too wet for a trench, two parallel sod walls answered the same purpose, and two trenches, 10 feet long, 9 inches broad, and 12 inches deep were allowed for a company of 120 men.

The medical arrangements were as elaborate as could be made consistent with the limited means of transport, but what was deficient in quantity was made up in excellence of detail. Medical officers and stretcher-bearers usually moved in front of the camp, and the temporary hospital was always placed in the least exposed position near at hand, while the field-hospitals were always in rear. One medical officer was allotted to each battalion of infantry, regiment of cavalry, or battery of artillery—more could not be spared. One bearer company and two field-hospitals were allotted to each division. This bearer company included 206 men, part natives, 101 mules or horses, and 30 waggons. The field-hospitals had each 75 men, 52 mules, and 10 waggons, while each field-hospital had equipment for 200 sick. Fortunately, the health of the troops was exceptionally good.

Instead of an advance from Rorke's Drift, it was now determined to take a line from Kopje Allein to Blood River, across the more northern spurs of the Ingutu hills, and endeavour to ultimately strike the road laid down in the maps, between the Alarm and the Isipizi Hills. This route was to be taken by General Wood's flying column in advance, and General Newdigate's division, of which actually it was intended to form an integral portion. The former consisted of the 13th and 90th Regiments of Light Infantry and five companies of the 80th Regiment, all of them in splendid and hard-working condition, and devoted to their brilliant leader. Wood's cavalry consisted of 900 mounted men belonging to various corps, and commanded by the Rupert of South Africa, Redvers Buller, whose men were ready to follow him anywhere, and die for him to a man, after his splendid self-devotion at Zlobani and elsewhere.

Wood, who made friends wherever he moved, had some valuable allies in Oham's people, who, hating the tyranny of Cetywayo, were invaluable as scouts and spies to the flying columns. The arrangements for the line of advance were as follows:—Wood's flying column was to keep in advance of Newdigate's division by about five miles, while in front of the former a veil of cavalry was to keep in advance about ten miles, connected by intervening files. Each morning orderlies were to report whether the front and rear were perfectly clear, nor was an advance to be made until such was known.

In case of any enemy attacking Wood, the latter was to be at once supported by Marshall, who could circle round and take the Zulus in the rear, a principle of strategy they strongly object to. Crealock, with the aid oi the naval authorities, was at the same time to push forward from Fort Chelmsford, and, if the landing at Port Durnford was reported practicable, force the Umvolosi and operate in conjunction with the 2nd column from his base at Port Durnford.

Lord Chelmsford had long seen that the best method to obviate the almost overwhelming difficulties of transport would be to form some seaport on the Zulu coast. Delagoa Bay was at first selected; but considerable difficulty was found in arranging with the Portuguese Government as to our landing a force in the neighbourhood, and that scheme was consequently abandoned. It then became evident that if a seaport, or even ever so small a landing-place could be provided at the mouth of the Umlalasi, it would be at once the nearest and best base of operations for any force moving from the Tugela upon Ulundi or Cetywayo's other stronghold.

Furthermore, as far back as December, 1877, Sir Theophilus Shepstone wrote to Sir Bartle Frere, informing his Excellency that two gentlemen—Mr. E. Rathbone and Mr. H. W. Taylor—wished to call attention to the fact that, from personal observations they had made, they were satisfied that a practicable landing-place on the Zulu coast could be found. These gentlemen, it is true, as Sir Theophilus pointed out, differed as to the precise spot on the coast, but both agreed that it was. near the Tugela mouth, and but a very few miles intervene between the one place described and the other. This discovery was made twenty-seven years ago, in the year 1852, and, so far from being kept a secret, was published for general information in the *Natal Mercury*.

H.M. gunboat *Forester* was accordingly despatched to thoroughly explore this part of the coast; no less than three minute and careful surveys were made, and finally, on May 26th, she returned with the welcome intelligence that a fine lagoon existed close to the mouth of the Umlalasi, with a sheltered outlet, and that, from the soundings taken for five miles on either side of the river, there was no actual obstacle to a landing being practicable at all tides and all seasons.

There was, however, at the mouth of the river, a bar on which the surf broke heavily; and in bad weather experience proved on more than one occasion that this formed an impassable barrier even to the most determined attempts to make a landing.

This spot was christened Port Durnford, and steps were immediately taken to form there a fort and depot of supplies for the 1st column, in command of which was General Crealock.

To Commodore Sullivan, Major Barrow, and the captain of H.M.S. *Forester* principally belong the honours of the discovery; and while the sailors worked heartily seaward and along the dangerous and difficult coast, Barrow and his riders found out all the roads which led to the point selected. It had been arranged that General Crealock, with the advanced guard of the 1st division should move down the Umlalasi to a point carefully surveyed by Barrow, and which was subsequently, in compliment to the gallant young prince, called Fort Napoleon. Thence he was to proceed to Port Durnford, to meet the *Forester*.

Hitherto the advance had been slow; but when it is remembered that forts were constructed at every strategic point of defence— at

196

the Amatikula, the Inyezani (respectively Forts Chelmsford and Cre-alock), and the whole of the road between this place and the Tugela had been put into working order by fatigue parties and Engineers, it is clear there was no real ground for complaint of the delay. Every stream had been bridged, either with pontoons, casks, or trestles, and trees had been cut down, rocks and boulders blown up, as well as gradients eased and facilities for transport carried out. Forts Pearson, Tenedos, Chelmsford, Crealock, and Napoleon were garrisoned by the less robust men of the column. Six companies of the 88th, with the headquarters, held Fort Chelmsford, while a wing of the 99th per-formed the same office at Fort Crealock. The regular communications along this line of advanced forts were placed in charge of one of the best men out there, namely. Colonel Hugh Rowlands, 41st Regiment, whose eye for country, tact, and temper with the natives and incessant vigilance eminently qualified him for such a responsibility.

At this time the force of the 1st division stood as follows:—Gen-eral Crealock, Brigadiers Bray and Rowlands; two batteries of artillery and one ammunition column; Royal Engineers, 30th company and C troop; infantry, six battalions, viz.:—the Buffs, 57th, 60th, 88th, 91st, and 99th Regiments, two squadrons of mounted infantry, the Natal Horse, the native scouts; as pretty and compact a little division as any moderately ambitious general could wish to command, and it speaks well for the chief's admirable temper under difficulties that, chafed as he now was, and tied as it were by the leg, by want of transport, he kept working incessantly without a murmur at the forts, bridges, fords, roads, and other requisites.

In accordance with the above-mentioned arrangement, General Crealock, Commodore Richards, and Lord Gifford set forth on the 25th June for Port Durnford, taking with them the advance-guard of the 1st division.

At first the road was over a level and sandy plain, with numerous small granite hills in different directions, and although there was not much vegetation for the first two or three miles of the road, it opened on to a more picturesque-looking champaign country, where the soil appeared teeming with fertility, and the air was balmy and pure. The country here, however, is arid and parched during the dry season, but in the rains, which last from November till May, it is well watered, and large crops of maize are grown, which by the end of June are usually ripened and fit for cutting. Large crops of *malama* are also grown, and it is upon the stalks of this that the cattle are mostly fed in the drought, when they appear in good condition, notwithstanding its seeming want of nutriment.

Here a halt was made; vedettes were placed, and a meal was partaken of. Then, after half an hour's rest, they again pushed on, and soon came to an undulating and extremely romantic-looking valley, shut in on either side by some huge granite hills. Ascending the highest of these, they looked down upon the Indian Ocean, Port Durnford, and the *Forester*, standing off about a mile from the shore, and evidently on the look-out. From this point to the outlet of the Umlalazi the country was fairly open, and the landscape fertile and partly cultivated.

The only obstacle to progress was a rocky and rather narrow ridge, through which, however, ran a fairly open *kloof*, with a small and tributary stream winding its way to the Umlalazi. Here was the road, and another two hours saw them through the *kloof* without question or attack, and they cantered along the grassy slopes to the bright and shingly beach, upon which a couple of boat's crews, despatched when they were first sighted, were occupied in preparing a very excellent dinner of ship's rations for the tired and hungry men.

General Crealock highly approved of the position, and a fort and other works were at once traced out, thus rendering complete the cordon of posts that had been drawn all round the south of Zululand, right from the sea to the left attack (or 2nd column), and through which it was impossible for Cetywayo to force a way, and which rendered his capture or submission a mere question of time.

CHAPTER 9

Death of the Prince Imperial

We now come to an event which though it in no way affected the course or result of this war, was nevertheless so deplorably sad in itself, as well as to the British Army, and was, furthermore, of such world-wide interest, altering, as it undoubtedly did, the history of one of the mightiest nations of Europe, that no apology is required for a detailed narrative.

Ever since the arrival of the Prince Imperial in the colony he had continued to win the friendship and esteem of all ranks, and his unassuming quietude and modesty, genial humour, and readiness to learn the most minute details of the profession he had adopted, made him a universal favourite. It has been previously mentioned that the prince had been engaged in several reconnaissances, and only three days before his death he had been with Lord Chelmsford upon a patrol extending more than twenty miles into the Zulu country. On May the 28th General Wood received orders to move parallel to, but slightly in advance, of General Newdigate's column, from Kopje Allein, in a south-easterly direction towards the Itelezi hill.

After three days had been spent in carefully exploring the country, General Newdigate moved forward on June 1st with his division, as nearly as possible 10,000 strong, and with a baggage train of 480 waggons. The country had been carefully scouted by Buller's Horse for twenty miles round, and no Zulus were reported near. On the evening of the 1st the column *laagered* not far from the Itelezi, and on the following day the general moved south-east along a level country towards the Inguita range; and the flying column being one march ahead, a communication was kept up by the vedettes of General Newdigate and General Wood.

On Sunday, the 1st, General Wood with a small escort reconnoitred in advance of the column, which was about five miles in advance of General Newdigate's force. Away on the right and left were Buller's horsemen dotting the ridges of the hills on either side. In front lay green slopes, which were traversed here and there by watercourses, and bounded by the most singularly shaped mountains, flat at the summit and crowned with a sort of rocky dome. A good deal of rain had fallen in the night, and the morning was as clear and fresh as a May day in England. The general and his escort had ridden about six miles, when the path suddenly made a bend to the left, skirting a clump of trees, which grew near the edge of the stream. Pushing a way through thick thorny underwood mingled with date-palms and tall reeds, they at length looked down upon the still deep waters of a narrow river, flowing across a long red sandbank.

A ledge of granite formed a rugged barrier eight feet or ten feet high across the river, and down the hollows of this the clear water rushed and gurgled in fantastic rills, cascades, and rapids, bubbling and eddying among the great masses of rock above, in many of which great holes were worn by stones which during the floods had settled in small hollows. Traversing a sandstone hill, with a long spur stretching away to the eastward, and rising in cliffs of 300 feet to the south of the river, they came upon a grove of fan-palms and mimosa, where the banks of the stream were covered with golden-blossomed acacias. Crossing the river by an easy ford, they had ridden on about another mile, when they observed some of the vedettes on the high ground to the left signalling that horsemen were approaching.

Soon they came out upon an immense cultivated flat, terminating to the right, in a long, dark, and winding gorge, black with bush, and arched by huge precipices of sandstone and granite. Into this they turned, and, following a Kaffir path marked with tracks made by Buller's men, they came upon a bush of about six or seven acres, in the centre of which were the remains of a burnt *kraal* and marks of recent fighting. On the edge of a small stream they discovered a path to the extreme right, in fact quite on the hillside, and here the surface showed numerous boot-marks, where the scouts had evidently been. They had now reached a plain, from which they were divided by a broad and well-worn watercourse, and here they were joined by three or four vedettes, who came to report that they had noticed some horsemen coming at a rapid canter from the direction of the Tombalaka and the Iyuligazi Rivers, which were about equidistant between Wood's late camp and that of General Newdigate.

They had not long to wait for the solution of the mystery, for, riding in the direction of the horsemen, they were met by Colonel Buller and a dozen of his men, who was equally anxious with General Wood to discover who the fugitives could be. They all rode on together, and rounding the base of the cliff came up with Lieutenant Carey and four troopers of Bettington's Horse. In a few seconds more the terrible secret was revealed, and Lieutenant Carey, whose horse was almost dead beat, and covered with foam, was rapidly relating to General Wood the details.

"Where is the prince?" exclaimed Wood, as he breasted his horse at some fallen trees which intervened, and dashed forward to meet the fugitives. "Speak, sir; what has happened?"

"The prince, I fear, is killed, sir," said one of the men, Carey being at first unable to speak.

"Is that the case? Tell me instantly, sir," answered the general.

"I fear 'tis so, general," was the answer; upon which our chief exclaimed, "And what are you, sir, doing here?"

A veil must be drawn over the rest of the interview, which was of the most painful character. A short despatch was at once written while on horseback by the general, and in this a resume of the fearful tragedy was told, how English soldiers had had the unutterable shame of seeing an English officer and four English troopers unwounded and escaped from a Zulu ambush, in which a gallant young prince, the guest of England and the hope of France, had been barbarously slain. This letter was at once despatched by the general to headquarters, where he ordered Lieutenant Carey and his party to proceed and make their report.

The story elicited from Carey and the four men, in spite of a few discrepancies, was in the main as follows:—

On Sunday, the 1st of June, the prince learnt that a patrol was to be sent out in advance of the column, to choose the site for the camp on the following day, and His Highness at once applied for and obtained permission to accompany it. At six o'clock on Sunday morning the Prince Imperial sent for his groom, and consulted him as to what horse he should ride, and the man strongly advised him not to take the large grey horse, which was eventually one of the causes of his death.

This animal was not one of those selected for the prince by Sir John Bissett, who had assisted him in the choice of others. He was a big, awkward looking, but very powerful animal, but an inveterate buck-jumper, and, moreover, excessively timid under fire, a fault which in a charger is dangerous to the last degree. Two of the prince's horses had died, either on the voyage out or soon after landing, and upon the fatal Sunday the grey horse was the only steed not lame or upon the sick report, so he had to be taken as a case of "Hobson's choice."

At seven o'clock a note arrived addressed to the prince, in which he was informed that permission was accorded him to go with the patrol about to be sent on to choose next day's camping-ground. This note was from Colonel Harrison, the acting quarter-master-general, and the prince at once went over to his tent, and received final instructions from him verbally; which it must be assumed, were in accordance with the wishes of the commander-in-chief, who expressly stated that the prince was to be well cared for, to have no military responsibility, and yet, at the same time, was not to be interfered with, or in any way prevented from seeing the country.

Lieutenant Carey's account of these matters is somewhat at variance with this statement of Colonel Harrison, as he (Carey) says that he was told that the prince was to have the entire charge of the escort and the entire duty of selecting the camp. Lieutenant Carey says in his written statement, that it was by his express desire that he was named to accompany the escort, and he made this request in consequence of his knowledge of the country and, in some degree, of the language. Six men of Captain Bettington's Horse and the same number of Shepstone's Basutos were ordered to parade at half-past eight a.m. as escort, but for some hitherto unexplained reason the latter never appeared, and when Carey suggested they should wait for them the prince, with that utter contempt for danger for which he was always remarkable, exclaimed, "Oh, no; we are quite strong enough!"

At nine a.m. all was ready, a frugal breakfast of black coffee and biscuit had been partaken of, saddles, carbines, swords, revolvers, and accoutrements had been carefully inspected, and the word was given to "mount" and "away!" Before leaving the camp, however, a message was sent to Captain Shepstone to say that the escort would halt and wait for the six Basutos on the ridge between the Incenzi and Itelezi hills. A messenger was again sent to hurry on these natives, but it seems they never came, and therefore the patrol consisted only of the prince, Lieutenant Carey, six mounted men of Bettington's Horse, and one friendly Zulu. This was certainly not a fit escort for such a charge, and it seems impossible not to attach a grave responsibility to the staff officer who made the detail.

All the six Europeans were well armed and well mounted, their weapons consisting of the Martini-Henry slung across the back, ammunition in *bandoleer*, and a stout serviceable knife, which could be used for meals or on emergency as a weapon at close quarters. The prince and Lieutenant Carey had not rifles, but swords and revolvers, and unfortunately the latter were not worn upon the person as they invariably should be, but in the holsters. The prince had been on several visits to General Wood's camp, and was an enthusiastic admirer of both Wood and Buller, with the latter of whom he had become very intimate ever since the last two patrols he had made with him. With Lieutenant Carey His Imperial Highness had also an intimacy of some standing, and as Carey's skill as a draughtsman was well known in the camp, he had been selected on several occasions to assist His Highness in surveying operations.

The day had broken on this fated Sunday with all the glory of a real South African morning. It had been raining during the night, but this only served to give a more delightful perfume to the odorous plants that were crushed by the hoofs of the horses belonging to the escort. The rain of the previous day and night had refreshed the ground, and filled the various pools with water, and the plains were cheerful with the animals and birds coming out of the bush to feed. The patrol met with no adventure for some time, but continued its course along a valley running north-east, and narrowing gradually. The track in some places crossed bad *spruits*, and was undefined, and in parts obliterated by thorn-trees and bush.

It was also commanded here and there by projecting spurs and bluffs, where an enemy could have easily hidden in force, and have attacked them at an advantage, but on either side could be seen the friendly Basutos scouting in the distance. The watershed of the mountain was reached about an hour after the patrol started, and on arriving at the ridge the prince and Lieutenant Carey dismounted, as they wished to fix the position of some important hills with their compasses. Here Colonel Harrison overtook them, and remarked that the whole of the escort was not with them, adding that the patrol had better wait for the Basutos to come up. The prince said, "Oh, we are quite strong enough. Besides, we have all our friends around us, and with my glass, I can see General Marshall's cavalry coming up."

Lieutenant Carey, as soon as he had finished his sketch, proposed to off-saddle and breakfast; but he states that the prince overruled this suggestion and expressed a wish to push on to the river. The patrol accordingly proceeded on for about four miles, where for some distance the way was along the bottom of a deep sandy *nullah* with very precipitous sides, which they were forced to take as the only practicable place. This at length debouched into an open space, from which there appeared to be an entrance to a disused *kraal* some two miles up the ravine. Here the escort found that there was good drinking-water in some pools under a large kopje in front, situated in a complete amphitheatre of hills, and upon this *kopje* were some of our Basuto skirmishers. After watering the horses, the party advanced for a mile and a half along a commanding and rocky range of hills a short distance beyond the Ilyotosi River.

Here Carey again proposed to off-saddle, but the prince did not approve of the spot, and after some more sketching and surveying the country with telescopes and compass, the valley was descended as far as an isolated *kraal*, and the order was given to off-saddle. The prince, who did not appear very strong, now complained of being tired, and while coffee was being prepared lay down beside the door of a hut.

The place where this halt was made would appear, from the statements of Lieutenant Carey and the surviving men of the escort, to be about as ill-chosen and suspicious a locality as could be found. The *kraal* where they now were consisted of about half a dozen huts, and was situated about three hundred yards from the River Moazani (so called by the Zulu who accompanied the party). Between the *kraal* and the river stretched a tall and luxuriant growth of that most dangerous cover, five, six, and seven feet in height, Tambookie grass interspersed here and there, as is customary, with equally tall mealies and Kaffir corn. The plains beneath this spot afforded every temptation to the artistic eye of the prince, and here again another sketch of the panorama was quickly made.

The bright glowing tints of the foreground, whose colours were lit up by green and fresh grass and wide-spreading acacia and flowering shrubs, well mellowed away in the middle distance, while far away towards the horizon were to be seen the shadowy outlines of the blue Itelezi hills. The *kraal* was not completely surrounded, for in front there was an open space where broken cooking utensils and burnt-out embers, bones, and other debris, showed that the place had not long ago been occupied. Some hungry-looking dogs came out and snarled at the intruders. Here the fatal order was given to off-saddle, and, in defiance of the most common and ordinary precautions, which the merest tyro should have taken, the horses were knee-haltered and turned out to graze, while coffee was prepared, and not the slightest search made in the cover around.

The friendly Zulu was sent down to the river for water, and also to see that the horses did not stray too far. All this time a party of Zulus, supposed to have been about thirty or forty, were concealed and watching the doomed party, who, utterly unsuspicious of an ambush, were seated around, chatting and sipping their coffee. A deep *donga* lay right across the path subsequently taken by the fugitives, and this served to screen the enemy as he stealthily crawled to his prey. Stealing noiselessly along, hidden by the rank vegetation, and unheard by the unwatchful escort, the savages came nearer and nearer to their quarry, but while creeping along were descried by the watchful eyes of the Kaffir, who, not losing a second, darted back to the prince, and gave the warning of danger.

A little delay now occurs, for His Highness fails to understand the native, who has to appeal to Corporal Grubb, one of the escort, to interpret. The corporal explains to the prince, who looks at his watch, and (we are told) seeing it was ten minutes to four, says, "You can give your horses ten minutes more." But this must have been countermanded, for the horses were at once collected, and in a few moments were prepared to start. The prince is carefully and calmly examining his bit and bridle, and, it is surmised, had not sufficiently tightened his girths. His grey horse is a fidgety, troublesome animal to mount, and now appears to be nervous and anxious to break away.

Meanwhile all the escort stand to their horses and await the word, which the prince now gives, "Prepare to mount." But this was the death-signal, for hardly had the order escaped the lips that gave it, and that spoke no other word on earth, than the fearful traditional "*Usulu! Usulu!*" awoke the echoes of the valley, and a tremendous volley was poured in from the favouring cover of the grass and mealies. All the horses swerved instinctively with terror, and some broke away. Private Rogers was shot before he could mount, and the prince's tall grey, half mad with fright, became impossible to mount. Where is the English iron nerve that is proof against the panic of a moment? Where are the guardians of England's princely guest? All have lost their courage and their sense of manhood. *Sauve qui peut!* is the craven spirit of those who had they rallied back to back could have probably saved a noble life and preserved a nation's honour.

Not a carbine was loaded, not a sentry placed. Surprise, the most unsoldierlike crime, was allowed, and white with fear each trooper galloped away to save himself, nor drew bridle-rein till miles of country placed safety in his path. Meanwhile, the gallant and unfortunate prince is losing every chance of escape which the slightest attempt at succour would have given. One friendly hand to steady the scared and ill-broken steed; one carbine, even unloaded, presented at the bush—for the savages had not dared to come forth—or one gallant heart like Buller, Leet, or Wood to have shown the chivalry of France that England's sons were worthy of their ancient fame, and the prince would have been alive today.

There is, it is true, the testimony of one man, borne away by his frightened and possibly wounded horse, who says that not being more than half in the saddle, and having no control over his mount, he could not stay to aid the prince. "*Dépêchez-vous, monsieur!*" he cried, as he swept by at a racing gallop, and that was all the warning he could give. And then—oh, shame and humiliation!—this young lad, schooled to arms with English soldiers' sons, wearing an English uniform, and escorted by British soldiers to a bloody grave, was left alone to be speared to death, without a sword being drawn or a shot fired, even from a distance, in his defence.

The Zulus, seeing only one man unable to mount, burst at length from their treacherous cover, and with fiendish yells rush upon the prince, who, holding the stirrup-leather with one hand and the holster-flap with the other, must have made one final and desperate attempt to spring into the saddle. But all is in vain, the untrustworthy leather gives way in his hand; his feet slip from under him; he falls beneath the horse, which treads upon his body and gallops away! The last that was seen of the empress's beloved son was, that he was alone and on foot, with some dozen Zulus poising their *assegais* within a few feet from him, and his body was afterwards found pierced in front with some eighteen or twenty thrusts, and stripped of all but his mother's amulet.

It cannot have escaped the reader that there are some discrepancies and anachronisms in the accounts given by Lieutenant Carey and the survivors of that fatal and ill-omened day, the 1st of June. These contradictions were not unnoticed by General Wood when he took down the report and forwarded it to the headquarter camp. In the first place we are told that the prince was too rash and venturesome, and that he nearly lost his life on the day when, accompanied by Major Bettington, some of his men, and a party of Basutos, he visited a Zulu *kraal* in the neighbourhood of the camp, and was fired upon by the enemy. Now, on this as on former occasions, when the prince went out with Colonel Buller, Lord Chelmsford, and other officers in charge of patrols or reconnaissances, he was perfectly well aware that he was merely incurring the same risk as were other English officers, whose lives to the British Nation, if not to France, were as valuable as his, and whose temerity—if such it can be called—was absolutely necessary to the conduct of the campaign.

But on the last fatal occasion His Highness was allowed to go alone, or virtually alone, for Lieutenant Carey does not seem to have taken his honest and proper share of responsibility, or looked after the most ordinary precautions which a subaltern of a week's standing would have carried out in a time of profound peace. We are told that the prince gave all orders and words of command during the day, that he selected, approved of, and disapproved of each halting-place that was arrived at, and that when Lieutenant Carey wished the escort to muster and leave the deserted *kraal* at a certain hour the prince demurred, and gave the order to stay much longer.

Now this, if authentic, indicates a lack of military knowledge which it is difficult to understand as appertaining to an officer of Lieutenant Carey's standing. The rule of the service is imperative, and no civilian, no volunteer, and no guest, whatever his rank, may, can, or should at least be allowed to give a word of command when an official authority is present. If Lieutenant Carey, out of compliment or out of courtesy, allowed the Prince Imperial to choose the halting-places and to give the words of command to the troopers, whom he and not His Highness commanded, he betrayed an ignorance of the customs, duties, and etiquette of his profession which renders him totally unfit for the possession of Her Majesty's commission.

If he did not allow our deplored and gallant guest to select these halts, to choose the places for "off-saddle," and to give the necessary cautions and words of command in regard to mounting, why, then, he is still more to blame, as knowing, as he should have known, that he and not the prince was in command, his first and transparently obvious duty was to post vedettes and keep a soldierlike look-out on all sides. Lieutenant Carey was specially ordered to take half a dozen Basutos with him, in addition to the scanty escort allotted by the quartermaster-general of six of Bettington's Horse. He says that the escort of Basutos never came, and that the prince, when told of their absence, would not wait, but insisted on pushing forward.

The captain of a ship who, at the instance of an impatient pas-

207

senger, puts to sea with only half his water and provisions on board, endangers the lives of those under his command, and for ever forfeits his claim to future confidence in his conduct and prudence. We are told that as the first division and the flying column of General Wood were on converging lines, and were rapidly approaching, and that as the ground over which this fatal reconnaissance was made had been previously explored by the prince, Lieutenant Carey was justified in arriving at the illogical conclusion that it must be safe from an enemy.

A more preposterous assertion was never before made to hoodwink and blind justice. Why, not a day passed during this unhappy war when the troops, in all their camps, were not dogged and followed by parties more or less numerous, whose duties were to lie in wait for and cut off any imprudent scouts or stragglers from the camp. The officer in command of the escort should have been aware of this, and should have known that the fact of a particular neighbourhood or *kraal* having been searched a week previously and found deserted afforded no presumption that the locality would not be full of Kaffirs some days further on.

After the word "Mount" was given by the prince, a fact which is to most minds somewhat doubtful, we are told that the volley of musketry was fired, and that some of the horses broke away, while that of the prince became so frightened that he could not be mounted. "One by one the party galloped past the prince, who was in vain endeavouring to mount." Where was the friend and associate of England's guest? Where was the officer who had specially applied for this sacred and most honourable duty? Where, we want to know, was the English officer in command of the "escort"? His place was with his men, not leading them away with their backs to the paltry handful of Zulus, which, it is now known, were in the mealies, but holding the ground, and covering the body of his charge.

The captain of a sinking or waterlogged vessel is not the first man in the boats, leaving passengers and crew to sink without him. His place is upon his deck, trumpet in hand, and even if death-doomed, sinking like an Englishman under the shadow of the British flag. Such, comparatively, was the place and the devoir of the officer in command of the prince's escort, and had he devoted one brief half-moment to see and aid our guest to his saddle he would, even if killed or wounded in the act, have earned a name in every English and French household more cherished and lustrous than the star of valour which our queen gives to her bravest men.

We now come to the statements of the survivors, and here we are at a considerable loss to reconcile the accounts. It is distinctly mentioned by one witness that the abandoned prince was seen vainly endeavouring to spring into the saddle by the aid of the holster and the cantle. The story must be received with considerable reservation, if not utter mistrust. The prince, it is well-known, was a most accomplished horseman, and especially distinguished by his proficiency in all the arts and minutiae of the *manége*, and he therefore would be most unlikely to attempt to mount in the way described. Almost the first lesson given in the riding-school to a recruit is the one which teaches the method of mounting the horse. The merest novice in military equitation must be aware that the first motion with the left hand is to grasp a lock of the mane, before placing the right hand upon the cantle of the saddle, or horse's back if not saddled.

The prince was too well-drilled a cavalier to think of mounting by grasping either the saddle-flap, holster, or stirrup-leather, either of which would tend to turn a loosely-girthed saddle round under the horse. If the witnesses had sufficient time to minutely describe the details of the prince's desperate struggle, they undoubtedly had equal time and opportunity to have drawn rein and assisted him to mount. From all that can be gleaned of a reliable nature, it would appear that the one exception of devotion and courage displayed in this otherwise disgraceful affair was exhibited by the friendly Zulu who was with the party. He it was who first discovered the proximity of the enemy, and who, not being mounted, might have had some excuse for trying to save his life by timely flight. But he stayed loyally and gallantly with his white comrades, and came back with quiet and deliberate consideration to give warning of the concealed Zulus.

Even then it would appear that he did not attempt to fly, but fought with his breast to the foe until overcome by numbers. This poor fellow's body was afterwards discovered not far from that of the prince, riddled with wounds, and in a pool of his own and the enemy's blood, together with a number of his own *assegais* broken, but reeking with the gore of his assailants. Doubtless, the first and real great error was committed by the prince and his party advancing without the Basutos detailed to accompany them. Had these native scouts, whose powers of observation and eyesight so far exceed those of any white man, that no reconnaissance was considered complete without them, paraded as they had been ordered to, it is beyond question that they would have detected the vicinity of the concealed Zulus, and a fearful tragedy would have been averted.

The sad news thrilled the whole camp. In every tent, and amongst each group of old and young soldiers around the bivouac fires, the tidings were discussed during the whole of the evening, and late into the night. General Newdigate was applied to by General Marshall for permission to take out a cavalry patrol, during the night, to recover the body of the ill-fated prince, but the former thought it would be more prudent to wait for the daylight. At four a.m., however, two squadrons were paraded in front of the camp, and, under General Marshall's command, proceeded in the direction of the plateau three miles above the junction of the Tombolaka and Ityolyozi Rivers—about equidistant between the cavalry camp at the Incetu Neck and that of Wood at the Munhla hill, and some twelve miles from either.

About eight miles from Incetu the horsemen came to a bend of the river, and after crossing the *spruit*, which in the rainy season helps to fill the Ityolyozi, they came to the base of one of those flat-topped hills which are so common in this country. With some considerable difficulty they ascended to the summit of this *kop*, from which was obtained a splendid view of the river below as it wound along the valley, and at the further end fell over a ledge of rock by a directly perpendicular descent of 150 feet high and fifty feet wide. Here the water whirled down into the abyss beneath, and seemed to be carried off in a serpentine form through a deep channel between great red scarped rocks. In the ascent to the *kop* several small but well-built Zulu *kraals* were passed, and it was noticed that the huts were very neatly built. The wickerwork was made of wattles, light and straight, and bent over at regular distances. The *kraals* were well plastered and very neatly thatched, while the doors were made rather small, with the flooring hard and smooth.

At the upper end there was a raised ledge running right across the hut, which served as a cupboard where all utensils are placed. Firewood was neatly packed inside between two grass copes which were fastened against the wall. The furniture was scanty and all of native manufacture, and some large clay pots to hold native beer were, in several of the huts. Looking down over the ground dividing the lower ground from the higher range, a fine view broke upon the eye in the foreground. Mount Munhla stood well out of the range upon the plain like some huge bastion, while behind it endless grassy slopes filled up the foreground of the picture. The hill ascended was one of the spots selected by the prince for his sketches, and here it was that

210

the party had made their first halt. Here they could be in no danger of surprise, and well would it have been if the party had chosen an equally safe position to off-saddle on Sunday.

There is no doubt that the prince's talent with the pencil and the pen, combined with his remarkable proficiency in military surveying, while making his services so valuable to the army, contributed in no inconsiderable manner to the risks which on several occasions he ran. From this spot, the prince, when he had finished his sketches, pointed out to Lieutenant Carey the *kraal* at which he had been fired at on a previous occasion. From here might be seen the Umbazini, about two miles farther on, and the *kraal*, consisting of five huts, where the Prince was killed. Vedettes were now ordered to push along the ridges to right and left, and to signal as they advanced, while the main body of horsemen, in sections of fours, were led by the general down the north-eastern side of the *krantz*.

It was an interesting sight to see the long blue and white hue of horsemen winding like a huge serpent round the sides of the mountain; the steel-topped bamboo lances and fluttering pennons glistening bravely in the morning sunlight, while the horses' hoofs, noiseless upon the soft and elastic *veldt*, were in harmony with the silence and sad expression that were maintained in the ranks.

From the general and all the officers to the rear-rank files there was a subdued and solemn determination of countenance which was far more eloquent in sympathy for their dead comrade than any words could speak, while might be seen, at the same time, in every eye and on every lip, a stern resolve of retribution should opportunity occur. The cry of "English cowards!" so often hurled at our men at Ekowe, at Zlobani, at Kambula, Ginghilovo, and, above all, on the fatal Sunday, was rankling in the hearts of our men, as they longed to find themselves in the presence of a Zulu force.

As they rode cautiously yet speedily down the slopes of the mountain and came nearer and nearer to the place of blood, low whispers and murmurs in subdued accents were heard in the ranks, bronzed and bearded faces seemed to grow more ironlike and hard, weapons were grasped with a tighter clutch, and every eye scanned and searched the horizon for a hidden enemy. No trumpet was sounded, but lance signals were employed to tell the vedettes to close in upon the column as it advanced nearer to the *kraal*. Now could be seen the long and luxuriant patches of Tambookie grass and mealies intermixed which gave shelter to the foe, and whose proximity was so strangely and unaccountably ignored by the escort of the prince.

In front, with General Marshall and two other officers of the 17th Lancers, rode Captain Wyatt-Edgell, their eyes fixed on the *donga*, where the massacre—for it is difficult to give it another name—took place. Would the lifeless remains of one whose bright spirit was part of a widowed and stricken life, whose pure and Christian nature ennobled the profession of strife to which his heart was devoted, be left intact by the savages or mutilated by the instincts of their brutal superstition? Would the young, calm, and somewhat sad eyes so well remembered by each be torn or defaced by the vulture, or his still more repugnant rival the common *aasvogel* (*gyps tulvus*), and would that lithe and graceful form which used to lounge at evening into the homely bell-tent and interchange camp gossip and pleasant badinage with glad and devoted comrades—would all these be gone to human sight and ken? Were they to have the mournful and defeated joy of bearing those poor shorn relics back even one stage on the way to a broken-hearted mother's hearth; or had the wild dog and the eagle feasted upon all that once was the pride and the hope of Imperial Gaul?

As they neared the horrible pit, for it was nothing more, where the boy so well loved by all had given his spirit to Him who gave it, they were startled and horror-stricken at the sight of some bearded vultures, hawks, falcons, and secretary-birds, which mounted on the wing from the long, dank grasses as the advance was made; and they shuddered at the thought of the ghoul-like banquet of which they might have partaken. But a deep and impassable *kloof* had to be crossed, and although time was of the greatest importance at that moment. General Marshall was too good a *sabreur* to hazard the lives of the living without precaution, in order to recover the relics of the dead. Consequently, as it was quite possible that the foes might have discovered how valued was the life which had been so carelessly squandered, and that a large force might be hidden in other and neighbouring ambush, the usual simple but most effectual precautions were taken while the advance was continued.

Vedettes were again thrown out, lance in sling and carbine on thigh. Oh! what a moment of pride for Drury-Lowe, for Boulderson, for Edgell, for Cooke, or for "Dick" Boyle (had he been there to see). Every trooper's eye gleamed with excitement, every thigh pressed the horse's flank, and every heart throbbed with unspeakable rapture at the thought that a chance might be gained to dash as an *enfant perdu*

212

at the Golgotha where the dead friends should be, even though the living enemies were waiting to wrap and twine them in their grim embrace. Twelve men were selected to ride to the right, left, and front, and report. They had orders to dash at once into the bush should a Zulu appear.

To run away in the open before these people is not only madness, but almost certain death to those whose misfortune it is to be left behind; but the merest tyro in North American, South African, or, indeed, any bush warfare, must know that once in the bush the assailed well-armed is more than a match for the antagonist ill armed. But a ravine yet intervened between them and the scene of slaughter, and they were compelled to make a somewhat wide detour, during the passage of which, however, each eye and ear was on the *qui vive* to the slightest rustle of branch or bough.

A group of officers were riding in front; but one topic could be discussed—a sad and yet a cherished and welcome theme. There is that peculiar temperament and idiosyncrasy about the soldier, a mixture of sentiment, poetry, and practical common sense, which makes up a philosophy all its own, and a measure of life and death, which no man who holds not his life in the hollow of his palm can pretend to comprehend. "*Dépêchez-vous, s'il vous plait, monsieur,*" rang in every ear, and seemed to be echoed through the eldritch and ghostlike solitudes of the greystones and caverns above. The ravens, disturbed at their approach, screamed as they passed on, while the monkeys, nestling among the luxuriant clusters of *imporotla* or *peopisi*,—fruit whose pods, three feet long, full of large broad beans, hanging from the branches like cucumbers or sausages, gave a singular, a cultivated, and almost civilized aspect to the scene,—seemed as wishing to point out the spot where the gallant young Prince was slain.

Some Zulus, about one hundred in number, were now seen hiding in bushes and caves; but they were quickly dislodged by a party of dismounted lancers under Adjutant Frith, a smart officer and worthy follower in the old traditions of his corps. The line then brought its shoulders sharply round to the left, and covered the five huts forming the *kraal*, while the officers in front galloped through the *tambookie* grass and maize, and posted vedettes at each angle of the plantation. Taking open order, General Marshall now advanced and surrounded the *donga*, and, dismounting himself, with three other officers, descended the slopes of the worn and steep shelter that held what once was a bright and gallant spirit.

A small bank of sand, over which the sparse and struggling wild flowers were striving to blossom and flourish, gave a pillow to the young prince, whose body divested of all clothing, and stripped bare save for a charm or locket round his neck, lay extended, not in writhed contortion, but graceful as in slumber. The face was composed and almost smiling, and looked up to the sky towards which the pure and unselfish spirit had soared. No trace of a violent and bloody death could be seen on the fair and unwrinkled brow, where the lines of thought, care, and sorrow, were as yet unploughed. The eyes were open, and seemed to gaze up with human sympathy, though one was injured by a cruel wound which gashed the lid and eyebrow.

The body was not mutilated, and save for the eighteen *assegai* wounds in the chest and front, no desecration of the clay had been committed. The left arm lay across the chest as if striving to shield the heart from some cruel thrust, while the right grasped in deathly rigour a tuft of human hair, which showed in conclusive evidence that the boy must have had time to close in the last death-struggle with one at least of his assailants.

Beyond this fact, the ground near where the body lay was trampled and tossed, while here and there, in the direction towards which the Zulus fled, dark congealed clots of blood were still to be seen. Hence the conclusion that the generous and high-souled boy, whom all loved so well, had preserved, if not his revolver (which probably was left in his holster), at least his sword, and that, accomplished swordsman as he was, even in his mortal agony he had been able to sell his life dearly, and strike as he fell. Hard-hearted and hard-headed troopers, impervious to danger and to hardships, bowed their heads in sorrow and shame to their horses' manes, while the fierce light of battle which is to be seen when the trumpet sounds the "charge" gleamed through the mist of tears, as these honest fellows looked upon the remains of him whose gashed body seemed to appeal to them.

But the sad duty was but half achieved, and, under the kind supervision of General Marshall, a soldier's bier was quickly improvised of 17th lances, covered with cut rushes and mealies laid above, while a horseman's cloak lay like a shroud to cover the whole. Tenderly and reverently as soldiers only can lift was the body lifted to its carriage, and it was carried in relays by loving and respectful hands back over the long and difficult road to the camp, where, on the same day, the whole of the division paraded to do honour to the dead. When the camp was nearly reached a messenger was sent on, and General

214

Newdigate and his staff came out to meet the sad cortege, and when inside the lines, a gun-carriage was brought, upon which, decently wrapped in linen clothes and covered with the Union Jack, the remains were tenderly laid, while the funeral service was impressively performed by the Rev. Charles Ballard, the Roman Catholic chaplain, Lord Chelmsford, who was deeply affected, being the chief mourner.

The same evening the corpse was enclosed in a rough deal coffin and conveyed by a mule waggon to Maritzburg. It was met bareheaded by the Lieutenant-Governor, the Colonial Secretary, General Sir John Bissett, and General Clifford, while minute-guns were fired from the fort, and all the flags were at half-mast. Here again there was an elaborate and impressive funeral, the coffin being carried by the representatives of every branch of the service, and followed out of the town by the whole of the large garrison, the civic authorities, and the Roman Catholic, Protestant, and Dissenting clergy. At Durban, where the remains arrived on the 10th inst., the body was received by the mayor and Corporation.

The streets leading to the Roman Catholic Church were lined by the garrison, leaning on their arms, reversed, and a requiem mass was celebrated the same day. The following morning the coffin was received on board Her Majesty's ship *Boadicea*, being escorted to the point of embarkation by the naval and military authorities, while the sad boom of the minute-guns accompanied the procession. The *Boadicea* then sailed for Simon's Bay. Arrived there, the relics were transferred to Her Majesty's ship *Orontes*, and so conveyed to England.

After identification and lying in state at the Woolwich Arsenal, the body was conveyed to the empress's residence at Chiselhurst; there, with all the pomp and pageantry of full military honours, it was laid in the tomb in the same chapel, where rest the remains of his loved father, Napoleon III., Emperor of France. The utmost sympathy was shown for his bereaved mother by the whole English nation, from highest to lowest. The queen in person attended the funeral at Chiselhurst, and amongst the pall-bearers were the Prince of Wales, the Duke of Cambridge, the Duke of Connaught, the Duke of Edinburgh, and Prince Leopold.

A court-martial was held on Lieutenant Carey, on the charge of having behaved in an unsoldierlike manner in face of the foe; but the sentence was kept secret, awaiting its confirmation by the commander-in-chief in England. Meanwhile Lieutenant Carey was sent home under arrest. On his arrival there the proceedings of the court-martial were declared null and void on account of some technical irregularity, and he was ordered to resume his duties. (It is untrue that he since received a high staff appointment).

It was generally understood that the sentence was dismissal from the service with ignominy, but that it was not confirmed by the special desire of the empress, who made a personal request to the queen that nothing should be done in the matter.

CHAPTER 10

March of the 2nd Column

Two special orders were issued by Lord Chelmsford's command in regard to this most melancholy affair. The first, dated Pietermaritzburg, June 5, was signed by General Clifford:—

The Inspector-General of Lines of Communication and Base has received from his Excellency the Lieut. General Commanding official confirmation of the calamity which has befallen the forces under his command, by the death, on duty in the field, of the late gallant young soldier, the Prince Imperial Louis Napoleon, who, having, in his military training, been lately associated with the British Army, came out to this country to take part in the Zulu campaign. The general feels that he is carrying out the wishes of his Excellency the Lieut. General Commanding now in Zululand, by thus recording the feelings of deep sorrow and sympathy, experienced by every officer and man whose duty keeps him at his post in the colony with the loss thus sustained.

The second order was issued by Major Butler to the troops at Durban, and expressed the feeling and sympathy of all the columns:—

In following the coffin which holds the body of the late Prince Imperial of France, and paying to his ashes the final tribute of sorrow and honour, the troops of the garrison will remember that he was the last inheritor of a mighty name and great military renown; secondly, that he was the son of England's firm allies in dangerous days; and, thirdly, that he was the sole child of a widowed empress, now left throneless and childless in exile upon English shores, deepening the profound sorrow and solemn reverence to those memories. The troops will also

217

remember that the Prince Imperial of France fell fighting as a British soldier.

On the 28th of May the second column or division quitted the camp at Landsman's Drift, and proceeded to Kopje Allein, which is near the Blood River, being about a mile to the north-east of it, at a point as near as possible to the junction of that stream with the Buffalo. The position of the camp there was all that could be desired, and the character of the country was much more favourable than most of the previously selected camps, inasmuch as no enemy could approach without being seen for several miles.

At Kopje Allein there was a further concentration, and several reinforcements were received, the consequence being that the whole force amounted to 2500 British infantry, 1100 British cavalry, 300 Artillery, 100 Engineers, 66 Colonial Horse, 1300 Native Infantry, and in all, with Military Train and Hospital Staff, making 5700 men. It was found impossible, for sanitary reasons, to form one undivided column, and much as General Newdigate objected to straggling, the exigencies of war compelled him to send his forces off in detachments. The King's Dragoon Guards marched on Monday, the 26th, and these were followed by Harness's Battery and a large convoy of stores on the following day, Tuesday, the 27th.

On the Wednesday the headquarter staff took the road, accompanied by the 17th Lancers, Le Grice's Field Battery, the field-hospital, and the 24th Regiment. They took with them fifteen days' supplies, and to accomplish this General Newdigate wisely cut everything down to the lowest possible limit, sixteen men being allotted to each tent, and one tent only to six officers. Tents were really superfluous; for the climate is simply magnificent, and no man out on a shooting expedition would dream of carrying about with him such extra luxury as a bell-tent. Of course the climate of this portion of Zululand being semitropical, the usual precautions to be used in tropical lands must be used here. The climate and diseases which prevail along the line, from the Tugela, by which Crealock was advancing, are thus alluded to by Dr. Jones, district surgeon, one of the most experienced authorities upon the subject.

He says that at a distance of fifteen miles from the sea the fever is not more prevalent than in the interior; that the high ground is comparatively safe in his district, and that the type of fever is mild, the attack lasting usually from five to twenty days. It begins about February, and is always at its worst in March, continuing more or less till the end of May, and appearing to be more or less influenced by the current of the north-east wind, which would, of course, carry the miasma of the St. Lucia swamps in this direction.

Dr. Dalzell, an equally good authority as Dr. Jones, says that the high lands here are remarkably healthy. The same holds good of the tract known as Oham's country, situated in the valley of the Black Umvolosi River. It is evident that the fever of this country has been greatly exaggerated, and that it is merely intensified in localities which are within reach of the poisonous malaria borne upon the wind. General Newdigate and General Crealock both gave orders, that when the troops had to bivouac, they were never on any account to pass the night either on a very low or on a very wet situation, on account of fever, or on the hill-tops, on account of thunderstorms.

The position of the Zulu *kraals* should invariably be noted, and a lesson taken from them in regard to choice of camp; while the neighbourhood of a river that has been lately flooded should, if possible, be always avoided. It is possible that a white man settling here for good would sooner or later be attacked by fever, but white men do not settle here, while a rapid march through the country appears to injure no one. Dysentery and rheumatism troubled the troops but little, and cases of sunstroke were rare. Sickness had prevailed certainly to a considerable extent in some corps; but it was, as a rule, confined to the young soldiers, unseasoned and of weak physique, who had been lately sent out from England.

The cause of our failures—and there were several of a palpable nature—are not to be found in want of generalship, want of organisation, or want of transport. They were due undoubtedly to the sending out of raw, sickly, unseasoned, and untutored boys, who, being the sweepings of half the regiments in Her Majesty's service, could not possibly have any feeling of communion, or traditional sympathy, with the corps into which, before a formidable enemy, they found themselves pitchforked. Most of the battalions out there had to draw their reinforcements not from its reserve battalion or depot at home, as was the case in former years, but from the army at large, and some battalions arrived on the shores of Africa so drenched and diluted with outsiders, that they had the appearance of a mongrel pack, unused to discipline and useless in the field.

That the destruction of the regimental system by Lord Cardwell has been the original cause of several of our reverses, surprises, and humiliations, there can be little hesitation in saying. The men at Isand-hlwana were not well handled, it must be admitted; but it has since leaked out that many of them would not rally round their officers, but attempted safety in flight. Dozens of the men, sergeants and other non-commissioned officers, have since declared they did not even know the names of their company officers, or those of their right or left-thand man.

Another instance of the evil effects of Lord Cardwell's system may be given. The 91st recruits in past days were the envy of all recruiting-sergeants, and so particular was the colonel, backed up by the surgeon of the corps, that a young fellow must have had chest, constitution, and stamina—qualities unfortunately not now insisted upon—before he could pass the sacred portals of the 91st barrack. Few regiments, however, have suffered from the present system more than, or so much as, this corp. On receiving its orders for Zululand, it could not muster 200 men, so denuded was the regiment of rank and file by the drafts it had previously given. The consequence was that to make up the 900 men which was supposed to be its fighting strength, volunteers and drafts had to be obtained from half the regiments at home, and the facings of the 91st on parade, until the master tailor had put matters a little straight, represented almost all the colours of the rainbow, while the men, drawn from all parts, neither knew one another nor the officers set over them.

Rumours of negotiations for peace, and the granting of an armistice, which were being circulated about this time, arose from the following facts:—In the middle of May, Zulu messengers, of some position, but not of the highest rank, had presented themselves to General Crealock, with a desire to know what terms would be granted to Cetywayo in case of his wishing to come to terms of peace. The general, finding they had no authority or commission from the king, sent them away, but believing from their statements that they were sincere, and knowing at the same time that Setewango, one of the king's most influential *indunas*, and Samapo and Panato, the indunas who commanded against Pearson at Ekowe, were in the neighbourhood of Ginghilovo, let Setewango know that he would not object to see him.

Setewango admitted that he had no commission or authority direct from the king, but added, at the same time, that many of the chiefs were sick of fighting, as they considered the English too strong. General Crealock then said he had no power to treat, but that Lord Chelmsford had, and if Cetywayo were first seen by Setewango something might be arranged. After this Setewango went to Ulundi, and after great difficulty he and the indunas persuaded the king to allow them to visit Lord Chelmsford, at whose camp they arrived early in June, having first presented themselves to General Wood. Lord Chelmsford saw these men three times, when they were distinctly told that before any negotiations could be entered into, as an evidence of the king's sincerity the whole of the spoil taken at Isandhlwana, especially the two captured 7-pounders, must be restored.

With these guns were to be sent accredited ambassadors and hostages of the highest rank. These Zulu messengers seemed much awed and impressed with the appearance of the camp, and particularly with Marshall's cavalry, and they left on the 6th instant. They had not long departed when much of their story was corroborated by Tongabena and Lampunda, two well-known friendly Zulu spies, who had just arrived from Ulundi, where they assured us there were few warriors, the men having declined to assemble. Dabulamanzi, whose death has been so often reported, was still there, and a large number of women, children, stores, and cattle. Umbelini was really dead, having been three times severely wounded, and was hit mortally in the back through the blade-bone as he was escaping on horseback.

On June 5th, Marshall had a very exciting little brush with the Zulus not far from Wood's camp on the Nondonini river. In this affair poor young Frith, a capital soldier, a good adjutant, and a general favourite, was unfortunately killed. He was sitting on his horse receiving an order from Colonel Drury-Lowe, when a Martini-Henry bullet struck him, probably to the heart, as he never spoke. The patrol was brought about by information brought into Wood's camp by the ubiquitous and indefatigable Buller, who had been out on the previous day and discovered the whereabouts of a large Zulu force.

The gallant 17th and the smart King's Dragoon Guards were delighted to see themselves in orders on the afternoon of the 4th, that they were to parade at four a.m. under General Marshall, who was also to take with him Shepstone's Basutos and Bettington's cavalry. It was not yet sunrise when they arrived at Wood's camp on the Nondonini, and then found that Buller, anxious to draw first blood, had already started in the night to scour the country and report what he could discover of the enemy.

After partaking of some excellent coffee, a little *beltong*, and some well-made and well-baked bread done in Wood's field-ovens, they were again in the saddle, taking a course towards the south-east, till the summit of a wild ridge overlooking a deep *kloof* was reached. In the plain below was a pretty little river, and near its bank a number of Kaffir huts all blazing, having been fired early by Buller and his men, who could be seen slowly retiring before a number of Zulus, who were keeping up a hot fire upon them, as well as from both sides of the valley. The order was given to advance, and Buller soon came on to meet them, making his report that he had been attacked by these Zulus as soon as he attempted to fire the *kraal*. Frith was the only casualty, and the order was then given by General Marshall to retire firing by alternate squadrons. As the Zulus were posted in clefts and caves of the ridges on either side, it was impossible to get at them, and so the troops were brought steadily off without further loss.

Lord Chelmsford had intended having a large depot formed on a portion of the Ibabanango range; but owing to one of the principal staff officers losing not only his own way, but his head, his lordship was compelled to change the venue, and form the principal depot upon the Upoko River, not far from the spot where the prince met his fate. This was called Fort Newdigate, and was held by four companies of infantry, and a detachment or two of cavalry to keep up communication with a still more advanced depôt afterwards formed at Umsenguini, near the source of the Upoko, where the main road from Utrecht and the Transvaal forms a junction with that leading through Rorke's Drift and Isandhlwana.

How arduous were the duties of the cavalry in convoying large trains of supplies from the bases to the front through the enemy's country may be surmised, when it is borne in mind that Lord Chelmsford had to feed 7000 whites, 2000 natives, 350 English draught-horses, 860 saddle-horses, 2000 colonial horses and mules, and 10,634 oxen. From these figures also may be formed an estimate of the work thrown upon the commissariat.

In previous wars out in South Africa blame has been, and not unjustly, thrown upon the commissariat for the manner in which stores have been wasted and frittered away while the troops have been without rations. But in this war it would be impossible to cite any such instance of want of management, as the troops were invariably well fed and cared for. Want of success, therefore, could in no case be attributed to want of supply. Great praise is due to Commissary-General Strickland for the excellent manner in which all his plans were laid and executed. Another instance of good work may be given. On the 4th instant Lord Chelmsford had occasion to send a sudden order to

Commissary-General Brownrigg for the immediate furnishing and delivery of rations equal to six weeks' supply for 9000 Europeans, 2500 natives, 1200 English horses, and 3000 cattle, and all these were sent in by the 10th.

On June 10th Sir Evelyn Wood's column received a valuable addition to its force; *viz.* 450 men of the 80th Regiment, all old and seasoned campaigners in South Africa, together with four splendid Gatling guns. On the same day a report was made that Zulus had been seen near the Inyezani, and on the following morning a patrol was sent out, consisting of twenty Mounted Infantry, thirty Mounted Basutos, and fifty Light Horse, under the command of Captain Brown, who had with him Lord William Beresford, and Captains Cochrane, D'Arcy, and Berry. A reconnaissance for fully twenty miles from the camp was made, and the patrol returned about six the same evening, having made several sketches and surveys of the country, but without seeing any Zulus.

Meanwhile grumblers and incompetent critics had kept so incessantly bringing all sorts of reckless charges against Lord Chelmsford, of incapacity as a soldier, that the home government thought it wise to give way, and accordingly, to please the *vulgus pro-fanum*, recalled Sir Garnet Wolseley from Cyprus, and appointed him Governor of South Africa, High Commissioner in Natal and the Transvaal, and commander-in-chief of Her Majesty's forces in Africa, thus superseding Lord Chelmsford. This news reached the troops actively employed against the Zulus about the middle of June, and was received with considerable dissatisfaction by both officers and men.

It seemed to them unfair that their general should be superseded just as a final advance was being made, and just as he was about to reap the fruits of all his anxiety and labour. He had at that time on the way to Ulundi a perfectly-equipped force of 9364 Imperial Infantry, 3957 Colonial Infantry, 1190 Imperial Cavalry, 1877 Colonial Cavalry, 775 Artillery, with a proportionate number of guns (36), and 385 Royal Engineers. Generals Crealock and Newdigate had received full instructions with regard to the concentration and movement of this force, and all the organisation had been planned and carried out under the personal supervision of Lord Chelmsford, who had worked night and day to get matters to a state of efficiency. It seemed, therefore, rather hard and disheartening that the new general, who had had none of the anxiety or the toil, should appear as the *Deus ex machina* upon the scene, and reap all the credit and glory of the campaign.

A great deal of rubbish was talked about the inhumanity of burning down *kraals*, and accusations of shooting down women and children were not unfrequently brought against the troops. Now most people in England do not know that there are three distinct species of *kraals*. The king's or royal *kraals*, the military *kraals*—*i. e.* the respective barracks or official homes of the different corps—and, finally, the tribal and domestic *kraal*, a sort of village of cabins, built together for convenience and safety. Now, Lord Chelmsford and all his lieutenants were too good soldiers to allow England's honour to be disgraced by wanton cruelty or barbarous conduct even in fighting a barbarous enemy.

Military *kraals*, being the fortified depots of the king's troops, their mustering rendezvous and rallying-points, were attacked and destroyed without compunction, as they represented the arsenals and strongholds of the enemy. The king's royal *kraals*, on the other hand, were the places where Cetywayo got together cattle, mealies, and other commissariat supplies, wherewith to tempt or reward his warriors. These were destroyed as a matter of course, as one would capture a convoy or destroy a hostile magazine.

It has been stated on apparently good authority that the destruction of a royal or military *kraal* was considered by the Zulus as scarcely any loss, and that the rebuilding of such was a matter of the greatest ease. This is a totally erroneous view, as all the *kraals* belonging to Cetywayo and his great chiefs which had been destroyed were most formidable as regards defence, and must have taken great time and trouble to construct. All these *kraals* of the kings, princes, and principal chiefs are protected with high wooden stockades, pierced here and there with low entrances, large enough to admit only one person at a time. The *isigodhlo*, or inner enclosure, where the chief huts are situated, is guarded by zigzags of the same description of stockade work very strongly put together.

There are altogether about forty military villages or *kraals* scattered through the country, of from 400 to 3000 huts each, in which for a portion of the year the troops are quartered, averaging 2000 men in each. There are, however, other military *kraals* not fortified, and used only as barracks. These consist of a dry stake and wattle fence, generally oval in form and about five feet high. Inside this fence are the huts of the men in single, double, or treble rows, according to the size of the *kraal*, while inside the huts is another fence similar to the one outside, and the central space is invariably the cattle-pen.

The king's *kraal* at Ulundi (afterwards destroyed) was 800 yards in diameter, and had a normal garrison of 5000 men. The Umhlabatini plains, upon which it was situated, are fifteen by twenty miles in extent, and completely shut in by hills studded with thick bush. The White Umvolosi runs through this plain, in which were also established the other *kraals* forming the headquarters of regiments. These, too, were subsequently destroyed. Here in these *kraals* the principal regiments were wont to assemble annually at the great national military festival held in honour of the king, which is now a tradition. of the past. Some years ago, when Cetywayo was full of ambition in regard to his military power, and anxious in every manner to consolidate it, he had a new magazine or depot of arms built at the junction of the Black and White Umvolosi Rivers.

This magazine and *kraal* is called Amanzekanze, and is surrounded by a dense bush. The Amanzekanze *kraal* had, up to this time, held the reputation of being impregnable, and its approaches, it was said, were so difficult that they could only be forced at immense loss. The name of the *kraal*, Amanzekanze, translated is "Let the enemy come now."

Coming now to the farming and domestic *kraals*, it may without fear of contradiction be asserted, after minute and careful inquiries, that no single instance can be adduced in which Her Majesty's troops ever attacked or molested such unless first attacked and fired upon.

A few words must here be said concerning the helioscope, which on more than one occasion played a prominent part in this war.

One of the great features of the occupation of Port Durnford was the establishment of mirror-signals from the "*kop*" at Port Durnford, and at the post on the Inyezani down to the mouth of the Umlalasi. The use of mirrors as a means of communication had been so fully demonstrated in Afghanistan, that it seemed astonishing that army officers at Natal were supremely ignorant of, and, indeed, indifferent to, the system. When it is remembered that by this simple process it was found possible to flash intelligence and words of sympathy and kindness to the half-famished garrison at Ekowe, and that by means of this admirable invention, many important items of intelligence were from time to time instantaneously and surely communicated from one part of the British force to another, which through the position of the enemy it was only possible to send by messengers, who were compelled to take the most circuitous routes, thus causing great delay and sometimes even failing to reach their destination at all, the value of this simple yet grand discovery cannot be too highly considered.

Its importance in some respects may indeed be declared to be in advance of the electric telegraph, for that necessitates apparatus of delicate mechanism and a friendly, or at least non-hostile territory, over which the messages are sent. A predatory or hostile tribe may at any time sever the line of telegraphic wire, and cut all communications between neighbouring columns who are anxious to make their whereabouts and intentions known; but this cannot be done to the mirror system, where with no more apparatus than a small hand-glass telegraphy is established which no mortal agency can interrupt. No invention, no discovery can surpass in value this mode of silent yet eloquent communication, and only the interruption of the sun's beams by clouds or fogs can interfere with the transmission by signals, noiselessly, and in a manner almost imperceptible to all save the two interlocutors, who may be distant ten, twenty, thirty, or even forty miles.

At Gibraltar messages are by this process constantly sent across the Straits; and in Australia, Mauritius, Singapore, and even Canada, the invention has obtained for its discoverer the greatest reputation and *kudos*.

Some four years ago Lieutenant Parrott, of the Volunteer Engineer Corps of New South Wales, conducted a series of very successful operations in mirror telegraphy, using discs, about six inches in diameter, of polished metal covered with glass. At first the distance separating the two mirrors was from six to ten miles, but eventually the system was tested from the Kumagong mountain, about 2000 feet above the sea level, to the lighthouse at the entrance to Port Jackson, 400 feet above sea level, a direct distance of nearly forty miles. Now, when we consider that the only apparatus required is a small hand-mirror, and that no skill beyond the faculty of reflecting the sun's beam in the required direction, and of flashing "dots" and "signals" by means of a simple turn of the wrist, in the same way as the Morse telegraph is presented by flag-signals, are necessary, we must allow the vast importance of this discovery to the soldier and the sailor, more especially in savage or uncivilized warfare.

Of course the whole method is dependent on the presence of sunshine, and, fortunately. Natal is seldom without this great boon. In South Africa the sun's beams are more constant than in almost any other clime, and they may be counted and depended upon during the major portion of the dry season. It is not unworthy of notice that a system of sun-signalling, not dissimilar to that established between Port Durnford and General Crealock's column, has been known and practised for some considerable time among the Nez Percés Indians of North America. Mr. F. C. Browne, of Sydney, Australia, however, gives a still more remarkable method of signalling, and states that successful feats have also been accomplished by moonlight for distances of from four to six miles. He considers, and doubtless he is correct, that it would be quite possible to supplement this sun-and-moon telegraphy on very dark nights by an analogous system of alternately obscuring and displaying at longer or shorter intervals a powerfully reflected light.

Lately at Portsmouth some highly successful experiments in night-signalling have been made by casting the electric and other powerful lights upon columns of steam; a method evidently suggested by the helioscope and use of reflecting mirrors.

CHAPTER 11

Advance of 1st Column

The actual advance of the 1st division may be said to have commenced on the 17th of June, when the gallant bluejackets and Marines (the Naval Brigade), one troop of Lonsdale's Horse, and one troop of Royal Engineers effected an important though short movement from Fort Pearson, the so-called base, to Fort Chelmsford; while the 57th Foot and Barton's Contingent pushed on to Fort Crealock. General Crealock, with his headquarters, arrived at Fort Crealock on the following day, and on the 19th reached Fort Chelmsford.

The road at starting from Fort Pearson led up a steep ascent and across a table-land, gradually sloping towards the west, with occasional slight undulations, until it came to the steep and almost cliff-like descent into the valley of the Amatikula. Here frequent outcrops of sandstone and quartz were noticeable to the engineers, whose professional enthusiasm was excited at seeing before them the materials for building a permanent fort in the district. Crystalline pebbles were plentiful, and the soil, which was in some places of a reddish hue, was at other points a pure white silver sand, both, however, being covered by a considerable layer of vegetable mould.

Many beautiful flowers gladdened the eye on the march, amongst which were tiger lilies, convolvuli, primulas of a rich deep yellow, and another species having the appearance of a foxglove opened back. In the valley of the Amatikula were some thorn-bushes of osier-like growth, which the natives use for fencing their kraals, and these bore large purple bell-shaped flowers. On the coast grow some of a similar nature, and a full mile further on were white primulas, large yellow daisies, and small red and blue flowers not unlike forget-me-nots. After this came some rough marching, excessively trying to the waggons and oxen, over very steep hills, through patches of tiger-grass, and across ravines forty and fifty feet deep, with almost precipitous sides, at each of which it became necessary to unload the more heavily-laden waggons and carry the contents up by hand.

All the hills were exceedingly rocky, being composed mostly of granite, but in some instances of nearly pure quartz, thickly clothed, however, with trees whenever the inequalities of the ground and surface allowed the soil to accumulate. The greater number of these trees were acacias in full bloom, their red, white, and yellow blossoms, and those of other flowering trees standing out in rich masses of gorgeous and Turneresque colour. Late in the afternoon the column arrived at the camping-ground near Fort Crealock, where the works were proceeding rapidly towards completion, and every preparation was being made to reconnoitre on to the Umlalasi. The *laager* was formed above a rocky pass, having at the bottom pools of water in splendid granite basins. Out of these two small streams issued, one running west and the other east, and falling ultimately into the Umlalasi and the Umlatoosi.

The next day a patrol was sent out to explore a deserted *kraal* five miles distant. Barrow, with about 100 horsemen, also went out scouting; but after riding a couple of miles found the hills so closed in on either side and the path so blocked with bamboo cane grass that his men were compelled to dismount and lead their horses. The thick growth also shut out most of the view of the hills, the prospect of which, however, when a peep was obtainable, was delightful.

By the side of the path was a torrent bed more than twenty feet deep, with nearly perpendicular sides, and over this slope went one of Barrow's men, horse and rider rolling over each other until the stream below was reached, luckily without causing any injury to the trooper—a Dutchman, whom Barrow congratulated by telling him he suffered no injury as he fell upon his head. A little hair rubbed off a remarkably sun-browned forehead was all the damage done, while the horse had only a few scratches.

The latter part of the pass, the same afternoon, when the march was continued to Chelmsford, was very slippery sandstone and quartz; and at one point, where the waggons had to wind round in single file, the hills, clothed to their summits with trees, rose to some 300 feet in height. These heights were scouted as the troops advanced, but nothing but old women and children were seen.

The valleys through which the column passed were very fertile, with pleasing alternations of open wood, jungle, grass, and cultivation. The torrents, however, from the hills in the rainy season must do great injury to the crops of mealies, and several *spruits* and streams were crossed, flowing knee-deep between thickets of bamboo and tall rushes, which, when flooded, would have been impassable.

The second brigade was behind encamped on the Inyezani, and included the Buffs, Naval Brigade, 88th, and Sandham's battery, and came on to Chelmsford as the first brigade marched into camp at Napoleon hill.

The two main causes of the seemingly protracted delay in the advance of General Crealock's division were want of transport beasts, among which a severe epidemic had broken out, and the large amount of fort-building and road-making requisite in and around Port Durnford. Still, the time taken up in regard to this new base was by no means wasted, as it sufficed to keep a large and well-armed portion of the Zulu Army idle in this vicinity, and thus gave Lord Chelmsford immense facilities for pushing on his men to the left front, whilst General Crealock was able to utilise his force towards the coast while waiting for transport to move up into the interior.

The sick-list still continued somewhat heavy, a very large proportion of officers and men being *hors de combat*. Much of the malaria, the medical authorities considered, arose from the effluvia caused by the decomposition of the numerous carcases of oxen and horses which lay all along the road, and literally tainted and poisoned the air. These carcases lay where the convoys had to pass, and the consequence was that whenever a detachment had to come or go to or from the fort, some portion, often a large percentage, reported themselves ill with fever. The remedy seemed easy, but was not so. The men were worked so hard at digging and entrenching, that it was impossible to detail fatigue parties to bury or remove the carcases, which, therefore, were left to breed pestilence in the camp.

On June 22nd General Crealock decided to make another strong reconnaissance towards the sea on the following day, and orders were given overnight that the entire cavalry force, consisting of two squadrons of mounted infantry, the Natal Horse, and the native Basuto scouts, should parade at daybreak with the whole of the 91st Highlanders. The general's object was to utilise his stay at Fort Napoleon by doing as much to open communications with Port Durnford as possible, and particularly to effect what improvements could be made in the road between the fort and that place.

The only result of this expedition was that the troops accidentally came upon a body of 250 Zulus, driving away a large number of oxen; of which, after a sharp skirmish, though without the loss of a man, they captured 192 fine head, as well as numerous women and children, who came to the general imploring protection. This was of course assured to them; and as they appeared hungry and half starved, biscuits and mealies were served out to them upon the ground.

On the homeward march to Fort Napoleon they were overtaken by two very good-looking young Zulus, fully armed and equipped in war panoply. These men stated that they belonged to Cuzame, a powerful Zulu chief, who was now on his way with his wives and head men to Fort Napoleon to surrender. On arriving at the fort later on in the evening, this was found to be the case. After a long interview with General Crealock, in which Cuzame gave some valuable information in regard to Cetywayo's army then collecting for the defence of the big *kraals*, the chief was ordered by the general to leave his family and some of his warriors, and return to his *kraal* for his arms and cattle. This he expressed himself most willing and anxious to do.

It was now discovered that it was an error to suppose that the Zulus were a united nation, all regarding Cetywayo as their supreme autocrat and head. On the contrary, there were other chieftains with objects and ambitions of their own. Thus, a chief named Umsintwanga (or the "Old Fox") came in on the morning of June 26th, with the usual ivory tusk and proposals for peace. He and his party were seen at daybreak about two or three miles from the camp trying to ford a small stream, tributary to the Umlalazi. The vedettes could not quite make out their proceedings, as, when halfway across the stream, they turned back, ascended a neighbouring *kop*, and spent a considerable time in reconnoitring the position of the fort.

This naturally excited the suspicions of the patrol, to whom the mounted vedettes reported, and a small mounted body of men was sent to make a circuit and cut them off in case they attempted to retire. Whether this movement was observed is uncertain, but eventually, after considerable delay, and after approaching the camp from several different points, the chief and his attendants, four in number only, came boldly up to the patrol, and requested to be brought into camp, to the presence of the great chief.

At eight o'clock, Umsintwanga, who is a rather finely built, elderly man, inclined to be corpulent, was brought into the presence of General Crealock, who treated him with the greatest courtesy and respect. The countenance of the chief showed a curious mixture of dogged

231

determination, savage cunning, and treachery. His hair was frizzed, and plastered elaborately with red clay and grease, while he wore a belt with some foxtails round his waist, and a species of garters of smaller tails tied below the knee. His mantle seemed to be an old and much-stained horse-blanket, and above this was a small tippet of leopard-skin, worn something like a herald's tabard. He carried no weapon save a stout knobkerrie, and his attendants, who were four splendidly stalwart Zulus, carried the tusk with the greatest ease and dignity.

Care had been taken that the place of conference should be out of sight of the fort, and for this purpose the base of a small hollow near the camp had been chosen, where the rising ground intervened and prevented any observation of what was going on in the trenches and about the lines. The conference was not of long duration, for after waiting a reasonable time to allow the chief time to collect himself, the general at once and shortly asked what was the meaning and purport of his mission, and why he had come into camp.

To this Umsintwanga, through an interpreter, replied that he was sent by the king and his *indunas* to sue for peace, and in proof of their overtures being sincere he desired to present the immemorial symbol of peace and friendship, the ivory tusk. He said further, that he was deputed to ask the stoppage of the 1st Division, the proceedings of which had much grieved and astonished the king, and he, therefore, was desired to ask that it should advance no further towards the king's *kraal*, while he, the ambassador, might be allowed to go through our division to Natal.

Umsintwanga spoke tolerably well, and seemed not to have learnt his speech off by heart, as he occasionally hesitated, stopped, and now and then exchanged words and phrases for others which he thought more suitable. General Crealock, who listened with the utmost deference and patience to the somewhat long tirade, then rather abruptly said, "Am I to understand you distinctly, and without any reservation, that you, Umsintwanga, *induna*, come direct and with full authority from the king?"

This query seemed to astonish and somewhat confuse the ambassador, who, after some little circumlocution, admitted that he had come, if not quite with the king's authority, at least with his knowledge and sanction. On being pressed a little more, the old chief further admitted that it was principally by the desire of the *indunas*, more than by that of the king, that he had come, and he still most positively adhered to the statement that his proposals were official and in good faith.

Umsintwanga was then informed that he had not come to the proper camp with his proposals, that it was to Lord Chelmsford, and no other, that he must apply, and that even if he went to Lord Chelmsford he would not be listened to unless the demands specified in his lordship's ultimatum were complied with to the letter. The whole of the interview did not occupy more than a quarter of an hour or twenty minutes: and when it was over, it would have been quite impossible to have told, from the imperturbable countenances of the *induna* and his suite, whether they were disappointed or not. They seemed to take their rebuff, as if they expected it, and were then conducted by a circuitous route away from our camp, and left, with the tusk, two miles upon their road.

It must here be remarked that Lord Chelmsford had throughout the campaign shown the greatest suavity and patience to any attempt at peaceful proposals, but he had by this time seen the necessity of a certain degree of firmness, and General Crealock, although he doubtless would have given a similar answer had he not been instructed, had a complete understanding with the commander-in-chief that no proposals were to be listened to unless accompanied with the fulfilment of the conditions laid down in the chief's message to the last messengers. Brigadiers Bray and Rowlands, together with the whole of the general's staff, were present at the interview, and the induna and his attendants, although unwilling to manifest any surprise, were evidently impressed with the quietude and promptitude with which every wish and order of the general were carried out.

Again on June 21st. General Crealock, then engaged in completing the fortifications at Napoleon hill, rode out across the Umlalazi River with a small staff and escort, to interview a chief named Umguelumgwizi, who had just made friendly overtures and expressed a wish to consult the general as to what his future line of conduct should be. Umguelumgwizi's *kraal* was some miles off, but the chief said he would come and meet the general; and not more than two miles in his direction had been traversed when he was seen coming, accompanied by several of his sons and head men.

The Zulu chief was known to be rich in cattle, and possessed of considerable local influence. He was a man apparently about fifty-two or fifty-three years of age, and, in spite of a somewhat sinister expression, had a tolerably open and apparently honest manner of speaking. He was not by any means long in coming to the point, declaring emphatically that he had no quarrel with the English, or, for the matter of that, he added, with the Dutch. He had heard of and understood the award given by the English Commissioners in regard to the Dutch boundary, and he thought "Sompsen" and "Bartle" had behaved most generously to Cetywayo. He had been obliged to go out to fight on Cetywayo's side, but neither he nor his young men wished to go out again. If he refused, he would be accused of witchcraft, "smelt out" and "eaten out." What was he under these circumstances to do?

General Crealock, who had listened very patiently to this somewhat long harangue, said he had spoken honestly and well, that as a soldier he did not wish to advise any man to desert his king or his chief, but that he could not be doing wrong in refusing to fight in what he considered an unjust cause. If he chose to come in and surrender, with his arms, his cattle, his wives, children, and his tribe, all should be protected, and all should be held for him in trust till peace was made. The chief, who seemed much pleased with General Crealock's kind and manly advice, consulted a few moments with those of his advisers who were with him, and then asked the general to give him one day for consideration.

"Willingly, my friends," said Crealock, "and I will meet you on this side of the river tomorrow, when you can tell me your decision."

Upon the Monday (June 22nd), therefore, directly after the general had made his usual tour of inspection among the road fatigues, he crossed over, this time with a couple of troops of Barrow's men, and met Umguelumgwizi with an immense following, consisting of his wives and children. The general, however, explained to the chief that he could only accept this surrender in part, and that it would not be complete until all his cattle and all his fighting men came in. This the chief promised to attend to.

On the 25th the 1st Brigade, under General Rowlands, crossed and moved down the river, encamping about six miles from here. The day following this brigade moved on to Port Durnford, and reinforced the small force there. On the 27th Clarke's Brigade started from this place, and moved on to support Rowlands', encamping and *laagering* up two hills in sight of the 1st Brigade. From this encampment a splendid view of Fort Durnford can be obtained.

The long ranges of mountains, which completely. separate the coast-line from the interior, here stand out in magnificent relief, and although they are at a distance of fifty to seventy miles, they present a sharply defined outline in the morning air, their ravines, watercourses, and terraced heights appearing with almost supernatural distinctness.

Here is a country where the light is rich and brilliant, where the atmosphere is surpassingly bright and clear, and the scenery bold, spacious, and grand. The characteristic beauty of light in South Africa is not seen in its blending with manifold forms of cloud so much as in the full and even splendour with which it penetrates the air.

Distant objects, that in a less brilliant atmosphere fade away in hazy outline, stand out with perfect distinctness. Let a spectator place himself at a distance of twenty or thirty miles from the Drakenberg, or any of the big ranges of this country, and contrast the effect he will obtain with that he would experience with Snowdon, Mangerton, or any of our home mountains at a similar distance. Small boulders, cavernous hollows in the rocks, patches of bush at the head of the *kloofs*, at an elevation of 2000 or 3000 feet, are seen with the naked eye without difficulty. A northern mountain at home, at either of these elevations, will appear in more or less of hazy outline with all details of face and profile obscured, but here in the clear atmosphere of Zululand, the very direction of the watercourses, the curves of the *kloofs*, and, indeed, every bold wrinkle on the face of the slopes of the mountains can be most clearly discerned.

We must now leave Crealock building his forts and making his roads, while we turn our attention to the movements of Newdigate and Wood.

Every facility had been given to Crealock's (1st) Division to make the first forward movement on the king's *kraal*. Lord Chelmsford considering that after the difficulties General Crealock had encountered it would be only fair to him and to those under his command to give him every chance of winning first blood in the final attack. However, the coast sickness proved so fatal to Crealock's transport train that he was utterly unable to take advantage of Lord Chelmsford's generosity, and it was to the 2nd column that the final honours of Ulundi fell. On Saturday, the 21st inst., General Newdigate with this column reached the right bank of the Umlatoosi, while Evelyn Wood, with his strong flying column, had slightly preceded him, and had encamped a little lower down on the left bank.

Newdigate's brigadiers were Glynn and Collingwood, with Marshall in command of the cavalry; and his corps were two batteries of artillery and an ammunition column, the 2nd company of Engineers, the King's Dragoon Guards and 17th Lancers, the 21st, the 1-24th, 58th, and 94th Regiments, Shepstone's Horse, No, 3 Troop, and the Mounted Natives. This force made up 1870 Europeans, 530 Natives, and eight guns. Wood's field state of this date gave the Gatling Battery, the Engineers, the 13th, 90th, and a wing of the 80th Regiment, with Buller's Cavalry, consisting of the Mounted Infantry, Frontier Light Horse, Transvaal Rangers, and Wood's Irregulars, making a force of 2192 Europeans, and 573 Natives, four guns and two Gatlings. These two columns, therefore, gave Lord Chelmsford a compact and admirably-welded and homogeneous body of 4062 Europeans, 1103 Natives, 12 guns, and two Gatlings, and with this force he justly considered that he held Ulundi in the hollow of his hand.

On the day following (the 22nd), while Newdigate, whose oxen much required it, gave the division a holiday in camp. Wood pushed on about four miles, taking care to note every bush, rock, stream, and salient point *en route*. The march was through a mixture of jungle, long grass, and occasional outcrops of granite, mixed with unpleasant-looking boulders of grey sandstone, but which would have been well appreciated by an engineer for the construction of a permanent work of defence. Ten small streams were passed, besides tributaries of the Umvolosi, and many tracks of buffalo and elephant were seen, while some of Wood's enthusiastic sportsmen were positive they could at times hear the well-known trumpet of the latter in the jungle. The road then led along a narrow valley, flanked by rocky hills on either side.

On the banks of the stream which flowed in this spot some deserted *kraals* were seen, with broken utensils, stone fireplaces, and small pits where mealies were stored and still left. The huts which composed these *kraals* were not built in the same way as others they had seen, but seemed constructed with more skill and an eye to greater comfort. First of all were stout posts planted in the ground, and the interstices filled up with clay. The roof, instead of being of the general umbrella shape, was flat, and with a slight slope to the front; and the rafters were covered either with sheets of bark or with bushes and grass, over which was spread a thick coating of earth. Sweet potatoes, cut in slices, pumpkins and gourds, and other vegetables of a succulent nature, were laid on some of the roofs to dry for the winter's provision.

The interior of these huts had, instead of one, as is usual in Zululand, two, and sometimes three divisions. The first contained a small raised space for a bed-place, covered with hides, and here was the almost universal African fireplace, consisting of the three cones of clay, which in many instances are hollow, and form a most ingenious oven. The only cooking utensils were earthen pots, nearly everything in this part of South Africa being prepared for eating by boiling.

In the next division lambs and goats were kept, and the innermost one was used as a granary, where corn is stored in *"lindo,"* band-boxes made of bark, with the lids carefully luted on with clay. These *lindo* are sometimes of enormous size, and are sufficiently large to contain a dozen or more sacks. Light is admitted only through the one door, which also provides the sole means for the escape of smoke, and as a consequence the rafters and walls are black and shiny, and the cobwebs with which they are festooned are loaded with soot. Among the rafters walking-staves, and *knobkerries, assegais,* and other primitive weapons of war, are usually stored, so as to get them good and due seasoning by the smoke.

The largest of the villages was clean and surprisingly well-built, said to be after a model one made by the late King Panda. It was surrounded by a stockade, in addition to the outer walls of houses, and the part where the chief had evidently lived was divided off from the rest of the village, and was also the gateway. The gates were heavy slabs of wood, hewn out of the solid trunk, and those wanting to enter could only go up to the principal gate one at a time, as a wing of palisading projected on either side in the form of a long U, with holes to use assegais through, so that it would be no pleasant attempt to try to force an entrance against the will of the dwellers therein.

There were some other smaller doorways in the outer walls of the house, forming part of what might be termed the enceinte, which closed in a sort of portcullis fashion. A number of heavy logs had holes in their upper ends, and the wall plate was rove through them. When the doorway is open, these logs are triced up inwards and out of the way, and when closed the outer sides of the lower ends butt, as it were, against a strong fixed log, and are secured by a strong movable log inside.

On the 23rd, Brigadier-General Wood halted, still on the left bank of the Umlatoosi, for the purpose of building a fort, which was to be held by two companies of the 58th, two of Harness's field-guns, and some irregular cavalry. The outlines and profiles were soon traced by experienced though not professional engineers, and on the evening of the same day the place was securely defensible.

The spot chosen by Wood to build the fort is on the Umlatoosi, and in a position naturally of great strength, for the river there makes a rapid bend and affords a ready means of both banks being swept and commanded from the work. A rude and most insecure bridge, formed of a couple of huge trees, already existed, but this was now under water, while the strength of the current was so great when the survey was being made that several of Wood's men were washed off, and only saved themselves by catching at bushes on the bank. In the centre of the stream there is an island, and upon this an outwork was constructed. This island is situated amongst numerous rapids and cascades, breaking out from the rocky hill-side. The difficulties of getting across seemed at first sight almost insuperable, but after a time it was discovered that there were places where it was possible to jump from rock to rock, and then to wade through the rapids themselves on narrow shelves, holding meanwhile "like grim death" by ropes of creepers, stretched from side to side for that purpose.

It will be, of course, understood that a single false step, or the snapping of the creeper-rope, at these points would be fatal, for nothing could save the traveller in that case from being dashed to pieces amongst the rocks beneath. The stream below this was about fifty yards wide, very deep, and running like a sluice. Happily, a passage was effected without any casualty. Looking back from the other side a most striking sight is presented by this mass of water bursting out of the precipitous hill-side, and broken by the rocks and little bushy islands into foaming cascades. Many small streams are passed, which occasionally flow for some considerable distance in subterranean channels. They work in amongst loose stones, covered with soil and vegetation, the underground portions of their course being sometimes not more than forty yards of their length, while in other instances they seem to have disappeared altogether, and no doubt help to supply those mysterious fresh springs which are known to exist even on the beach at Port Durnford.

The eastern portion of the Umlatoosi district, and that leading to the sea is moderately level, with rocky hills, on the summits of which are situated the villages of the chiefs; but as the western portion is reached, the country breaks into mountains of every shape and form, amongst which the more numerous are needles and cones of granite. In the foreground the hills are of red sandstone, crowned with groves of magnificent trees, festooned with jasmine and other sweet-scented creepers. Many of the rivers appear to have been crossed in former days by bridges, constructed either by the Zulus or by the missionaries, or possibly by both. Poles were planted in the bed of the stream, and upon others lashed at the top smaller poles and branches were laid to form the footway. When first constructed these were doubtless secured to the cross-pieces by lashings, but by this time they had rotted away, and consequently afforded but a very precarious foothold.

Between the 24th and the 26th both columns—that is to say, the headquarters and Wood's—advanced but six miles, but Buller was not more idle than Wood, as, while the latter was building a fort to hold a couple of hundred men in the heart almost of a formidable enemy's country, the former had patrolled in almost every direction to the front, rear, and both flanks. On the 25th Buller and his "merry men" were in the saddle and away more than nine miles to the front, and by noon there came an orderly, "bloody with spurring, fiery red with haste," who brought news that "Redvers," with his usual good fortune, had pounced upon about seventy or eighty Zulus busily engaged in grass-burning, to bother the advance in regard to grass for the horses and oxen. Buller made extremely short work of these fellows, whose surprise was so complete that the whole lot might have been annihilated if humanitarian principles had not interposed. As soon as the grass was effectually saved, Buller proceeded on a few miles, and, although watched here and there, suffered not the slightest molestation.

The same evening (25th) Buller came back from his own camp to the headquarter camp with full information in regard to the five *kraals* that had been observed on the 24th in the district of Usipexi, which he reported were guarded by a tolerably formidable Zulu *impi*. A small and select council of war was at once held in General Newdigate's tent, under the presidency of the commander-in-chief. After a very short conference, in which Lord Chelmsford, Generals Newdigate and Marshall, and Colonels Drury-Lowe and Buller were the principal speakers, it was finally decided that an attack in force should be made upon the five *kraals*, and any others that could be discovered at an early hour on the following day.

At daybreak accordingly the force was drawn up in line for Lord Chelmsford's inspection, which, as was usual with him, was, though rapid, most carefully minute. On the right were two guns and fifty men of Le Grice's admirable battery, and next came two of Drury-Lowe's splendid blue-and-white squadrons. These fellows would have won the heart of any light cavalry colonel or adjutant, and it seemed almost a pity that such glittering panoply of crest and spear and plume should have to abide the thrust of a hidden *assegai* from behind a rock or bush.

Four hundred and fifty of Buller's best men, though not so smart nor so well mounted as Drury-Lowe's gallant fellows, were not despised or looked down upon by those who were present, and the more brilliantly decked trooper, with his uniform and glittering apanage, felt proud to ride with the men who had fought so well at Zlobani and conquered so grandly at Kambula. Two companies of natives made up the force, which perhaps was the largest patrol ever furnished in this war for such a duty as the burning of *kraals*. The guns and part of the cavalry were sent by a circuitous path which led to an eminence near the largest *kraal*, and part of Buller's Horse bearing a little to the right, the main body advanced along the road by which Buller had yesterday returned.

They first came to the large *kraals* of Udugwoosu and of Udlumbedlu, which were found deserted, and shelled and burnt without opposition; and when this was effected, the cavalry and natives descended into the plains, to Uxixipi, which was also destroyed, after shelling out about a thousand natives, who were at once pursued by the Basutos and Frontier Light Horse. Not many Zulus were killed, as some were old men and boys, and strict orders had been given to spare these.

On the 27th the flying column, under Wood, advanced nine miles on the road to Ulundi; while the main division, under Newdigate, with Brigadiers Glynn and Collingwood, and Marshall in command of the cavalry, moved on eleven miles, both columns encamping at a place called Amhlabatini, within a mile of each other. They carried no tents, but took with them 200 ammunition-waggons, and ten days' full rations, which on emergency could have been spun out to double that number. Soon after the halt all the brigadiers were assembled by Lord Chelmsford, who briefly but succinctly expounded to them his intentions and future action.

His lordship said the time had now arrived for a final blow to be dealt, and he purposed, having first established a base of operations by constructing a small depot *laager* at Amhlabatini, pushing on at once to the attack of Ulundi. Buller would clear the front and mask the columns as they advanced, and would do all he could to provoke and entice the enemy to attack in the open. The question now was what details were to be left at the laager as a garrison, and it was decided that these should be furnished by three companies of the 1-24th Regiment, and some other contingents, making up 500 men. Soldiers, as a rule, must accept all commands without question; but although no open word is spoken, there are times when the bitterness of disappointment will show itself without speaking. Such was the case when

240

the order-book proclaimed the duty detailed for the 24th.

The entrenched *laager* was most artistically made in an incredibly short space of time. Within a radius of 600 yards all trees and bush were cut down and cleared away. In the centre a rectangle of waggons was formed, with earth thrown up above the axletrees, and at 15 yards' distance from these a trench and an embankment three feet high were constructed. Again, about 100 yards beyond this, strong and well-made abattis were placed. These consisted of whole trees and stout branches 12 and 15 feet long, felled and placed side by side, with their butts inwards and boughs interlaced, while the twigs and small leaves were stripped off and the boughs sharply pointed. The butts were strongly picketed down, and in some cases fastened by logs laid across several butts.

These abattis were fully five feet in height, and as green wood— not easy to burn—was selected, they made a formidable obstacle. It took 200 men only eight hours to construct 200 yards of abattis, and this, considering that many of them had never done such work before, was most creditable. All the officers were in the highest possible spirits, and no inconsiderable amount of banter was carried on between the two columns during the visits paid from one to the other. One of the most fertile subjects for "chaff" was the increasing weight and sleekness of Buller's men as compared with the visibly apparent attenuation of their horses, and the joke was to affect to believe that these "African Cossacks," as they were called, devoured all the oxen they captured, while making their horse-rations into oatmeal cakes for themselves! This story, if *ben trovato*, was singularly devoid of fact, for Buller's horses presented a most favourable contrast to those of Marshall, as the former would eat almost anything, and the latter were only just commencing to put up with mealies. The constant work of the former animals had naturally kept them devoid of superfluous flesh, but, for all this, they were as hard as "nails" and good in their wind.

On the afternoon of the 27th, vedettes signalled the approach of some natives, accompanied by a large number of cattle. These proved to be further messengers from Cetywayo, bringing 150 of our oxen captured at Isandhlwana, together with a pair of elephants' tusks and a letter, written in English by a captive dealer. The letter was fairly expressed, and said that the king could not comply with all Lord Chelmsford's demands, as the arms taken from us at Isandhlwana were not brought to him, and that it was beyond his power as a king to order or compel any of his regiments to lay down their arms.

The letter also said that Harness's guns should be sent, and on receipt of the cattle and these weapons the English must retire from Zulu territory. Whoever had written the letter must have been a bold and plucky fellow, as he had added in a corner in pencil a few words of warning, and an intimation that Cetywayo had with him at Ulundi and the neighbouring *kraals* a large and picked *impi*, amounting to 20,000 men. Even without this message Lord Chelmsford would have considered these overtures as suspicious; but, as it was, increased precaution against surprise or treachery was taken. Lord Chelmsford accordingly declined the tusks, and told the messengers in the plainest language that, before he thought of retiring, all the original conditions must be complied with, more especially as regards the formal laying down of arms by the regiment.

The messengers were then escorted from our column, and later in the day several large bodies of Zulus, amounting to some thousands, were noticed moving in a lateral direction from the side of Ulundi, and passing along by the left flank. The following day was a busy one for all. Lord Chelmsford was so anxious to complete the main details of the depot *laager* that he deferred his march till sundown. Wood, however, moved on in the morning as far as the left bank of the White Umvolosi, where he bivouacked and waited for the main body. After waiting until all the more prominent and essential matters were completed in regard to the garrison left in the depot, Lord Chelmsford ordered the parade for 5.30 in the evening, and they then marched on to the next bivouac in a compact and well-organised column.

It was still daylight when the White Umvolosi was reached, and they saw across the river, on the left bank, the flying column and the lancers already bivouacked. The scene as on the right bank of the river was most picturesque. On the left bank of the Umvolosi Wood had admirably chosen the ground for his bivouac. Here was a firm, wide plateau, bounded on the east and north by a hilly country, broken up by knolls and tall cone-like eminences, whose slopes here and there were covered by patches of dense jungle or bordered by young forests, whose shades seemed to invite shelter during the fierce heat of the day.

Away in the extreme distance the landscape differed materially in aspect from the country near. Mountains of loftier altitude, rising peak upon peak, tier upon tier, and range upon range, met the eye everywhere. Green trees covered their slopes in apparently endless expanse of vegetation. Immediately behind the lancer camp, and sheltering it

242

from the night breezes that swept across the plain, was a massive buttress of rock covered with richly and delicately-hued velvety mosses, while down the hard, steep, rocky beds of granite and sandstone, with here and there basalt and porphyry, flint and quartz, foamed sparkling little streams, which always seem so refreshing and so tempting on a South African march.

A deep gaping fissure in a high jutting wall of rock, through which bubbled the clear water in volumes; a great towering rock with perpendicular walls, to which clung, in spite of apparent impossibility, ferns and plants and moss, thick and velvety; and a huge conical hill which ambitiously hid its head in the clouds; these were wild and rugged forms of nature to be treasured up long after their marching days were gone and past. The camp was situated on a wide terrace or shelf of ground rising above a body of water, which more resembled a long narrow lake than a river. This part of the White Umvolosi, indeed, like many other African rivers, loses its current in the dry season, and becomes a series of long narrow pools, which in some places may be compared to lakes for their length, according to the nature of the ground in which depressions are found.

If the ground is rocky or of clayey mud the water is retained, instead of being absorbed, and here swarm multitudes of *silurus*, or bearded mud-fish. Wherever mud-fish are abundant, crocodiles, the great fish-eating reptiles of the African waters, are sure to be found, and, singularly enough, wherever crocodiles are found one is almost sure to find the hippopotamus—not because crocodiles and hippopotami have any affinity for each other, but because the soil which retains the water during the hot days of the drought season is almost sure to produce in the vicinity of the pools abundance of rich grass and tall cane, the favourite food of the hippopotamus.

Two miles further in the plain Wood's bivouac fires were seen in glittering and regular ranks, marking out the exact ground which each regiment or corps would occupy in order of parade or march. Far away, but in a line with each angle of the bivouac, were the outlying pickets; while, again, beyond these were those vigilant and unsleeping patrols which made this column so secure and impossible to surprise.

At daybreak on the 29th the main body crossed the river and joined the flying column on the left bank. They now were but fifteen miles from Ulundi, and all the king's *kraals* were visible to the naked eye. On the far slope of the hills that bound the plain were the two round *kraals*, Likasi and Undabakawazi; next, and built in the shape

243

of a crescent, were Unodwengo, Panda's old palace, Ulundi, built by the present king, while farthest of all was another, making five, called Umpanibougwena.

On the 30th Lord Chelmsford was ten miles from the Umvolosi; and he sent a despatch to Sir Garnet Wolseley, to say that the king's messengers had just left with an ultimatum for Cetywayo, to the effect that his lordship must advance to a position on the left bank of the river on the 1st July, but that if no opposition were offered the troops would wait there without any hostile movement until twelve at noon on the 3rd, when, if the original terms sent to Cetywayo, namely, the delivery of the guns taken at Isandhlwana, and the cattle, were complied with, 1000 captured rifles would be received instead of a regiment laying down its arms, and peace negotiations would be entertained. On the following morning, accordingly, the main body marched at an early hour, and, preceded by the flying column and Buller's men scouring the country in front and flank, arrived at the river and took up the position named above.

CHAPTER 12

Raid across the Umvolosi by Buller

On the morning of the 3rd of July, the last day of grace, so far from any compliance with Lord Chelmsford's demands being made, all sorts of hostile demonstrations were shown by the Zulus, who were gathered in large numbers about eight miles off. All day long, on the 1st and 2nd, there had been a dropping fire at long ranges upon our men; and on the 3rd the enemy, growing bolder, pushed his skirmishers down to some rocks on the opposite side of the river, and fired upon the men as they were watering their horses in the stream. One horse was killed and several men wounded, and then it was that Buller asked and obtained permission to make a raid into the enemy's country.

Early in the afternoon Buller was waiting impatiently to cross, looking, as was said of Picton, "*in a heavenly humour, because someone was likely to be killed.*" A couple of guns were brought into position on the banks of the river, to cover Buller's crossing, and, if necessary, to assist his retreat if hard pressed on his return. A couple or three rounds of shrapnel made short work of a crowd of Zulus who had approached on the opposite height in a most impudent manner; and hardly were the echoes of these heard along the shores before Buller and Beresford, dashing into the stream with a cheer that made the rocks resound, were followed over the river by Buller's horsemen, the Mounted Infantry, and Baker's Horse.

A good billiard or racquet player likes a gallery, and if the very dashing rifleman and *beau, sabreur* were at all anxious for an audience, they certainly had a large one on this occasion. In fact, the whole camp—if camp you can call a bivouac without tents—turned out literally in its shirt-sleeves to see the fun. The fatigue parties stopped their wood-cutting to take a look at the two camp favourites as they raced like schoolboys at a paper hunt after the Zulus, who were scut-

tling away like prize pedestrians to gain the shelter of a friendly *kraal*.
Buller being in command, however, was not forgetful of his men; and,
though galloping at a steeplechase pace, kept them well in hand, and
raced with about a score of his fellows at the military *kraal* Dalwayo,
on our right front. Beresford, however, being a sort of chartered liber-
tine, and having no separate command, "went for" the Zulus entirely,
as he subsequently expressed it, "on his own hook."

Meanwhile, by Buller's order. Baker's men, guided by their leader,
had inclined to the left front, to carry and hold a favourable hillock
which commanded the best part of the ford. This piece of thoughtful
strategy proved invaluable at the close of the day, when the horsemen
had hard work to get back. On galloped Buller's men past Nodwengo,
Lord William well to the front, now sabring a Zulu, now stopping to
aid a wounded comrade; while Buller, having picked a hundred of his
best-mounted men, pushed on with the intention of exploring and, if
possible, firing Ulundi.

There was nothing impossible in this project. Buller had good
information that the bulk of the king's army was away upon Lord
Chelmsford's right flank, and that the *kraal* would possibly have a slen-
der guard. It was well, perhaps, that this somewhat hair-brained ex-
ploit should not be carried out, and it was stopped as follows:—The
contour of the ground between this point and the king's *kraal* was
formed by a succession of undulating (at rather a steep angle) plains,
which in the hollows gave admirable cover and concealment to the
Zulus. These large dongas in two places formed positions where bodies of men could be massed at right angles, and so take an incautious
enemy on the flank.

Here the Zulu general, whoever he was, had admirably disposed
his reserves, and here, but for the steady conduct of all hands, Buller
might have met his fate. As suddenly as the mountain warriors of
Roderick appeared above the heather to James Fitz-James, did the tall
Zulu warriors put in an appearance, and from front and flank a very
well sustained fire was poured in upon the daring Buller and his men.

But Buller, with all the dash of a Rupert or a Murat, had much of
the prescience and caution of a veteran, and invariably adopted the
principle which may be indifferently expressed as "*having two strings to
your bow*," or "*not having all your eggs in one basket.*" He had, previously
to his daring advance in the enemy's country, ordered Commandant
Raaf to halt near Nodwengo, with his horsemen as reserve and supports. At the imminent moment, therefore, when the Zulus appeared

in the hollows, these gallant fellows came up and saved the day, and it is more than probable many valuable lives.

As Buller and his splendid marksmen retired by alternate ranks, and as each man fired, dropping his man, Raaf and his well-trained fellows covered the slow retreat; Baker's Horse also held the hillock of which mention has been before made, and did excellent service by the manner in which the Zulus were held in check. Tremlett's little battery on the right front of the camp kept back the enemy on the left line of retreat, so that the raid into the enemy's country, although not productive of any palpable advantage as regards booty or prisoners, was eminently well carried out as a reconnaissance in force.

The Zulus were exceedingly well led, and it was impossible not to admire their admirable skirmishing, and the magnificent manner in which they charged right down to the river's edge, amidst a storm of grape and shrapnel hurled against them to cover the retreat. Buller, of course, was wherever hard knocks were most to be obtained, while Beresford distinguished himself as much by his capital horsemanship, daring valour, and perfect coolness, as by the noble chivalry with which he galloped, under a heavy hostile fire, to bring off, on his tired and overweighted horse, a wounded sergeant of the Mounted Infantry.

It happened thus—Just after the volley had been poured in by the Zulus on either flank. Lord William Beresford, who had literally cut his way through about fifty Zulus who had tried to surround him, turned in the saddle to see how his men were getting on, and saw upon the ground a dismounted and wounded trooper about to be *assegaied* by half-a-dozen Zulus. Wheeling his horse round like lightning, he swept like a thunderbolt on the group, knocking three of the savages over with his horse's shoulder, and placing the other three *hors de combat* with a front and back-hander of his long, heavy sabre. In another moment Beresford had the wounded man safely *en croupe*, and carried off from what would have been a cruel death. Commandant D'Arcy, with equal gallantry, was not so fortunate, for seeing a wounded man on the ground he sought to carry him off, but his horse, being restive, reared and fell back, so that the unfortunate trooper was overtaken and *assegaied*, while D'Arcy was so severely bruised by falling on his revolver, that, although able to get back safely, he was unable to take part in the next day's fight. Three men killed, four wounded, and thirteen horses killed, was the total loss to our men.

A little before daybreak on the 4th, Wood, with his flying column, crossed the White Umvolosi, leaving the 1-24th Regiment in laager with all the heavy baggage and supplies. Lord Chelmsford was so pleased with Buller's magnificent reconnaissance, that he determined to advance at once upon Ulundi, giving every temptation to the Zulu Army to attack, upon the plain which had been admirably surveyed two days previously by Colonel Buller. Nothing could have been better considered, nothing could have been better planned, and nothing could have been better worked out, than the details of this splendid action. Every punctilio had been observed by Lord Chelmsford as regards his answers and promises to Cetywayo. The general had said he would not cross the river, thereby placing himself at some considerable disadvantage in a strategic point, and yet up to noon of the 3rd instant no act of submission was made.

On the 4th, therefore, the main body crossed after Wood's column, and knowing that the Zulu Army were somewhere between the river and Ulundi, had good reason to hope that they would show fight. Lord Chelmsford therefore advanced boldly, and without any undue show of caution, across the plain. They had nothing in the shape of baggage with the exception of ammunition and water-carts; but each man carried in his haversack biscuit and preserved meat for four days.

The crossing of the river was made without any opposition, although the movements of our troops were carefully watched by a body of Zulus from a neighbouring hillock on the left, and a more brilliant and picturesque sight could not be imagined. The banks of the river were covered with tamarinds and acacia, growing right down to the water's edge; while creeping plants, such as the convolvulus, the jessamine, and the deadly nightshade, were festooned from tree to tree. The wild guava, the pomegranate, and many a sweetly-scented bush, pushed upward their luxuriant undergrowth, and gave out faint odours as they were crushed by the horses' hoofs.

Bees were humming among the sweetly-scented *dholiocs*, and the ripple of the stream as it rushed and bubbled over the clear pebbles below made a music that seemed out of place with thoughts of bloodshed and strife. With Buller scouting far in front, Wood's division led the van, Newdigate next, and Drury-Lowe, with his gallant lancers, brought up the rear. The fortified camp on the right bank of the Umvolosi had been left with a Gatling gun, 900 Europeans, and 250 natives, under Colonel Bellairs. As soon as favourable ground had been reached. Wood was signalled to halt and wait for the main body; and the order was then given to form a large hollow square, with the

248

ammunition, two Gatlings, and the entrenching tool -carts and bearers in the centre.

Inside this square were also two companies of Engineers and some native Pioneers attached, under Major Chard and Captain Ainsley, together with the *impedimenta*, consisting of watercarts, ambulance-waggons, and stretchers. The square, although large, was not unwieldy, and the steady marching of the men prevented the slightest noise or confusion. The flying column under Wood held the post of honour in the front half of the square. Major Tucker, with the 80th Regiment, and Major Owen and two Gatlings in the centre, held the front face. On his right flank were two 7-pounders of Major Tremlett's battery, under Lieutenant Davidson, with seven companies of the 13th Light Infantry, under Major England, supplemented in continuation of the right face by two more of Tremlett's guns, in charge of Captain Brown and Lieutenant Slade; then came one 9-pounder of Major Le Grice's battery, under Lieutenant Crookenden; four fine companies of the 58th making up the remainder of the right face.

The rear face was composed of one gun of Le Grice's battery, two companies of the 21st Fusiliers, under Major Hazlerigg, and three companies of the 94th, under Colonel Malthus. On the left or west flank were the remaining three companies of the 94th, two 7-pound-ers of Major Harness's battery, under Lieutenant Parsons; eight companies of the 90th, under Major Rogers; and two guns of Major Le Grice's battery, attached *pro tem*, to Major Harness, under Lieutenant Elliott. Buller's Cavalry were away scouring the front and flanks, while Colonel Drury-Lowe, with two squadrons of the 17th Lancers, and Captain Shepstone's Basutos, formed the rear guard. The numbers of all ranks were as follows:—Flying Column, 2192 Europeans and 573 natives; Newdigate (2nd Division), 1870 Europeans and 530 natives; making a total of 5165 men.

Lord Chelmsford and his staff rode in the centre, in rear of the front face. He, of course, assumed the chief command; and his clear, sharp, soldier-like voice rang out like a trumpet to the men: "The square will wheel to the right." This order was taken up by the division as quickly and calmly as though by a brigade of Foot Guards at Aldershot or the Curragh. After moving on for a few miles they began to approach the smaller *kraals*; and Buller, with his advanced and seemingly ubiquitous riders, could be seen dashing here and there in every direction to tempt the Zulu columns, which could now be discerned along the horizon towards the left front.

BATTLE OF ULUNDI, INSIDE THE SQUARE

At the extreme end of the plain the sun glanced down upon a long line of white shields marching in a sort of double column, with skirmishers thrown out in European fashion in front and on the flanks. The square was now halted, while the first *kraal* was fired. This, some of Shepstone's Basutos said, was named Umlambo-Bogivimo, and Buller's men having applied their flints and steel to the task, the flames and smoke ascended to the sky. Next they came to the great *kraal* of King Panda, called Unodwengo; but although this was at first fired, it was found the smoke acted as such a screen to the Zulus that Lord Chelmsford ordered its extinction. Strong columns could now be seen moving out in quick though good order from Ulundi, and as they seemed bearing down upon the right front, the square took ground to the right and was halted in a capital position, pointed out to Lord Chelmsford by Buller.

Our troops were now assailed by a dropping but harmless fire from the Ulundi column on the right front, and from a strong Zulu force operating in some broken ground from Unodwengo, now on the left. It was now half-past eight, and by nine o'clock the Zulu attack was fully developed. Buller's men then made a strong demonstration on the left, driving the Zulus from the hollow where they were sheltered, back to the Unodwengo *kraal*. This movement was well supported by Shepstone and his Basutos, who skirmished splendidly on the left and rear face of the *kraal*. While this, however, was going on, a Zulu on a white horse was seen leading strong reinforcements from his proper right to assist in the attack upon the cavalry on the left.

The scene was now most exciting. Buller and his men fought in two ranks, the first mounted and ready to dash at a moment upon any weak point in the enemy's line; the second, dismounted, and making capital practice at long ranges, with their saddles as a rest for the rifle. As soon as the front rank became too hardly pressed, they cantered to the rear, dismounted, and relieved the second rank. This is the old Dutch mode of fighting the Zulus, and it has rarely been found unsuccessful. Colonel Lowe, at this juncture, asked Lord Chelmsford's permission to send out a squadron of his lancers, or even a troop; but the general wisely declined, as the ground was broken, and the Zulu line too powerful to be charged. Nothing could be finer than the way in which Buller and Shepstone retired, bringing the Zulu columns and their horns under the deadly hail of our Gatlings and Martinis.

Now, thought the Zulus, was the time for their grand attack. Were not the mounted men, under the terrible Buller, flying before the

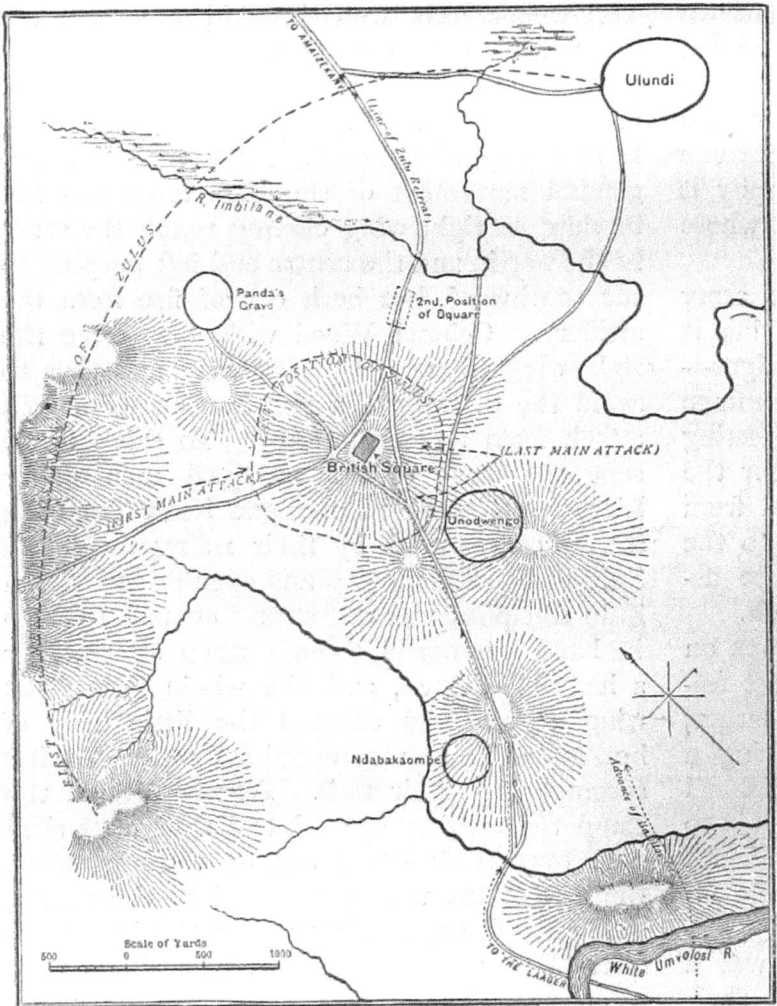

PLAN OF THE BATTLE OF ULUNDI: JULY 4, 1879.

fierce onslaught of the Zulu braves? Still the line of white shields came roaring on, like the big white billows that roll on to and break into foam upon the South African shore. The ridges on the front and left were now swarming with Zulus, fierce, stern, and terrible, as with fiendish and maniacal shouts they swept over the soft and springy *veldt* to be shattered, bloody and broken in their pride, by the leaden tempest that now whistled from all sides of the square.

"Steady, my lads; close up, fire low, and not so fast!" cried Evelyn Wood, who had his men under splendid control.

"Are the mounted men all in?" said Lord Chelmsford to General Newdigate.

"They are, my lord," replied Buller, who was just lighting a cigarette.

"Then give the enemy a round or two of shrapnel," said the chief.

Shells from the right and left were now poured in; but still on came the line of white shields. File-firing from the Martinis was poured in, but the Zulu columns were deployed, and, regardless of the *mitraille*, still came on in half-open order. But, under cover of their strong lines of skirmishers, the Zulu attack was now changed and further developed on the rear face, where Malthus and Hazlerigg held post. Hazlerigg, whose tall and stalwart form was conspicuous above the files of his men, made his front rank reserve its fire till the Zulus had arrived within sixty yards, and then the word was given to fire low and steady. The *kraal* of Unodwengo was, it has been said, upon the left, and it proved rather a thorn in the side.

Behind the rising ground from which the Basutos had been driven now came a stream of thousands of Zulus sweeping round the left flank from Ulundi. Their wild yells and unearthly war-cries smote upon the air, and were heard through the ping and rattle of the rifle-fire. Under cover of the Unodwengo *kraal*, and sweeping over the ground beyond, this strong body, led by the chief on the white horse, formed a hollow square, and after a few moments' pause to collect themselves, dashed like a whirlwind upon the right rear angle of the square. Now everyone knows that the angle of a square, like the salient angle of a bastion, is its weakest point, and for a moment it seemed a question whether the attack would succeed. The angle was held by two of Hazlerigg's companies, and although Le Grice's solitary gun, admirably served, poured forth its most deadly shells, and Hazlerigg kept his men firing in the most steady manner, at one moment it seemed as though it would come to close quarters fighting.

But one terrific volley from the 21st, the 94th, the 58th, and Royal Engineers, shattered their order, their square was broken, and after a moment's pause they sought shelter from so terrific a fire. Meanwhile the front attack had again developed, and here the gallant 80th were placed at a certain disadvantage. That awkward dip in their front enabled the Zulus to make their formation for attack out of sight and out of fire, so that Major Tucker's men had to reserve their fire until the tops of the enemies' heads were seen above the mound. But the 80th behaved so coolly and so steadily that the front attack at length slackened, and the Zulu line wavered, and finally ceased to fire.

It was now a quarter to ten, and as signs of wavering were remarked in every face of the attack. Colonel Drury-Lowe at this juncture had been allowed to file his men out from an opening in the rear face, and was just forming them in squadrons, when a spent ball knocked him off his charger. He was stunned, however, only for a moment, and was again in the saddle, smiling at his mishap. Now was the moment for which the gallant lancers had so long waited. Now every man gripped his weapon with stiffened sinews and determined heart. "Go at them, colonel, but don't pursue too far!" shouted Lord Chelmsford, as he raised his helmet to the men.

Moving first at a walk to steady his men, Lowe advanced in column of troops from the right, and as soon as the ground was favourable gave the words in succession, "Trot!" "Form squadrons!" "Form line!" "Gallop!" "Charge!" Away across the broad grassy slopes, and greeted by a burst of cheering from the square, went the splendid blue-and-white line, then pennons fluttering in the morning air, and their bright and deadly steel-topped bamboo lances in rest. On they went, driving the flying Zulus headlong into a *donga*, where sweeping round it the pursuing squadrons forced the enemy out into the open to fly for safety towards the mountains northward.

But flanking the *donga*, and hidden by the long grass, half of a Zulu regiment was posted to cover the retreat, and as the squadrons of Drury-Lowe's men came on a volley was poured in, which emptied several saddles, and was fatal to poor young Wyatt-Edgell, who was gallantly leading on his men. His men, almost maddened as they saw him fall, spurred more furiously on to take immediate and bloody vengeance.

A moment more and the bristling line of steel meets the black and shining wall of human flesh, rent, pierced, and gashed by a weapon as death dealing and unsparing as their own *assegai*. Still, though crushed

254

and stabbed by the lances, and though their firm array was scattered like sea-foam, the Zulus fought on in stubborn knots, nor cried for quarter, stabbing at the horses' bellies as they went down, and trying to drag the men off their horses in the melee. The lance was now relegated in most cases to its sling, and the heavy sabres of the troopers became red with gore. Never was a cavalry attack better timed or more effective, and never did that oft-abused arm, the lance, better vindicate its reputation as a weapon of pursuit.

But now a troop of the King's Dragoon Guards, under Captain Brewster, and some irregular cavalry, are let loose from different sides of the square, and, with Lord William Beresford full six horse-lengths in advance, charge full and fair upon the flying savages, who are cut down in scores until they gain the crests of the hill; but even there no safety or rest is found, for shrapnel, fired with time-fuses, scatters them like chaff in the wind.

The attacking force consisted of twelve regiments, and could not have been less than 23,000; 15,000 surrounding the British square, and 8000 in reserve. Their loss has been estimated at 1500, but it should probably be put down as double, for during the whole of the action they could be seen carrying their dead and wounded away. The total loss to our troops was not heavy—some dozen killed and about eighty wounded. Amongst those killed was one officer, of whom might well be said, "We could have better spared a better man."

In the gallant white-and-blue line of squadrons that swept like a torrent upon the scared and flying Zulu hordes, there rode no braver, no more knightly spirit than young, gallant Wyatt-Edgell. The scion of a noble house, and a soldier by hereditary tradition and birth, he had all the accomplishments and chivalrous attributes of his race. His loss was a great blow to all, and his premature though glorious death cast a deep gloom not only over his own regiment, but over the entire camp in which he had spent so many cheerful days, esteemed and loved by officers and men alike, from highest to lowest.

After the Battle of Ulundi and the destruction of the king's five great *kraals*. Lord Chelmsford marched his division back to Entonyani, where they remained some days, having had a storm of rain and thunder lasting thirty-six hours. As they had no tents the first night, the state of affairs may more easily be imagined than described. The rain came down in perfect torrents, sweeping away the bivouac fires and pouring through the camp like the overflow of a mighty river. The men behaved admirably, taking all the discomforts of their situa-

THE BURNING OF ULUNDI

tion with the good humour and jocularity of disciplined troops. The horses naturally suffered most, although every attempt was made to picket them in a sheltered spot. On arriving at Entonyani they found tents waiting for them, and were thus enabled to get dry and refit.

The nights were exceptionally cold and with heavy dews, causing some little sickness amongst the men. In fully estimating the importance of this battle, we must not forget the surroundings, nor the associations of the place. The valley of the Umvolosi is essentially the heart of Zululand. It is the richest and most fertile portion of the country, and as such was chosen as the royal abode. The two branches of the river, named after the district, converge through it towards the main stream which flows on to St. Lucia Bay. The one by which the king's great *kraal* but lately stood passes through a comparatively open country; and its waters, gleaming clear in the sunlight, arc called "White," just as the waters of the other branch, which run through a more bushy and broken district, are called "Black."

In the basin drained by this extensive water-system the Zulu nation was originally cradled. Thither Dingaan retired after he had slain his brother near the Nonoti. There the brave and bustling Dutchman Reteef and his companions were treacherously murdered in 1838; and there, again, Bongore, led into a trap the unsuspecting Boers, who were again duped by his representations, they believing that the king was alone at Mahlabatini. The valley where this last battle was fought is with the Zulus a sacred and historic spot. It is rife with what is most dear to the Zulu pride—legends of bloody massacre, treacherous surprise, and savage revenge.

Dingaan fled from thence; Panda died there; Cetywayo was first recognised and crowned there. Could the tall and wooded grey cliffs that looked down upon the combat speak, they could tell, in a direful tale of tyrannous cruelty and wrong, most of the annals of the Zulu nation. Year by year they witnessed the periodical gathering together of Cetywayo's legions, and watched the steady outgrowth of the savage power whose overthrow, by British troops and British discipline, they beheld but a few months since. But signal and satisfactory as this victory was, it could not be accepted as final until Cetywayo had completely submitted, though some of its effects were immediate and important.

The day after the Battle of Ulundi, and before the victory was known to the troops of the 1st Division, about 700 Zulus, with all their cattle, women, and children, came into the camp at Richard's

Cove, near Port Durnford, to tender submission and to claim protection. There is not the slightest doubt but that they had heard of the battle, although there was not a whisper of the engagement heard amongst these people. General Crealock, to give importance to the ceremony, ordered a general parade of the division at mid-day, and it was impossible not to be struck with the attenuated condition of his battalions, although every available man was put on parade. Both brigades made up rather a weak division.

The 1st Brigade was made up of the Buffs, two companies of the 88th, two companies of the *Shah's* and *Active's* bluejackets, and one of the marine artillery; while the 2nd Brigade was composed of the Royal Artillery, 57th, 60th Rifles, and 91st—in all twenty companies. At half past twelve the general, surrounded by his staff, rode on to the ground, and the division was wheeled into line. Then a galloper was sent out to the Zulus who were halted on the crest of the neighbouring hills, and they were told to advance and lay down their arms. Three hundred fine-looking fellows then advanced in good order, and arriving at the prescribed distance, made the customary obeisance while they deposited *assegais* and guns, in number about seventy, firearms mostly of the old pattern.

However, time proved that the results of Lord Chelmsford's engagement and victory on the 4th (July) were of far greater importance than had been at first imagined. Chiefs and tribes came pouring into the various camps, not by dozens or by scores, but literally by hundreds, and the only two questions they asked—and these kept invariably recurring—were "Why was not the victory of Ulundi followed up vigorously? and why was Cetywayo allowed to escape?"

It was this great error of immediately retiring from Ulundi which made us again ridiculous, not only in the eyes of Zululand, but also in those of military Europe. It was due, not to Lord Chelmsford, nor those under his command, but to extraneous influences beyond his control; and public opinion never arrived at a more true or just conclusion than in saying that the arrival of Lord Chelmsford's successor, no matter how valuable or how necessary it might have been, came at a most inopportune time, for it was well known that Lord Chelmsford's plans were so perfectly matured, that had he been left free to carry out his own designs, instead of being hampered and constrained by the orders of the new commander-in chief, he would have followed up Ulundi with the utmost possible activity, and would in all probability have secured the person of the king. Terms for the final pacification of the whole of Zululand could then have been dictated on the spot, and there would have been an end to the entire business.

Under these circumstances therefore Lord Chelmsford determined to resign all command; and within three days of the brilliant victory of Ulundi it was known to the soldiers throughout the camp that their General was about to leave them, and that with him were going Sir Evelyn Wood, General Crealock, and Colonel Redvers Buller. Accordingly, a grand parade of all arms was ordered on the morning of the 8th (July), that the general might take a formal leave of his men. At nine a.m. the bugle-call for coverers was sounded, the staff officers marked the alignment, and the various corps moved like clockwork upon their respective pivots. The division was then wheeled into line by General Newdigate, and the flanks, bringing forward their right and left shoulders, three sides of a large hollow square was formed, with the front ranks facing inwards.

Lord Chelmsford, his staff, and three brigadiers formed the fourth side of the square, and in a few warm-hearted, well chosen, and soldierlike sentences the commander-in-chief, under whom the troops had seen so much good hard work, honest service, and from whom all ranks had received at various times some recognition of their conduct in camp and on the field of battle, bade them farewell, and thanked them for the manner in which their duty to their queen and country had been performed.

For the courage, the coolness, and the devotion you have all displayed wherever I have been with you, I give you my best and my warmest thanks. For the unselfish devotion and untiring energy and good-humour with which you have encountered hardship, fatigue, and privation I find it hard to sufficiently express my gratitude. In all senses you have done your duty as English soldiers.

Such were the concluding words of a leader whom all loved, respected, and all regretted.

On the following day the camp bivouac was broken up, and the cavalry, the 2nd Division, and the flying column, marched *en route* to Intanjaneni and Kwamagwasa, thus beyond doubt leading Cetywayo and his indunas to suppose that their losses at Ulundi and want of military skill caused them to forego the advantages they had won.

Despatches from General Crealock fully demonstrate that his inability to effect a junction with the 2nd Division before the action at Ulundi was due to no want of energy or organisation on his part, but solely to those causes which will impede the movements of all bodies of civilized troops in uncivilized lands. But although sickness amongst the oxen and other impediments to transport caused General Crealock to lose his share of the victory gained, his time had not been wasted, for much valuable work was done in the nature of road-making and raiding over the enemy's country, thus affording a diversion which considerably weakened Cetywayo's chances of inflicting a defeat upon the other column.

The task of establishing the new base of supply at Port Durnford and the building of Fort Napoleon was thrown entirely upon the 1st Division, and naturally interfered with its rapid advance. The work, however, that fell to the coast column was fully and admirably carried out, and a pontoon and a trestle-bridge were built over the Tugela, without which no important advance could have been made along the coast. The ford over the Inyoni was rendered permanently practicable, and can, now that the descent is made easy for waggons, be passed at all seasons. The same work was effected at the Umsundusi and Amatikula rivers, whose approaches were made safe for wheels. The Umkusi and Inyezani hills and drifts were also made passable by improvement in the roads.

Along the Umlatoosi valley numerous small but difficult streams had drifts made over them. From the Umlatoosi to St. Paul's Mission Station used to be a bad and most difficult road, but all the dangerous places were now levelled, and a strong and defensible position was given. Fords were secured across the Uvulu, the Entonjaneni, the Umvolosi, and the Umlalasi, and there no physical obstacle was allowed to remain to delay the march of a European column with its baggage in any part of the coast and the south of Zululand, while forts had been completed or erected at Tenedos, Pearson, Crealock, Chelmsford, Napoleon, and Durnford.

The result of this was that Sir Garnet Wolseley, in taking over Lord Chelmsford's command, found a complete chain of military posts, the like of which was never before seen in South Africa, extending along the Zulu frontier from the Blood and Buffalo Rivers to the Umvolosi mouth and Port Durnford, and, in fact, encompassing three out of four sides of Cetywayo's kingdom.

In addition to the formation of the new base and the seaward communications the later operations of Barrow's cavalry fully vindicated the reputation they had obtained for activity, Barrow's Irregular

Mounted Corps, although not so numerous as those of Buller, were equally worthy of praise, alike for their admirable discipline, courage in action, and skill in patrolling. They consisted of about fifty enrolled volunteers under Captain Addison, forming a body called the "Natal Guides," three troops of Lonsdale's Mounted Rifles, three of the Mounted Infantry, the Natal Horse, and a very useful contingent of mounted natives. These, under such leaders as Colonel Barrow, Major Lord Gifford, Captains Barton and Nettleton, were at once the eyes and ears of the column. On July 6th Barrow's men made a forced march, during which they were thirty hours in the saddle, and, reaching Ondini, the king's old *kraal*, burnt it to the ground.

The patrol paraded overnight, and started some two hours before daylight, making its way through a valley district over fifteen miles in length by three or four in breadth, though here and there narrowing in parts to only one mile, over lofty spurs and ridges running into it, forming a series of densely-wooded and impracticable ravines. The weather was intensely hot, and although the men and horses were both distressed at times, the troops did their work in a manner which reflected great credit upon all present. From this valley the road or trek ran for ten or twelve miles through an open but rather broken country, the hills in the distance being covered with dense bush. The patrol then turned eastwards over a table-land which stretched away for about twenty miles, till the edge of the plateau is reached, and the path descends abruptly into the great thorn valley to the west of the White Umvolosi; at the edge of this plateau the coast road joins.

From this point the patrol marched a few miles, and halted for off-saddle and breakfast on the right bank of the river. The road is fairly good, but passes through thick thorn-bush, and the country is very broken and contains a number of small streamlets tributary to the Umvolosi. The drift here is good, and is commanded by a high stony hill to the north and upon the right of the road, and within rifle range of one of the smaller royal *kraals*. The Ondini *kraal* was reached about noon. It was occupied by some Zulus, who made away as the troops advanced at a canter; the place was fired, and in half an hour was utterly destroyed. The return to camp was made by another road, which was long and tedious; several of the horses were completely knocked up, one dying from exhaustion and several having to be abandoned on the road.

CHAPTER 13

Arrival of Sir Garnet Wolseley

It is now time to turn attention to the movements of the new commander-in-chief and governor. On the 28th of June his Excellency Sir Garnet Wolseley and his staff landed at Durban from the C.R.M.S. *Dunkeld.* The whole town was that day *en fête*, as the Durbanites like a sensation, no matter of what nature. At daylight the whole of the military and naval authorities were astir, and various coloured bunting began to appear all over the town. Crowds of well-to-do shopkeepers and farmers went down to the point on horseback, while hundreds went by the train. All the ships in the harbour and the bluff were gaily decorated, and the men-of-war, transports, and merchant-vessels were gallantly dressed in bunting from stem to stern. Sir Garnet brought with him many of his old staff, and others joined later on. Colonel Pomeroy Colley arrived by the next Zanzibar steamer, and took up the duties of chief of the staff, and Captain Lord Gifford joined from his regiment, the 57th. Sir Garnet Wolseley was not only to be Governor, Commander-in-Chief, and High Commissioner in Natal and the Transvaal, but also to exercise the functions of the latter office in the countries to the north and to the east.

The changes ordered by the new commander-in-chief were numerous and important. In the first place all military operations against Secocoeni were to be discontinued. This order gave great dissatisfaction, as several highly successful patrols had already been made against this chieftain; and Colonel Lanyon, after great delay and difficulty having completed his arrangements for the attack, was actually on his way to the front, when instructions reached him to stop and send his men to Derby, to protect that part of the border from Zulu raids.

The troops were to be immediately consolidated and reduced, and with them the expenses of the war.

262

The landing of the marines was countermanded, and they were to be sent back with all possible speed to Simon's Bay; the Natal Carabineers, the Durban Mounted Rifles, Bettington's Horse, and the Frontier Light Horse were to be forthwith disbanded: the 1st Division and the cavalry brigade were to be broken up; while the forts along the coast were to be abandoned. The following troops were also named for immediate embarkation:—1-24th, the 3rd (Buffs), the 99th, the 88th, the 1st battalion 13th, and two batteries of artillery, to proceed to England; the 17th Lancers to go on to India; Ellaby's and Tremlett's batteries to proceed to St. Helena, Lord Chelmsford, Generals Marshall, Wood, and Crealock, Colonels Crealock, Downe, Dawney, and Buller, Captains Buller, Molyneux, Frere, Milne, Grenfell, Beresford, and Reilly were going home, either by order or at their own request. Indeed, almost the only officer of high position who elected, or was selected, to remain was General Clifford, who still retained his post of Inspector-General of the lines of communication.

Sir Garnet's plan of operations for the future was as follows: a military post at Durnford with 400 men; another at St. Paul's, with a brigade; and a third at Intanjaneni with 400 men; a regiment to remain on the Umlatoosi, and a battalion of the Native Contingent to guard the line of the Tugela. Colonel Baker Russell was to start at once with a flying column from St. Paul's and co-operate with Oham in the west. Colonel George Villiers was to proceed to join Oham and organise various bodies of *burghers*, Natal natives, and Zulus, to hem in Cetywayo in that direction, whilst McLeod (late 74th Regiment) was to raise, equip, and command 5000 warriors of the Amaswazis, and, if necessary, lead them right into Zululand. Colonel Clarke (67th) meanwhile was to march straight on Ulundi, there to await Sir Garnet's arrival, with a force consisting of the 67th, 60th, five companies of the 80th, two troops of Lonsdale's Horse, one battalion of the Natal Native Contingent, and some mounted natives under the chiefs Jemptse and Mafionge, together with a battery of Gatlings and the Natal Pioneers.

Meanwhile Sir Garnet had convened a great council of Zulu chieftains to be held at St. Paul's, July 19th, to arrive if possible at some definite arrangement for the temporary government of the country. Such were the main features of the new commander's programme, and though severe strictures were at first passed thereupon by the majority of the colonists and old soldiers experienced in Kaffir warfare, time proved that his calculations were just and well-founded.

Leaving Durban on the 2nd of July, Sir Garnet and staff embarked on board Her Majesty's ship *Shah*, and proceeded to Durnford, where several attempts to land were made, but without success. On the morning of the 3rd, the steam-tug *Koodoo* came alongside, and Sir Garnet and his staff, including the two Colonels Russell, Captains Buchanan, Maurice, Braithwaite, and Baynes, Dr. Russell, and Mr. Herbert (private secretary), were with great difficulty and no little risk embarked on her and subsequently transferred to a surf-boat or lighter. While towing the lighter towards the shore the hawser broke, but most fortunately a sail was hoisted at once, and the boat, getting clear of the breakers, was again taken in tow by the *Koodoo*. After several ineffectual attempts to get the lighter made fast to the warp, the recall was fired from the *Shah*, and Sir Garnet returned to the man-of-war.

As the day wore on the surf became worse, and towards evening Captain Bradshaw, commanding the *Shah*, deemed it no longer safe to remain at anchor off the bar. Sir Garnet therefore returned to Durban, and hastening on overland *via* Forts Chelmsford, Pearson, and Crealock, reached the camp of the 1st Division at Richard's Cove, Port Durnford, on July 6th.

On the 14th an advance column, consisting of Buller's Light Horse about 100, two guns, the 57th Regiment, the whole under Colonel B. Russell, C.B., left camp and marched in the direction of St. Paul's, as far as the Umlatoosi, where they entrenched themselves on the right bank, the cavalry and Dunn's scouts forming an advanced guard on the left. This position commands a path about ten miles from the mouth of the river, and the site is very picturesque, overlooking the valley to the north-west. His Excellency and headquarter staff accompanied the column, and the next morning pushed on to St. Paul's with an escort of cavalry, where were the headquarters of the 2nd Division.

A parade of the troops, including the 17th Lancers and some 500 irregular cavalry—the celebrated Buller's Horse—was held, and the general, after taking leave of Lord Chelmsford, Brigadier General Wood, Colonel Buller, who with their staff, were leaving for England, returned to the camp on the Umlatoosi. It has been already said that the 19th was fixed by Sir Garnet Wolseley for the meeting or durbar of the principal chiefs, all of whom were expected to attend. By noon on that day the camp presented a curious sight. Outside the general's tent a guard of honour, with the queen's colours, was drawn up, while a large space was railed off for the reception of Zulu visitors, who came winding in bands over the slopes of the neighbouring hills from an early hour in the morning.

As each deputation from its respective tribe came into camp, preceded by its principal rulers, it was formed up in a sort of column, sixteen or eighteen feet deep, in the space set apart for the visitors. The gathering was a numerous one, upwards of 250 chiefs and their followers having attended, and evidently considering the occasion as one of great importance, as each man was attired in his most gorgeous manner. The enclosure was at the same time council-chamber and reception-hall, and although no seats were required, skins, mats, and canvas were put down for the principal chiefs to sit upon. Some of the chiefs had a covering of cow's tails and other skins round the waist, while broad rings of copper were worn round the arms and ankles of others. Plumes of feathers adorned the heads of the principal men, and hanging behind, somewhat after the fashion of a Hungarian *pelisse*, each warrior wore a panther or other similar skin.

The array of dusky savages looked fairly imposing, although none of them were armed save with the *knobkerrie* of place, which as they squatted was laid methodically in front of each man. Upon the hills in the distance were a number of boys and women who had accompanied the chiefs, but who preferred to remain outside spectators of the conference. The enclosure was marked out by branches of the mimosa, cut in convenient lengths, and forming a sort of palisade, which kept the crowd from intruding. When all were reported present. Sir Garnet and his staff, accompanied by Mr. Fynny, border agent, came out of his tent, and the guard having presented arms, the proceedings commenced. The two principal chiefs were the king's brothers, Dabulamanzi and Magwendi, who both replied to Sir Garnet's speech.

Dabulamanzi was a fine-looking man of large size, apparently in the full vigour of his age, and of great muscular development, presenting in this regard a striking contrast to his brother Oham, who was simply a large fat man. There was an air of considerable thought and command in his face, and, unlike the other chiefs, who wore their hair closely cropped, except with a black band round the temples, his hair was thrown back and his broad forehead was encircled with a fillet of ostrich feathers terminating with a single plume behind. Heavy rings of highly polished copper spanned the thick part of the arms of Magwendi, a much shorter and more common-looking man, and whose neck was adorned with a necklace formed of monkey's teeth and small shells. Both these chiefs held in their right hands the same kind of short stick carried by their warriors, while their left hands rested on their naked knees.

Mr. Fynny, the well-known border agent, who was considered to know almost as much about Zululand and the Zulus as Mr. John Dunn, and that is saying much, performed the duties of interpreter with remarkable skill and fluency, translating Sir Garnet's speech, sentence by sentence, as it was uttered, with due emphasis and point. Sir Garnet Wolseley spoke as nearly as possible to the following effect:

I am very pleased to welcome you to my camp, because your coming in answer to my invitation shows you are as anxious for peace as I am myself, and as is the great queen in whose name I now speak. We came to make war with Cetywayo, not with the Zulu people, and to put an end to his cruelties and his military system, which with his marriage laws made life and property unsafe in your land. We want peace with the Zulus, and that they shall be at peace with our people in Natal. We have beaten the king in open fight and burnt his *kraal*, so that he is now a fugitive and shall never more reign in Zululand.

We might now take all Zululand, but we do not want any of it, and we wish that all of you should have your property and land. I rode to St. Paul's the other day, and found all the people on the way living quietly in their own *kraals*, and with their cattle in them. All may do the same, but all must first give up their arms and the king's cattle in token of their submission. The old laws of Zululand shall be restored, and you shall be ruled by your own chiefs, whom you all know. I shall divide the kingdom into four or five districts, and all men shall be free to come and go, to work, to marry, and to become rich.

The great queen, who sends me, wishes the Zulus should be happy, but those who continue to bear arms, and will not submit, must be given up. On the north the Swazis and the Amatongas are only kept by my orders from invading Zululand, while Oham and his soldiers are moving upon the west. I am going myself to Ulundi on the 10th, where I shall tell the Zulu people my arrangements for the future government of the country.

This address was listened to with great attention, and with the most respectful silence, and several of the chiefs replied, one in particular making the naive and rather sarcastic remark that he and his friends could not see what fault Cetywayo had committed, but as the

266

English chiefs had seen it they were satisfied. Dabulamanzi did not speak, except to Magwendi, who rose and complained that his cattle had been taken from him, and that some of them had been sent in as belonging to the king. Redress was at once promised by Sir Garnet. The meeting then broke up, the chieftains undertaking to meet Sir Garnet again at Ulundi on August 10th, to arrive at a final settlement of affairs.

It has been before mentioned that General Crealock had determined to resign his command of the 1st Division; it was in pursuance of this resolution that he ordered a general parade on July 21st, on which occasion he made a short but appropriate speech to his men.

There were on parade the Buffs, 60th Rifles, 91st, the naval brigade of the *Boadicea*, one company of Marines, two troops of Lonsdale's Horse, one troop of Natal Horse, and a battery of 7-pounders. This little army was drawn up on the usual parade-ground, not far from the river, and in the midst of a scene of the greatest natural beauty. The banks of the stream are thickly wooded, and the valley is the resort of large species of game. Crocodiles frequent the river, and make it dangerous to bathe. Thick, thorny underwood, mingled with tall reeds and date-palms, grow close down to the waters, which reflect the tall green trees that overarch above. Trees, with branches bearing bright green leaves and yellow fragile flowers, drooped nearly to the ground around the plain. Pre-eminent in splendour shone out the brilliant *combretta*, whose masses of bloom gleamed like torches amidst the dark green of the thickets, whilst the golden sheen of the fruit intensified the marked contrast of the tints.

At the drinking place used for the horses the water flowed in streamlets over the rocks and along a long red sandbank. A ledge of granite forms a rugged barrier eight or ten feet high across the river, and down the hollows of this the clear waters rush and ripple in rills, cascades, and rapids, bubbling and eddying among the great masses of rock below, in many of which, like those of the Zambesi, great holes are worn by stones which during the flood perhaps had settled in small hollows. Dark lines of trees border the river on the right, and on the left there is a fine grove of baobabs with large dark green leaves and wide-spreading branches. Crossing a sandstone hill with a spur stretching away to the eastward, and adorned with some splendid specimens of the *encephalartoas*, or Kaffir bread, and then descending into the valley of the Umlalasi, one comes to sandstone and gneiss, rising in cliffs of 600 feet on the south of the river, but sloping away gradually on the north.

The banks are covered with verdant and golden-blossomed acacias, some of them with yellow bark and the sweet gum, which is said to indicate the presence of the tsetse fly. Away to the north are to be seen groves of palm and mimosas, with stems forty feet to the lower branches. Far away beyond the plain can be seen the purple outlines of the great Libomba range of mountains. These are to the east of the Drakenberg, and intervene between it and the sea. Stretching northward from the Pongolo River, this range crosses the Oliphant and touches the Limpopo. Its highest elevation is about 2150 feet high, and at the point at which the Umvolosi passes through the range to Delagoa Bay there is a lofty peak which reaches to 1900 feet, the river bed being there only 300 feet above sea level.

Further north the range declines, and is cut through by the Pongolo and the Usuta, tributaries of the Maputa; also by the Umvolosi, the Umcomazi, the Sabia, and the Oliphant, all of which run into the Indian Ocean. Such were the features of the landscape, and such was the background to this farewell parade.

After the division had wheeled into line a very creditable march past was performed, and the troops then wheeled into a square, and were addressed by General Crealock, who told them that, in obedience to orders received from Sir Garnet Wolseley, the column was to be broken up and dispersed. The general said that he took this opportunity, before separating, to thank all hands for their good conduct and constant hard work, carried on without a murmur and in the midst of many difficulties.

The task allotted to the 1st Division was to establish a series of posts along the coast of Zululand with an advanced depot of supplies, to open a base of supplies at Port Durnford, from which to feed a force operating against Ulundi, and finally to destroy the military *kraals* and clear the district of Zulus. All these instructions were fully carried out by the 1st Division by the 5th of July; and the general, in wishing them a hearty goodbye and success and prosperity, thanked all for the good conduct and zeal which enabled him to do so much.

Lord Chelmsford, who was now on his way home to England, received most enthusiastic receptions at Maritzburg, Durban, and Capetown. The banquet given in his honour at Pietermaritzburg was, perhaps, the most brilliant affair of the kind ever achieved in the colony, but there were those who considered the ball in Durban as a still greater, for there were more ladies and officers present who had come long distances to assist at the festivity. Sir Garnet Wolseley and the Lieutenant Governor, Sir Evelyn Wood, and his *Fidus Achates,* Colonel Buller, Major-General Clifford, and all the fighting and dancing men within a hundred miles of the place responded to the call.

Durban never before saw such a display of "rank, beauty, and fashion." All the *belles* of Natal were there to welcome the winner of Ulundi, and to sympathize with him in his efforts, under adverse criticisms and untoward fortune, to do his duty as a soldier of our queen. The general feeling of the colony may be gathered from the mayor's speech, who, in proposing his lordship's health, said that he felt doubly proud on the occasion, as he did not speak alone for himself, but in the name and with the voice of all Natal. Against difficulties which only colonial experience could realise, and against bitter and most vituperative criticism, Lord Chelmsford had worked steadily and patiently until he accomplished the object he was sent to perform.

The general, in reply, expressed in a soldierlike and impressive manner his deep sense of the kind feelings expressed by the mayor, and acknowledged that the reception accorded to him had quite overwhelmed him. But in giving his acknowledgments and thanks, his lordship made a happy allusion to the devotion and zeal of those who commanded and fought under him; and when he came to the mention of Evelyn Wood and Redvers Buller—two names which, he said, represented all that a soldier could show in loyalty and efficiency—his modest eulogium upon these, "his right hand and left hand supports during the war," was perhaps the most well received and telling point of his address. That Wood's services were appreciated by the colonists may be gathered from the fact that he was most warmly solicited by Mr. Gordon Sprigg, the Premier, to accept the appointment of Commandant-General of the Colonial Forces; and this request was made by the almost unanimous wish of the whole ministry. Sir Evelyn, however, did not feel at liberty to accept till he had consulted with the authorities at home.

On August 5th, Lord Chelmsford, Sir Evelyn Wood, Colonel Crealock, Colonel Buller, Major Grenfell, Captain Molyneux, and Captain Buller, embarked on board the Union steamship *German,* and sailed for England, where they arrived safely and were received with the honours they had so worthily deserved.

After the meeting of chiefs on the 19th, at the camp on the Umlatoosi, Sir Garnet Wolseley returned to Pietermaritzburg. Here he was engaged in arranging matters of detail until July 29th. Disturbances in Pondoland and the Transvaal also now claimed his attention. In the former the Pondos had attacked the Xesibes, a tribe in alliance with England and under British protection. Hither. Lieutenant-Colonel Bayley, with a detachment of Cape Mounted Rifles, was despatched from Butterworth, and soon succeeded in putting an end to this trouble. In the Transvaal the Boers were agitating for a repeal of the union, and threatening to assert their independence by force of arms. To render matters secure in this quarter Sir Garnet sent the headquarters of the King's Dragoon Guards, under Colonel Alexander, to Praetoria.

On the 30th the commander and his staff moved to Greytown and thence on, with a small escort, to the temporary camp at Umsingu. Travelling herefrom with all speed he reached Rorke's Drift early the following morning (August 3rd). Despatches were waiting here for the commander-in-chief, and determined the next week's movements. Cetywayo was still reported in a *kraal* in the Ngome, while letters were at hand from Villiers giving anything but a flattering account of his friend Oham and his promised Burgher and native levies. M'Leod also wrote to point out the difficulties under which he was labouring with his Swazis, and asking for some European troops to be sent to him to keep them under control.

Villiers was concentrating his heterogeneous gathering of levies at Luneberg, and hoped to be ready on or by the 6th; while M'Leod suggested that he should merely guard the frontier to prevent Cetywayo's escape, and not tempt his savages with the sight of their enemy's *kraals* or cattle; for to allow them to cross the border would be, he wrote, risking murder, rapine, and all sorts of atrocities, which, if once begun, it would be impossible to stop.

So little is generally known of the Swazis, that a short description of their persons and habits may here be acceptable. What are usually called Swazis are, in reality, somewhat a mongrel race, being a cross between the Zulu and the old race of Swaziland. The Swazis living along the borders of the Wakkerstroom, until late owed allegiance to Cetywayo, and some of them indeed had fought for him, notably Manyoyaba, a chief paramount in the Abakalusian district. But quarrels arose between the two races and they became most bitter foes; indeed, once the Swazis were near extermination at the hands of the Zulus.

The whole tribe possess characteristically broad heads with thick hair, which would be as frizzly as that of a negro were it not carefully dressed in the Zulu fashion with plaster of grease and red clay.

Their eyes, almond-shaped and somewhat sloping, are shaded with thick, sharply-defined brows, and are of remarkable size and fullness. The wide space between them testifies to the unusual width of the skull, and contributes a mingled expression of animal ferocity, warlike resolution, and, strange to say, ingenuous candour. A flat, square nose, a mouth of about the same width as the nose, with very thick lips; a round chin, and full, plump cheeks complete the countenance which may be described as circular in its general contour.

The bodies of the Swazis are generally inclined, like those of the Zulus, to be fat, but they are seldom wanting in muscular strength. They are fairly well proportioned, but the upper part of the figure is somewhat long in proportion to the legs, and this peculiarity gives a strange character to their movements, although it does not seem any bar to their agility in their war-dances. Nothing can be more simple than the ordinary headgear of the women.

It would, however, be a matter of some difficulty to find any kind of plait, tuft, or topknot, which has not been used by the Swazi men. The hair is usually parted right down the middle; towards the forehead it branches off so as to leave a kind of triangle, and from the fork which is thus formed, a tuft is raised and carried back to be fastened behind. On either side of this tuft the hair is arranged in rolls, like the ridges and crevices of a melon, while over the temples separate rolls are gathered up into knots, from which hang more tufts, twisted like a cord, that fall in bunches round the neck, three or four of the largest tresses being allowed to go free over the breast and shoulders.

A favourite decoration is formed with the teeth of a dog strung together under the hair and hanging along the forehead like a fringe. Another ornament not at all uncommon is worn by some, and this is ivory cut in imitation of lions' teeth, and arranged in radial fashion round the breast, the effect of the white substance in contrast with the dark skin being very striking. The weapons of the Swazis are much the same as those of the Zulus, but they have more variety in shape and quality of the *assegai*. The shields are smaller, and usually woven of stout reeds and then covered with undressed hide. They use also a heavy kind of lance which is adapted to the chase of large game.

A favourite amusement is a kind of war-dance, in which a warrior describes a conflict in which he was once engaged. Thus a chief may be often seen with his *assegai* s in one hand, his woven shield and *knobkerrie* in the other, with his knife in his girdle, and his limbs encircled by a skin, to which are attached the tails of the wild cat and other animals. Adorned on his breast and on his forehead by strings of teeth, the trophies of war or of the chase, his large keen eyes gleaming from beneath his heavy brow, his white and pointed teeth shining from between his parted lips, he alternately advances and retires before an imaginary foe, with a wild yet dramatic grace, which adds life and reality to the tale he is telling.

In describing these people, it is hard to determine how far they should be deemed a race of hunters or of agriculturists, the two occupations being apparently equally distributed between the sexes. The men most assiduously devote themselves to their hunting, and leave the care of the cattle and the culture of the soil to be carried on exclusively by the women. Now and then, indeed, the men bring home fruits, tubers, and funguses from their excursions in the forests, but practically they do nothing for their families beyond providing them with game. The agriculture of Swaziland, like that of Zululand involves but a small amount of labour. The area of the arable land is certainly limited, but the exuberant productiveness of the soil, scarcely to be surpassed in any part of the world, makes the cultivation of the country supremely easy, and provides the people with all they want.

The entire land is, besides, pre-eminently rich in spontaneous products, animal and vegetable alike, and these conduce to a direct maintenance in comparative ease of human life. Manioc, sweet potatoes, yams, are cultivated with little trouble, and all yield good crops. Plantains are rarely seen. Although the Swazis have a few carefully prepared dishes, of which they partake on high feasts and festivals, in a general way they exhibit as little nicety or choice in their diet as the Amaxosas or the Zulus. They have one dish, however, on which they pride themselves, and this most palatable mess is composed of the pulp of fresh maize, ground or pounded while the grain is soft and milky, cleansed from the bran, and prepared carefully, so that it is not burnt to the bottom of the pot.

The mode of preparation is ingenious. A little water having been put over the fire, until it is just beginning to boil, the raw meal, which has previously been rolled into small lumps, is very gently shaken in, and, having been allowed to simmer for a time, the whole is finally stirred up together. The acme, however, of all earthly enjoyments to these people would seem to be meat. "Meat!" is a watchword that one hears in all their campaigns, and beyond all doubt the alacrity with which these people responded to M'Leod's appeal was caused by the anticipations of devouring Cetywayo's cattle.

Amongst their other accomplishments may be mentioned the art they possess of making from malted *eleusine* a very palatable species of beer. This drink, which by the Swazis is prepared from the *eleusine*, is really capable, from the skill with which it is manipulated, of laying a very fair claim to be known as beer. It is quite bright, of a reddish pale brown colour, and is regularly brewed from the malted grain, without the addition of any extraneous ingredient. It has, moreover, a pleasant bitter flavour derived from the dark husks, which, if they were mixed in their natural condition with the dough, would impart a twang that would be exceedingly unpalatable.

How large is the proportion of beer consumed by the Swazis may be estimated by simply observing the ordinary manner in which they store their corn. As a rule, there are three granaries allotted to each dwelling, of which two are made to suffice for the supply which is to contribute the meal necessary for the household, and the other is entirely devoted to the grain that has been malted.

On August 4th Sir Garnet Wolseley left Rorke's Drift, and, after inspecting the several posts *en route*, reached Intanjaneni on the evening of the 6th. Intanjaneni is admirably situated for a central rendezvous as well as a depot of supplies. It is on the left bank of the Umlatoosi, or Slater's River, a stream which is constantly confounded by careless geographers with the Umlalazi, which is ten miles further to the south-west. Hither General Clarke and his column had preceded him; messengers also had already come in from Unihan, Cetywayo's prime minister, from Tyengwayo, who was second in command at Isandhlwana, and likewise from the headmen Usukame and Umkilebani; all these men said they would come in if their lives were spared and their property not confiscated. Many other chiefs were also in correspondence and treaty with the general, and all had promised to come to Ulundi on the 10th August.

On the 7th August messengers came from another chief of importance, by name Mbelebele, whose *kraal* was situated on the eastern bank of the Black Umvolosi, about twenty miles N.N.E. of the old *kraal* at Ondini. A party was sent, in accordance with his request, to meet him halfway between his *kraal* and Fort Victoria, the new post near Ulundi. The interview, which took place at the foot of the mountain range of the Lebombo, was short and satisfactory.

Mbelebele brought with him over 200 guns. He also brought information that Mangondo, another chief whose dwelling is near the Inkankla, would surrender if assured of safety against the vengeance

273

of the king. Mbelebele seems to have been a man much trusted by the other chiefs, as he had been in correspondence with the younger brother of Cetywayo, Tyami, Usmwelu, Usiteon, and with Sekatewayo, a northern chief, who all manifested a wish to come in and surrender their arms, cattle, and ammunition, provided life and safety were assured.

The chief, in speaking of the king, although somewhat reticent on some points, was certainly not so on others, and stoutly maintained that Cetywayo had doubled upon his pursuers, and so far from being, as was thought, on his way westward to Secocoeni, was in all likelihoods heading back towards a *kraal* beyond the Lebombo range, called Mussipulo. This information, of course, was at once sent to Lord Gifford and to Colonel Baker Russell.

Sir Garnet Wolseley's next move was on to Fort Victoria, Ulundi, where he arrived on August 9th. On the following day he received information which eventually led to the capture of Cetywayo; but of this we shall speak hereafter.

CHAPTER 14

Plans for the Capture of Cetywayo

Meantime the meshes of the net spread for King Cetywayo's capture were being more and more closely woven. Colonel Villiers, who it has been before mentioned had been sent to Oham's district, having got together a force of 65 Europeans and 3050 natives in a fair state of organisation, had by August 13th advanced as far as the Assegai River, so as to form a junction with M'Leod and his 5000 Swazis, at that time on the banks of the Pongolo, and thus complete the chain round that side of the Zulu country.

Lord Gifford, with a number of Jantjis, was following up the king, whilst 200 of the 57th were also in pursuit, carefully patrolling the hills that lay beyond Amansekranze, ably seconded by 500 of Barton's natives. The Intanjaneni district, from Middle Drift to Victoria and St. Paul's, was laid down with a line of piquets, whose orders were to keep strict watch by night and day. The escape of the Zulu monarch therefore appeared an impossibility. The Jantjis just spoken of merit a few words of description, not only on account of the good services they rendered, but also because in some points they differ vastly from other South African tribes.

The men of this race are fine, active, and well made, standing not unusually six feet in height. Their clothing consists simply of a blanket, worn in peace time in the manner of a Roman *toga*, but on the war-path invariably discarded for a simple belt of wild-cats' tails. Their weapons are the light *assegai*, or *umkonto*, and this spear can be thrown by them to the distance of seventy or eighty yards, when at that it will have sufficient strength to enter a man's body. Many of the men even brought their guns, and showing Lord Gifford how expert they were in their use, were allowed to carry and employ them, instead of the original native weapon.

275

The Jantjis, like the Kaffirs first, and then the Zulus, are beginning to find out that the *assegai* is not a match for a gun; consequently, as they have money, they procure a tolerably large number of them. Like most of the Zulu tribes, they build wickerwork huts, and thatch these with the long *tambookie* grass. These huts are, as usual, arranged in a circle, and thus form a village, or, as we should say, a *kraal*. The men, unlike the Zulus, are very fond of horses, and most of them can ride. This makes them most useful as mercenaries and levies. As they ride well, it is a pretty sight to see those who are chosen as orderlies dashing along with the letter-bag upon the smart little horses given them by government.

They utterly disdain the use of a saddle, and always gallop along at full speed, with an ostrich feather (if a chief) streaming in the wind, and some wild animal's skin worn hussar fashion, and floating behind. Even with their long black legs almost touching the ground, there is nothing grotesque in their appearance, though doubtless in London such a horseman would cause astonishment. Dashing up with a letter or heliographic message from Sir Garnet, these fellows bring their horses to a sudden stand, as Bedouins do, sending the mould and grit beneath the hoofs flying in the air. Saluting then most gracefully, with the spearhead to the earth, the messenger springs to the ground, and hands in his *paquet*.

To resume our narrative. On Sunday afternoon (10th August), as Sir Garnet Wolseley was walking with an *aide-de-camp* near the camp at Fort Victoria, Ulundi, a man on foot was observed, apparently lame and feeble, making the best of his way towards our camp. With glasses it could be made out that he came along with difficulty, limping much, and occasionally casting a furtive glance behind, as if in danger of being pursued. As ponies were ready at hand and saddled. Sir Garnet mounted and cantered out of the camp to see who the man was.

On coming to close quarters he found the wayfarer to be no less a personage than one Cornelius Vijn, a Dutch trader of Natal, who was known to have been a prisoner for some time at Cetywayo's *kraal*. His aspect and general appearance were, to put it mildly, more those of a badly-dressed scarecrow than those of a human being, and his haggard and hungry contour, his wearied look, lean and meagre, with eyes deeply sunk in their orbits, and his parchment-like cheeks, hollow and cavernous, all spoke with an eloquent voice of the ordeal he must have undergone while the enforced guest of King Cetywayo. The aide-de-camp, having with him a flask and some biscuits, was enabled to somewhat revive the fugitive, who then informed them who he was, and how he had managed to escape from the king's thrall.

As his information was considered highly important. Sir Garnet desired Mr Vijn to narrate briefly his story out of hearing of the camp in order that any future operations or measures, consequent upon the information given, might not transpire to the outer world. The necessity for this precaution had been of late forced upon the general, who had had many of his plans and movements made known by those upon whose discretion while at headquarters he thought he could vouch for. Besides, since his arrival in Natal, Sir Garnet had achieved all his successes by striking without warning, and by carefully concealing the movements of troops, stores, &c., from all but those actually in command where the movement was to be made; and there was but little doubt that the Zulus, in the earlier portion of the war, obtained much of their information from the Dutch, at least from that section of the Boers who thought it their interest to see the English army unsuccessful, and who consequently made known to the enemy the British weak points.

Mr. Vijn's narrative, although very long, did not contain many details of general interest. He left Natal for trading purposes as far back as the 29th of October, 1878, and about the middle of January fell into the power of the king, who, however, does not seem to have treated him at all rigorously, but allowed him to remain at one of his brother's *kraals* under a sort of friendly supervision. During this detention Mr. Vijn appears to have kept a sort of journal, which has a certain value, as showing the opinions of the king, his brothers, and the Zulu people in regard to the war. As Mr. Vijn's information regarding the movements and whereabouts of the king was both authentic and valuable, and as he volunteered to return to Cetywayo and persuade him to surrender.

Sir Garnet decided to avail himself of such offer. His presence near the camp was, however, kept entirely secret, and having been allowed to rest and refit, he was despatched on his return journey, pledging himself to return if possible by Tuesday evening with the king's answer. On the following Wednesday Mr. Vijn came back to the camp, and reported that his mission had been unsuccessful, as the king had left the *kraals* where Vijn had last seen him, and had fled away to the north towards the Ngome forest. As soon as this news was communicated to Sir Garnet, instructions were given to Major Barrow to take a troop of the King's Dragoon Guards, sixty mounted infantry, some colonial levies and natives, making in all a force of 220 whites and eighty natives, and to proceed into the territory of those chiefs who were still holding out, and where, it was supposed, the king had taken refuge.

Major Marter, K.D.G., Captain Maurice, Lord Gifford, Captain Hardy, Captain Hay, and Mr. Herbert accompanied Major Barrow, and they merely took with them, to be in as light marching order as possible, three days' preserved rations—their commander wisely assuming that they would find no great difficulty in foraging as they went on. Half an hour after the order to parade was given they were all in the saddle and ready for the road. Sir Garnet, accompanied by Colonel Colley, minutely inspected men, horses, equipment, rations, and ammunition, and, after addressing a few private words of advice to the officers, bade them "God-speed."

Proceeding north-eastward at starting they soon came to the little River Umbellan, which, flowing past the dense bush of the district, ultimately joins the Umvolosi. At this time of the year it is about twenty feet deep, and murmurs along a channel of from twenty to thirty feet wide, now and then forming deep basins, which were found to be full of fish. Soon after midnight the junction of the Black Umvolosi was reached, and the first night's camp was made near a fine tamarind-tree, which was noted as a landmark in case of a return that way. At this season there was a rather heavy dew towards daybreak, but the nights were calm, and, in comparison with the day, considerably colder than would be expected.

Just as the party was ready and preparing to start, after an early meal in the morning, some natives came from a neighbouring *kraal* with the information that on the previous night one of their best oxen, having strayed outside the cattle enclosure, had been seized and carried off by a lion. It had already been stated by John Dunn that the district through which they had to pass had been for some years infested with lions, and lately the casualties had been so frequent that the inhabitants were commencing to migrate. The Umvolosi at its junction with the Umbellan is about the same size as the latter river, and at this point makes a most remarkable bend from south-east to north-east, but its general direction for some distance in this district is due north, the stream flowing between banks twenty or thirty feet in height, with an average width of full forty feet and a depth of only three feet. The velocity of the current, however, was 120 feet a minute.

Leaving Amansekranze, they marched about nine miles towards the north-west, having on their left the Black Umvolosi, and on their right the huge terraces and wood-crowned ravines of the Lebombo mountains. The woods came down to the river as it flowed between its rocky banks; and farther north-west some wide meadow-like flats were crossed, containing water basins almost as large as lakes. Several kinds of antelope of the larger sort, waterbucks, and hartebeests appeared, and as the troopers managed to wound and ride down several, their nightly bivouac in the forest was solaced by a feast of excellent venison. Between the Umvolosi and the Lebombo range the previous uniformity of the rocks began to be broken by projections of gneiss and by scattered hills.

About twelve miles from the junction of the rivers at Amansekranze a remarkable illustration of this formation was passed, where huge blocks of stone rose in mounds from which colossal obelisks could be cut. These elevated places alternated with extensive flats as level as a table-top. In keeping with this weird and fantastic scenery and eccentric native architecture is the peculiarity of the conies or rock rabbits that have their dwelling among the crevices of the gneiss. Soon after the sun went down, and just before sunrise, they were to be seen all round squatting like natives at the entrance of their holes, into which at the slightest noise or sound of danger they darted with the most extraordinary snorts and grunts.

There is, however, a great variety of species—difficult for one who is not a skilled naturalist to distinguish the one from the other—scattered through the whole of Zululand, each district seeming to present its own representative. They appear to feed chiefly on the bark of trees, although they will occasionally devour young shoots and grass. Distinct from anything in the more civilized parts of South Africa was the aspect of the landscape presented to view on the second morning of the march. From the heights to which Barrow and his men had ascended, and as far as the eye could reach, there extended a wide, grassy plain, broken artistically by huge stones of the most fantastic outline and by thickets and single trees. Graceful and luxuriant palms of the fan species waved above the groves, while the russet autumnal tints gave a rich colouring to the scenery; every rock, with its wealth of covering parasites, being a picture in itself.

In the far north could be seen the Mussipulo and the distant portions of the Lebombo, whose purple peaks stood out in bold relief in the pale azure of the horizon. In the far distance, and in the direction of the Amatongas, the country had the deep and luscious blue of a Neapolitan sky, mellowed, however, as it came nearer and nearer into the most bewitching tints of grey and a golden brown that Titian would have loved to paint. In the foreground were the sturdy troopers of Marter's squadron grouped in picturesque disorder as the process of saddling went on. These with their bright uniforms, and the glint of steel scabbard, spur, and chain, were thrown out by the splendid hues of a foliage rich and alternating with the varied tints of red, yellow, and olive green, lightened up with the glad freshness of the sprouting shrubs, the deep red of the numerous ant-hills and the silver grey of the jutting rocks.

After leaving the river, the way at first led over what for horses alone, without wheels, was fair trekking ground. They then descended for about five miles, coming gradually down the slopes to a sort of rough trampled pathway, evidently made by a herd of driven cattle. Here could be distinctly traced the spoor, and here the king's cattle had evidently been driven. Now dipping into a deep hollow, where the grass grew in rank luxuriance, now topping a gentle rise and stopping to listen if they could hear the distant horns of the Zulu sounded when they announce the proximity of an enemy—the horsemen neared the forest-land at the foot of the steep mountain range. Troops of eland crossed their path now and then, and occasionally a herd of *koodoo*.

They now came to the end of the plain, and had to pass over a much more difficult country, where they could scarcely manage to get along two abreast, and sometimes in Indian file. The onward path at one portion of the *kloof* seemed completely barred by a closely set forest of underwood bush of dwarf acacia and creepers of the most tangled nature. Indeed, it seemed at one time impossible to pass, but Lord Gifford, after a search of some moments, found the dry bed of a stream, up which, he said, they might have a chance of progressing. They had now to dismount and lead their horses, and slowly and with the greatest difficulty made their way on, sometimes crawling on hands and knees, and having to drag their rifles after them, winning way patiently, yard by yard, and almost inch by inch. Sometimes they were fairly stopped by huge masses of rock, and even compelled to cut a road through the spiky branches of the mimosa, which were bound up tightly together with the wild vines and creeping cane-like plants. For more than a mile did the column toil on through this ravine, their clothes torn, and face and hands bleeding from the thorns.

The morning after the first day's march brought them to the *kraals* where the king had been a fortnight previous to his flight, as stated to

Sir Garnet by the Dutch trader, and it was no surprise to find these *kraals* burnt to the ground, and completely deserted. Therefore, after a brief halt, they pushed on, and did not draw rein until it became only too evident that the tired horses could go no further. They had been more than three and twenty hours in the saddle, and the weight of the dragoons had told severely upon Marter's horses, which, after the last ten miles under a most burning sun, and over rough and broken ground, were nearly all done up.

On coming to the next *kraal* they found they were still upon the right track, as they gleaned sufficient intelligence to know that the king had slept there on the day preceding. He had, however, been warned by scouts and signal-fires,—the latter had been noticed as they came along,—and had decamped in time to get a good start. At this point Major Barrow decided to leave the King's Dragoon Guards behind, and push on with the lighter portion of his mounted men, and this arrangement was carried out with the understanding that the "King's" should follow as soon as their horses were fit. Once more, therefore, Barrow set out, and, as he subsequently found, was upon the king's trail for two clear days, having by dint of bribery and threats extorted information as to the king's intentions. On Thursday the column had a fearfully fatiguing and at the same time disappointing day. They reached another *kraal* at sundown, having travelled over a most difficult and hilly country all day.

Major Barrow decided to bivouac at this *kraal*, and to start during the night should the moon give sufficient light. The moon, however, rose so late that it was really sunrise when they were on the move on Friday morning. Lord Gifford was now sent on ahead with a few men, and it was subsequently found afterwards that he and Captain Hardy chased and nearly caught one of the king's principal attendants. This man would have been caught had he not dexterously abandoned his horse, and, taking to the jungle, managed to elude further pursuit. Meanwhile the main body followed on, and on Saturday came to another *kraal*.

One of the king's personal attendants was here captured, who having been frightened by a little threatening, showed where the king had stayed and slept on Thursday. This fellow's statements were somewhat contradictory and improbable. He wished Major Barrow to believe that the king meditated changing the direction of his flight and endeavouring to gain the Inkhangla bush, which is as nearly as possible opposite the Tugela middle drift. But to make this point the king would have had to get through the line of posts stationed in this district, and this made the story seem improbable. Major Barrow, however, taking the remote chance of the man being truthful, and having no better information, allowed the Zulu to take him in a retrograde and southerly direction, until he met another Zulu messenger, who said he had heard nothing of the king along the road he came. Major Barrow therefore retraced his steps to the camp of the main body on the Black Umyolosi, and sent Lord Gifford and Captain Maurice on with eight men to get some cattle from a *kraal* and obtain what information he could.

The first destination of this party was a *kraal* with cattle and mealies, and this was said to be about seven miles from where they were then halted. On reaching the said *kraal* on Saturday afternoon they surprised some Zulu boys, and partly by threats and partly by persuasion induced them to come on to another *kraal*, seven miles off. These boys, after some pressing, confessed that on the previous day (Friday), the king had endeavoured to double back towards the south, and had slept within a mile of where they had bivouacked, and had actually passed the *kraal* where they then were. This intelligence confirmed the story that had previously been told by the king's attendant, and the information was at once sent back to Major Barrow.

On Saturday night they slept in the *kraal* they had reached in the afternoon, having during the day visited a number of smaller *kraals* and villages, in which they captured many assegais and other weapons. They thus had made a circuit and were now heading almost due south, and though they had now been four clear days in the saddle, had managed their three days' supply of rations so well that they had still a reserve to fall back upon. This feat of commissariat skill was accomplished by obtaining wherever they could such simple supplies as the *kraals* afforded—sour milk, Indian corn cakes made of mealies, pumpkin, sweet potatoes, and now and then a little Kaffir beer, which after a time, and when the taste is acquired, is not such very bad stuff.

Sunday, the 17th, was a most eventful day. Lord Gifford paraded his men, and they started, as usual, just before sunrise, their destination being an important military *kraal*, which they had every reason to believe the king must have visited. The gallant leader had on the previous evening induced two Zulu boys to accompany his men as guides, for the shortest way was through the forest and across country, where it was impossible to find the smallest trace of a trek. When they set out, the whole of the wood was veiled in mist, and the ground was yet reeking with the early dew. But as the light came on they were rewarded by seeing an immense variety of forest shrubs. Especially beautiful was the *Eucephalartus*, which grew in abundance; most noticeable too was a cabbage-shaped *Euphorbia*, as well as a large variety of conspicuous shrubs, many of them covered with such fine blossoms as to give the wilderness the aspect of an artificial park.

About three miles to the right, and to the south of the ford last crossed, rose several thickly-wooded hills, and in the *kloofs* could be seen the smoke of *kraals*. The guides had by this time become quite friendly and confidential, and by their advice more than one of these *kraals* were surrounded, in hope that if they did not see the king they might hear of his more recent movements. At three of these *kraals* they captured arms and ammunition, and filled their haversacks with mealies, but could gain no tidings of Cetywayo, although they knew he could not be far off. In one instance they thought they had discovered their prize, as coming out of the forest they saw a portion of open country before them and several natives on horseback and on foot about two miles away to their right.

The scenery they were now approaching towards the south-west assumed a character very different to the park-like landscape through which they had been passing. For many miles the eye rested upon treeless steppes and flats, broken by bamboo and mimosa jungles that seemed almost impenetrable, and standing in detached groups, their dark olive green contrasted admirably with the bright hue of the grass, giving a complete novelty of character to the general aspect. The moment the group of natives saw them emerge from the forest they quickened their pace, and endeavoured to gain the jungle to their left, while Lord Gifford detached three of his men round a small hill to cut them off. A most exciting race now commenced, two Basutos joining in the pursuit, and taking advantage of every rock and bush to dodge and intercept the fugitives.

Suddenly the Zulus became aware of the party sent round the hill to intercept them, and giving a shout of alarm ran back in the direction of the *kraal* the English troopers had left. This was exactly what was required, and galloping right across the plain the troopers caught them halfway. These men were found to be Zulus of the neighbourhood, and when they were satisfied that their pursuers had no hostile intentions they became quite friendly, offering milk and Kaffir corn, as well as food for the horses. They professed to be starting on a journey to a *kraal* about ten miles off, belonging to a chief named Isnabomlika, who, they said, was anxious for the capture of the king, as he had grievously oppressed him. Leaving these men, they continued their march, and soon came to a tract of country much better cultivated than any they had hitherto seen. Maize-fields (mealies) showed that the ground was fertile, and although no cattle was seen, the presence of several kraals on the neighbouring hills showed that the district was populous.

About midday they reached the large military kraal where it was thought probable the king might have stopped. His guides had served him with fidelity, and so Lord Gifford promised to reward them at headquarters with a present of cattle to each. These lads had made themselves great favourites with the men, who seemed quite to fraternize with them. Their delight was unbounded when the officers came across and killed with their rifles any description of game, and they seemed wonderfully impressed with the accuracy of the shooting. They said it had been currently reported in their neighbourhood that the king was lame and could not travel fast, and that his followers were leaving him every day.

Just before reaching the kraal one of the lads, an intelligent, sharp little fellow, as he was running a few yards in front of the horses, pointed out to Lord Gifford the track of cattle leading away to the bush on the right. They halted and had a consultation; but it was decided not to follow these tracks, but to continue on southwards, their object being, if possible, to hem in the king, and drive him on towards the pickets of Barrow's party or the scouts of General Clarke, who had four companies of infantry, the headquarters of the King's Dragoon Guards, and a number of irregulars (cavalry and infantry) encamped at the drift of the Black Umvolosi. As they knew that Clarke's patrols were scouring the country to the north and east, they had no fear of the king's escape in that direction.

But little information was gained at the big kraal, where they off-saddled for two hours, and fed their rather overworked mounts. At three o'clock they again started and now made a bend towards Entonjaneni, as by this course it was considered they would have the best chance of intercepting the king in his attempt to cut through the cordon now drawn around him. The range of hills which they now had on their right were the Umyati. They are a continuation of the Ngome Mountains, which shoot out from the Lebombo towards the west, and they form a portion of the ridge bordering the southern or right bank of the Black Umvolosi.

On the summit, as far as the eye could reach, there was an extensive plateau broken by detached groves and handsome trees, and sloping down towards the north to the stream. A few miles on they came to some fine tamarinds, under the pleasant shade of which another short halt and off-saddle was made. Before reaching the river they had to cross four little brooks that flowed in an easterly direction to join it. The first of these to the north of the hills was the upper course of the Enhlongana, and was full of water in a deep bed enclosed in an avenue of trees. A ridge of hills ran parallel to the path on the left, and after they had crossed the second brook a mass of red rock, rising to about 300 feet was observed on the right.

The long grass was now very troublesome, coming up in some places to the saddle-flaps, and tickling the horses in a most unpleasant manner. Towards five o'clock they entered the splendid forest of Enhlongana, through which, but ten miles to the west, they had passed some ten days before. After the forest came an open *steppe*, with a distant view of the hills in front, which they crossed, though more to the west than before. The passage of the Enhlongana having been accomplished without mishap, the road began to ascend and led through a wood, where the foliage was so dense that it was quite impossible to see many steps in front.

It will be observed that there were no less than twelve brooks crossed in the interval between the march in the morning and the final bivouac on Sunday night. These are all supplied more or less copiously with water, even in the dry season; at least so said the guides. Although all these streams have their origin quite close to the left bank of the Enhlongana, yet they take a very devious course before they actually join it; the last five, indeed, do not actually meet the river, but join another stream a little to the west called the Ivuma, which unites itself with the Black Umvolosi under the Ngome Mountain. On this watershed bamboo and mimosa jungles extend over an area of many square miles. The species of bamboo which is thus found in such masses is not so large as that one is accustomed to see in India, Ceylon, or the Mauritius; and in the manner of its growth it is not unlike an asparagus bed in the summer-time, hundreds of sprouts starting up from a single root, and drooping in the most graceful curves over towards the ground.

In other respects, the habit of the plant is similar to the Indian bamboo. The night was now coming on; they had ridden at the very least thirty-five miles, besides exploring *kraals*, examining prisoners, and galloping after wounded game. All knew and felt instinctively that the king was in the toils, that he could not have broken through the network spread for him, and that it was a mere question of days as to when he would be forced to surrender. The horses were indeed fatigued, but none as yet were lame, while the three days' rations of biscuit and preserved meats, with which they had started, were almost intact, so well had they been husbanded by the men living on what they could shoot or obtain from the *kraals*.

On Sunday night (August 17th) the bivouac was made at the wild mountain *kraal* of Unhlovani; some women, girls, and children were found here, who at first were terribly frightened at the approach of the troopers, but soon became reassured and friendly. Indeed, Lord Gifford had a wonderful faculty of ingratiating himself with the native races, and, after a little persuasion, made one of the chief's daughters confess that, although the king did not pass by this particular *kraal*, his attendants did but two days since. She also added information of great value, namely, that there were but two passes over the mountain they had now reached, and that three of the king's wives had passed over the eastern road the day before, carrying bundles and food.

They further learnt that this girl had no possible reason for sympathy for or loyalty to Cetywayo, inasmuch as an old Zulu, who stated that she was his niece, told them that the king, about two years ago, suspecting her father of some pretended conspiracy, had had him smelt out and killed, and that the children were at Cetywayo's disposal for sale or gift. On the following morning (Monday) the horses were tolerably refreshed. They had a good amount of forage given them, and a careful examination of each animal showed that no back sinews were strained, and that no sore backs had come on.

A small supply of sweet potatoes, pumpkins, and a quantity of mealies were given to them by the chief's daughters, whose hearts their leader had won by explaining to them that the king's reign of terror was at an end, and that henceforth they could marry any young warrior they pleased. Bidding these Zulu friends adieu, the party were in the saddle and on the road by five o'clock; and, ascending by a path pointed out by some boys of the *kraal*, they came to a lofty ridge dominating the valley below, and along which they pushed at a fast walk for about an hour.

From this ridge, which they were following as quickly as the rugged nature of the narrow ledge would allow, the view was magnificently grand. In the foreground, where they were compelled to march in single file, and where a halt was made every now and then to allow a straggler to come up, was a most inviting grove, with some of the most charming types of tropical vegetation—the large-leaved, blue-green *anona*, the purple *Gruvia mollis*, and a number of pretty little trees of the pine genus, that gave a Swiss character to the scene. Having risen in their march to an elevation of 2000 feet, they gazed down upon a fine view of the valley and its meandering rivers below.

The banks of each stream were marked by rows of tall reeds, and the morning sun gleamed upon the mirror of the numerous backwaters, while the distance revealed a series of woody undulations in the direction of the Norwegian mission station of Enhlongana. Turning sharply round a curve in the rocky path, they came suddenly upon a *kraal* nestled in a most secluded and difficult spot, and here they found two good-looking and very communicative Zulu girls, who fetched for them some capital milk, and, after a little coaxing, told them that the king's attendants had passed on that way the previous evening. These women, as far as could be gleaned from the interpreter, had also suffered some wrong and oppression, and whatever might be the political feeling or loyal tendencies of Cetywayo's male subjects, it seemed tolerably evident that the Zulu women would have no objection to a change of government.

These women at the *kraal* having shown them a short cut down one side of the ridge, they hastened on in the hope of overtaking some of the king's following, and their activity was soon rewarded by discovering a couple of figures making their way hurriedly along the lower ledge about a mile from them. One of the officers volunteered to proceed on foot to cut these people off by a sort of goat-path that seemed practicable down the side of the cliff; and, accompanied by one trooper, half-sliding, half-falling, and with a desperate scramble, the gallant fellow reached the next ledge at a point where it was evident the travellers must pass. In ten minutes they came up—a tall and stalwart Zulu with a bundle of *assegais*, accompanied by a lad carrying a sort of canvas bag. something in shape like those in which cricketers carry a bat and flannel suit.

At the word "Halt!" accompanied by a presented revolver, the couple of natives came to a stand, and on being questioned declared they were messengers from the chief Usibibo to a neighbouring *kraal*. As this story seemed rather doubtful, it was determined to search the cricket-bag, and they were not long in finding a trophy that almost repaid them for their many weary miles of travel. Inside was a very handsome Henry rifle belonging to the king, a small leather handbag, a number of cartridges, and a hand-mirror! As such articles do not form the travelling appendages of the ordinary Zulu, it was at once seen that they were getting hotter and hotter on the trail. While these two were thus carefully examining the captured spoil, the main party came winding down the *kloof*, having during their absence come suddenly upon and surprised some more of Cetywayo's attendants. A halt was immediately ordered, and the whole of the prisoners examined one by one.

Some of the people from the friendly *kraal* had, in the meantime, overtaken the English horsemen, and their presence seemed to act as a wonderful incentive to truth on the part of the prisoners.

"Tell them," said Lord Gifford, "that if they all speak the truth to our questions we will do them no harm and let them go free."

This had a wonderful effect, and, coupled with a private communication of a confidential nature, from the Zulus of the *kraal*, evidently to the effect that the white man's intentions were not hostile to them, it caused the prisoners to confess at once that they were of the king's following, and that the elder was his personal attendant. From further information then obtained from these people it was found that a mile further on, and hidden in a cave, were a troop of Zulu girls and other attendants with goods and chattels of the king. Guided by these not too faithful adherents of Cetywayo, the troopers soon came to where these people were, and they surrendered at once without any attempt to escape.

These latter prisoners appeared to have with them all the paraphernalia of the monarch's toilet. There were gums, wax, and unguents for the hair and face, brushes, combs, tweezers, scissors, and razors, together with old pocket-books, almanacs, gaily-coloured pocket-handkerchiefs, and charms and medicine, made of ground human teeth, and hair and skins of reptiles, reminding one irresistibly of the ingredients of the witches' cauldron in Macbeth.

A silk pocket-handkerchief was recognised as belonging to Colonel Degacher by the name in its corner, and this was almost the only article that could not be considered rags or rubbish. While Lord Gifford and his party were holding a solemn Court of Inquiry over this burlesque of human vanity a loud whistle was heard, and coming round the corner of the ledge, they saw Captain Hay and a Basuto approaching at a smart canter. Hay, flinging himself from his panting mount, and wiping the perspiration from his forehead, announced that he was sent on by Major Barrow, to say that, having himself failed in obtaining any traces of the king, and deeming it inadvisable to delay the others in waiting for him to catch them up, he had decided to increase Lord Gifford's little force with twenty Basatos, under their leader, Jantzi, and to leave the pursuit of the king in his (Gifford's) hands, while he (Barrow) made his way back to Clarke's camp.

Meanwhile, the arrival of these additions to the English force seemed to exercise a marked influence upon the ladies of the king's household, who immediately jumped at the conclusion that Cetywayo had fallen into the hands of the soldiers. This had a wonderful effect, as they now discovered from the women and attendants where the king had actually slept the previous day, and armed with this information, they pushed on, bivouacked for the night at the nearest *kraal*, and started before daybreak on the following morning. From these prisoners they learnt, moreover, several most important and invaluable pieces of information: first, that the poor king was almost deserted; secondly, that he had been obliged to abandon his horses; and, thirdly, that he was ill and footsore.

From Tuesday, the 19th, until Wednesday, the 27th, long marches were incessant, and to describe the adventures that befell this small party would be merely a repetition of those already told. The arrival of Jantzi and the timely reinforcements of Basutos enabled Lord Gifford to detach parties and hem in the fugitive monarch in a manner he could not have effected with only nine men. It was now almost a point of honour with Gifford that his men should succeed in capturing the king after the way in which Barrow had entrusted the pursuit to him; and although he knew that the king was pursued by Barton's Native Infantry, three companies of the 57th, and 150 of Marter's Dragoons, he still felt confident that his party alone were upon the right track.

Marter he had heard had gone back after losing three of his horses by lions in the district through which he had passed; and his only fear now was that the Mounted Police would take the wind out of his sails by a rapid move from the Transvaal, and capture the king should he attempt to escape towards the north. This he considered was not improbable, as he had news from Villiers up to the 12th, saying that the tribes in his neighbourhood were most unfriendly, and anxious to afford help to the king. Indeed, they had attempted an attack upon the mixed force organised by Villiers, but had been easily beaten off.

The movements of Gifford's party from the 20th (Wednesday) up to the 26th, were not of special interest. They marched and counter-marched, the king never far in front, but always managing to keep thirty or forty miles between himself and them, and their information sometimes right and sometimes wrong, according to the feelings of the natives whom they questioned. On the 25th they had tolerably authentic information that the king had decided to come in to Lord Gifford, and surrender. Dabulamauzi, however, a brave soldier although a double-dyed and scheming traitor, wrote or sent to the king, telling him the English would hang or shoot him if he surrendered. Dabulamanzi's object was most transparent. He hoped the king might be killed or die in the wilds of starvation, as then he might possibly be made the English nominee to the throne.

Jumping over the interval between Monday, 18th August, and that day week, during which the pursuer's movements merely resembled those of a pack of harriers when "pussy" will keep dodging and doubling over the same ground, we may come to the incidents which led up to the king's capture. On Monday night, 28th August, scouts came in, who kept Gifford and his party well in line with the king's refuge, and although their horses were nearly dropping from fatigue they marched on Tuesday and on through Tuesday night, until at daybreak on Wednesday they came to a large *kraal* situated close to the Ngome forest, where it was known the king had passed the previous night.

This *kraal* was situated in a most curious and out-of-the-way portion of the land that skirted the forest, and, hidden as it was between two high kops, it might have been easily passed unobserved had it not been for the information Lord Gifford had been enabled to obtain. They approached this *kraal* at dusk, and found that the king had left early in the morning. Some mats, two blankets, and a snuff-box were recognised as belonging to the king. A couple of lads were caught, who at first would tell nothing, but Lord Gifford, assuming a stern air, ordered them both to be blindfolded, and said in their own language, "Shoot first one and then the other!" A volley was fired, and the ruse succeeded, for one boy had been led away out of sight, and the other, thinking he was shot, exclaimed, "They will kill me next; I will confess!" He accordingly said, if his life were spared, he would conduct Lord Gifford to the king's hiding-place.

What was to be done? The horses had had a terrible ten days' "bucketing," the men were tired, hungry, and incapable of great fatigue; but when their chief said, "My lads, we must do it tonight!" every heart beat high with enthusiasm, and hunger, thirst, and fatigue, were at once forgotten. That night-march, conducted by the Zulu boy, was an event that will never be forgotten by those engaged therein. Scarcely had the sun disappeared below the horizon when the devoted little band started on their way, and the novelty of their position in the wilderness could hardly be realised by those who were not used to the country—the deep hum of hundreds of insect creatures signalling their presence to each other, the lizards and poisonous snakes that crawled across the path, the grim, gaunt figure of the beast of prey stalking near the projecting rock, the yells of the monkeys, and the howl of the wild dogs in the plain.

Busy, silent, spectral-like forms passed in the night, and, with a snort of terror or a growl of anger, moved out of the path, scarcely liking to let pass such defenceless creatures as men seem to be, yet apparently in awe of a certain presence which the brute creation can never thoroughly overcome. Tiny creeping animals crackled the crisp leaves as they scampered about in their fastnesses among the bushes, and sniffed the scent of the strange intruder, while the noiseless flapping of wings attracted for an instant the soldier's sight as some ghost-like moving night-bird flew around and examined the strange being that intruded in his domain. Having marched all Tuesday night, with men and horses almost dead with fatigue, they arrived at daybreak within four miles of the *kraal* where they were told the king was lying. He was, they knew, footsore, weary almost unto death, and so despondent that he would scarcely speak to those who still continued with him.

Lord Gifford, knowing the king could go no farther, deemed his capture more certain in the dusk, and accordingly sent back a message to Major Marter, who was known to be not far off, for him to come up on the opposite side to that on which he and his men were posted. Where Lord Gifford was posted was a splendid ambush, as they could see without being seen, and during the day they noticed that an ox was killed and preparations made for a feast. They also saw Marter's men appear on the opposite heights, and then they knew that their task was virtually accomplished. Gifford's ambush, it may be remarked, was on the south-east side, while Marter had posted his men on the north-east.

The king, it was subsequently learnt, saw Marter, but did not see Gifford's men, and he considered that the cavalry could not approach without his knowing. But Marter had wisely taken off his saddles, and made his men leave their steel scabbards, advancing only with *numnahs* and naked swords, and then, disappearing into the bush as if disappointed in his quest, the major stole up quietly by a circuitous route to the *kraal*, and surrounded the king's hut. The Native Contingent were actually the men first up, as they were on foot, and could move more rapidly than the horses. These fellows dashed at the *kraal*, saying to the king's attendants, "The white man is here, you are caught!" Major Marter then rode up quietly to the king's hut, inside the *kraal*, and called upon Cetywayo to surrender.

The king said, with a certain amount of dignity, "Enter into my hut; I am your prisoner!" Major Marter, however, declined this invitation, and prudently invited the king again to come forth. This was the final picture! A Zulu *kraal* is, perhaps, a refuge with as little of the picturesque or dignified as any known habitation, yet the poor king, somewhat bloated in appearance, weak, footsore, and evidently sick at heart, came out of his refuge with a royal dignity which could not be surpassed, and when a too heedless dragoon tried to touch him, said, in grave and majestic tones, "White soldier, do not touch me—I surrender to your chief."

Meanwhile Lord Gifford, to whom, beyond all doubt, the capture was due, as he alone tracked down the quarry, galloped in, and the king expressly said he surrendered to him, and not to Major Marter. With haughty gaze and supremely regal though savage dignity, with head erect, and the mien of a Roman Emperor, Cetywayo marched between the two lines of the 60th Rifles to his tent, while the men, by the order of Lord Gifford, presented arms to him as he passed. Such was the final scene of the Zulu War.

Notes

1: Narrative of Cetywayo's Wanderings after Ulundi, Taken from His Own Lips.

The following account of Cetywayo's movements after the Battle of Ulundi is of great interest as having been taken directly from his lips since he has been confined in Capetown:—

Cetywayo was not present at Ulundi; he was then at the *kraal* of a chief called Umbonambi, which is situated about three miles north of Kwamizekanze. One of Cetywayo's brothers, Uziwetu, in company with Vijn, the captured German trader, had posted himself on the summit of the Uncungi hill, and thus witnessed the conflict. Men, also, had been placed on the look-out, and they brought the news of his army's defeat to Cetywayo, who, at once crossing the neck of the Ntabankulu Mountains, retreated into the bush beyond, where he was joined by Umnyama and other chiefs.

Vijn and Uziwetu came to the king on the following day, but after a short interview withdrew to Uziwetu's *kraal* of Ematina. Cetywayo then retired to Ekushu Maileni, a *kraal* belonging to Umnyama, his prime minister, which is on the banks of the River Isiqmeshi. Arriving here three days after the engagement, he received news of the retreat of the English Army; this determined him to remain where he was; so he lived in this *kraal* for nearly three weeks.

When information of Sir Garnet Wolseley's advance was brought to him, Cetywayo despatched three chiefs to meet the general, and tell him that the king was getting together his cattle, and would send them on to Sir Garnet by his minister Umnyama, who was then personally engaged in collecting the royal herds. These messengers, having fallen in with a detachment of Clarke's column, were directed by them to Entonjaneni, where they met Sir Garnet on his arrival. Vijn, in the meantime, had, by the king's command, gone to Fort Victoria bearing a similar message, with this addition, that after the cattle had been received by the English commander he would give himself up.

During Vijn's absence Cetywayo moved on to Zonymana's *kraal*; here he was rejoined by Vijn, who told him that the English were thoroughly determined to capture him. Hereupon he sent Vijn a second time to Sir Garnet, with no definite proposals, but merely a complaint that he could not give himself up to any of the patrols, as he was apprehensive that he would be killed out of hand. And there was some ground for this fear, as Dabulamanzi had sent a message warning him that the English meant to put him to death, and so he had better not yield himself up until the cattle had been received and Umnyama made terms for him with the English commander. The three first messengers, after leaving Entonjaneni, fell in with Umnyama and the cattle near Ulundi, whither they betook themselves, in company with that chieftain, instead of returning to Cetywayo. The morning following that on which Vijn had been despatched on his second embassy the king moved on to the river Mona, and slept that night in a *kraal* upon its bank. On the next morning, having crossed the stream, he was ascending the hill that rose on the other side when a messenger from his brother Uziwetu came to tell him that soldiers on horseback had just visited Zonymana's *kraal*. He therefore concealed himself in the bush, and in no long time beheld the white men's scouts on the opposite hill; thereupon he descended the ravine into the Mona bush. The same evening, he travelled as far as the Black Umvolosi, and slept there.

On the following day they had scarcely finished killing and skinning a couple of oxen when scouts came in to say the white horsemen were coming through the hush. The king then bade all the women to escape as best they could, whilst he, going out of the bush, concealed himself in the long grass on the top of a mound just above the drift, whence he could clearly watch the patrol as they passed, and, indeed, could hear them speak and laugh. As soon as they had passed, he and the five or six followers, who were now all the retainers that remained with him, journeyed further up the Black Umvolosi, and lived for some days in various *kraals*. Remaining for three days in the same *kraal*, he was joined by one of his wives.

Finding the troops still on the trail, he now struck off across country into the Ingome forest, where news reached him that Umnyama had, instead of making terms for him, promised Sir Garnet Wolseley to use his best endeavours to capture the king and to deliver him up should he be found in any of the *kraals* of his (Umnyama's) district. Cetywayo was much grieved at this, and exclaimed, 'Why does Umnyama do this? Why does he act treacherously towards me? Why does he not send a message to tell me to deliver myself up?' He then moved on to the *kraal* of the Ingome, where four more women rejoined him. Here he was taken by Lord Gifford and Major Marter, and conducted by them back to Ulundi. On the way one of the women escaped into the bush.

2: Fate of Cetywayo and Final Settlement of Zululand.

Cetywayo was first taken to Sir Garnet Wolseley at Ulundi, and thence by that general's orders was conveyed, under an escort commanded by Captain Poole, R.A., to Capetown, where he still remains in an honourable captivity, treated with all the respect and indulgence due to his position.

After Cetywayo's capture no further opposition of any sort was encountered in Zululand, but the chiefs and people immediately assented to the terms of peace proposed by Sir Garnet, by which the country was split up into thirteen districts, each subject to its own chief, while supreme over all these was placed a British resident. Native laws and customs were to be respected, and European immigration was forbidden. Mr. Wheelwright, for some considerable time a magistrate of Natal, was appointed the first resident.

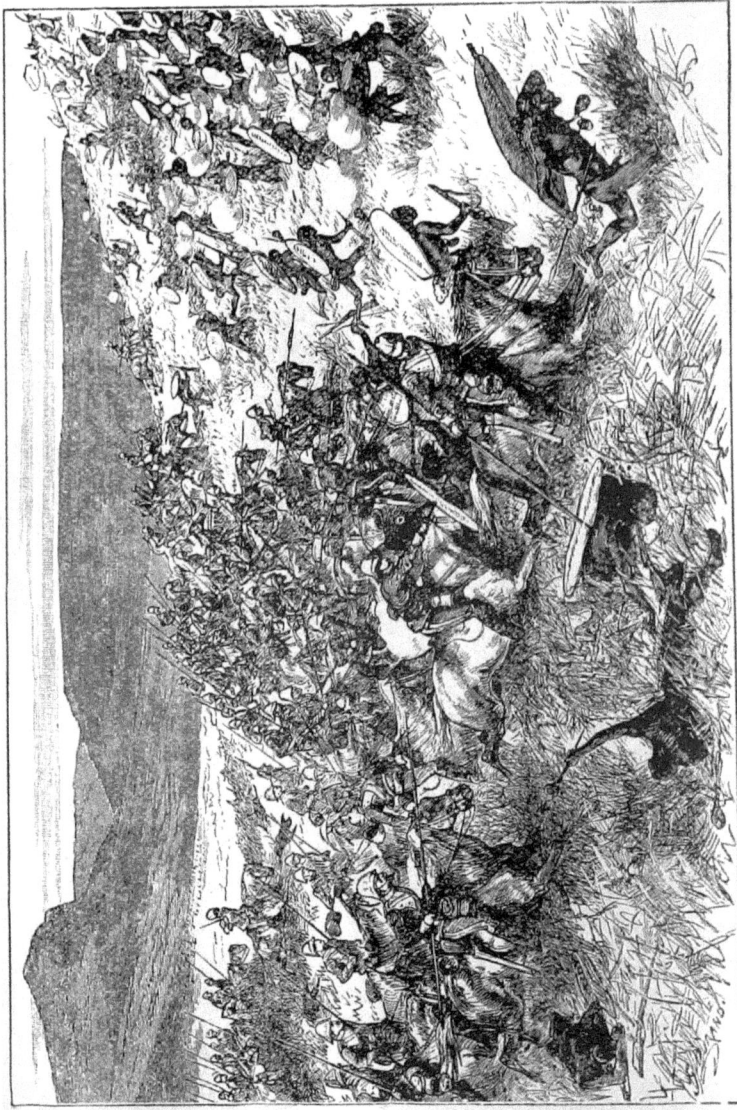

Charge of the 17th Lancers at Ulundi

The 17th Lancers or Duke of Cambridge's Own During the Zulu War

By J. W. Fortescue

At the beginning of February, 1879, England was shocked by the intelligence that one of Lord Chelmsford's columns, consisting of the 24th Regiment, had been surprised and annihilated by the Zulus at Isandlhwana (22nd January). The Seventeenth Lancers was at once warned, (10th Feb), to proceed on active service in South Africa, and the regiment was augmented by the transfer of sixty-five men and horses from the 5th and 16th Lancers.

In the short interval between the warning and the embarkation the commanding officer, Colonel Gonne, was accidentally shot while superintending the practice of the non-commissioned officers with the newly issued revolver, and so severely wounded as to be unable to proceed on active service.

Accordingly, on the 22nd February, Colonel Drury Lowe was gazetted as supernumerary Lieutenant-Colonel, and reassumed command of the regiment, his return being joyfully welcomed by all ranks, without exception, from the second in command downwards.

On the same day the regiment was inspected by the Colonel-in-Chief at Hounslow, and two days later one wing, under the command of Major Boulderson, embarked on board the hired transport *France* at Victoria Docks; headquarters and the other wing embarking on board the *England* at Southampton on the 25th.

A depot of 121 men with 30 horses was left under the command of Captain Benson at Hounslow. The strength of the regiment, as embarked, was as follows:—

	Field Officer.	Captains.	Subalterns.	Staff.	Total.	Rank and File.	Horses. Officers.	Troopers.	Total.
Headquarter wing —*England*	1	4	7	4	16	302	25	238	263
Left wing—*France*	1	3	9	1	14	238	21	238	259
Totals	2	7	16	5	30	540	46	476	522

Both ships arrived at St.Vincent, Cape de Verdes, on the 7th March, 1879, to coal; but owing to the great number of transports assembled at the same place for the same purpose, the *England* did not leave until the 12th, nor the *France* until the 14th. Both ships were detained again at Table Bay for a few days to coal, and arrived at Port Durban, the England on the 6th, and the *France* on the 11th April; five horses dead on the former, and six on the latter ship, were the casualties for the voyage. By the 14th both wings were disembarked, and the regiment then encamped for a day or two at Cator's Manor, near Durban—the right wing, under Colonel Drury Lowe, finally marching on the 17th April to Landman's Drift, and the left wing, under Major Boulderson, on the 21st April to Dundee.

The entire regiment shortly after marched up to Rorke's Drift together with the King's Dragoon Guards, the whole being under the command of Major-General Marshall. On the 21st May it visited the battlefield of Isandlhwana, buried most of the dead bodies, and brought back some of the abandoned waggons to Rorke's Drift. On the 23rd it joined the 2nd Division under Major-General Newdegate at Landman's Drift, on the 28th it marched with it to Koppie Allein on the Blood River, and at last on the 1st June crossed that river and entered Zululand.

On the 5th June the regiment came in contact with the Zulus for the first time at Erzungayan Hill. In a trifling skirmish which ensued the adjutant, Lieutenant Frith, was shot dead by the colonel's side. Two days later the division reached the Upoko River. A squadron of the Seventeenth was now detached to do duty at Fort Marshall, one of the posts constructed to guard the line of communication. The remainder moved up with division towards Ulundi, the *kraal* of the Zulu king. It was employed in the usual reconnaissance and outpost duties, varied by an occasional skirmish with the Zulus, but was never able to come to close quarters with the enemy. It was not employed, nor was any part of the strong force of cavalry available for the service, in a rapid advance upon Ulundi, as had been expected and hoped.

On the 2nd July the second division and flying column encamped on the south bank of the White Umvolosi River, about five miles from Ulundi, and on the 4th crossed the river and advanced against the *kraal*. The three squadrons of the Seventeenth formed the rearguard; but no opportunity occurred of attacking the enemy on the march. The column was now rapidly enveloped by the Zulus in great force, and the cavalry was ordered to withdraw within the hollow square into which the infantry was formed.

The Zulu attack began at 8.50 a.m., and was maintained for three-quarters of an hour within a hundred yards of a murderous artillery and rifle fire. During this time the Seventeenth stood to their horses under a heavy cross-fire, and suffered some casualties, Lieutenant Jenkins, among the officers, being shot in the jaw. About 9.30 the Zulus showed signs of wavering, and the Seventeenth was ordered out of the square to attack. As they rode out Captain Edgell was shot dead at the head of his squadron, and his troop farrier was killed at the same instant.

Once clear of the square the regiment formed in echelon of wings, rank entire, covering over three hundred yards of front, and charged. It was met by a hot fire in front and flank from the Zulus, who were concealed in long grass in a *donga*; but charging right through them the Seventeenth scattered them in every direction, and then taking up the pursuit hunted them with great execution for nearly two miles. The horses were fresh, and there was no escape from the lances, which the enemy now encountered for the first time.

The Zulu Army was not only defeated but dispersed by this pursuit, and never appeared in the field again. The casualties of the Seventeenth on this day were, one officer (Captain Wyatt Edgell) and two men killed, three officers, *viz.* Colonel Drury Lowe, Lieutenant James, Scots Greys, attached to the Seventeenth, Lieutenant and acting Adjutant Jenkins, and five men wounded; the two first-named officers slightly, and the third severely. Also 26 horses were killed and wounded. The regiment was highly complimented, both verbally and in orders, by the general for its conduct at Ulundi. The only matter worthy of note in this short Zulu campaign is the heavy loss suffered by the Seventeenth in officers as compared with men; and this through pure chance, for all ranks were equally exposed.

The regiment began the return march on the day after the battle, with the 2nd Division, and arrived at the Upoko River on the 15th

July. On the 26th it was ordered to march to Koppie Allein, to give over its horses to the King's Dragoon Guards, and to proceed dismounted to Pinetown, where it arrived on the 21st August. It was reduced a month later to six troops for Indian service; and 198 men then proceeded direct to England under Lieutenant W. Kevill-Davies. On the 1st October Colonel Drury Lowe for the second time took leave of the regiment; and Major Boulderson took command. The regiment then embarked for India; the left wing under Captain Cook sailing on board H.M.S. *Serapis* on 8th October, the right wing under Major Boulderson on board H.M.S. *Crocodile* on the 20th, and arriving at Bombay on the 28th October and 10th November respectively.

LEONAUR

ALSO FROM LEONAUR
AVAILABLE IN SOFTCOVER OR HARDCOVER WITH DUST JACKET

ESCAPE FROM THE FRENCH *by Edward Boys*—A Young Royal Navy Midshipman's Adventures During the Napoleonic War.

THE VOYAGE OF H.M.S. PANDORA *by Edward Edwards R. N. & George Hamilton, edited by Basil Thomson*—In Pursuit of the Mutineers of the Bounty in the South Seas—1790-1791.

MEDUSA *by J. B. Henry Savigny and Alexander Correard and Charlotte-Adélaïde Dard* —Narrative of a Voyage to Senegal in 1816 & The Sufferings of the Picard Family After the Shipwreck of the Medusa.

THE SEA WAR OF 1812 VOLUME 1 *by A. T. Mahan*—A History of the Maritime Conflict.

THE SEA WAR OF 1812 VOLUME 2 *by A. T. Mahan*—A History of the Maritime Conflict.

WETHERELL OF H. M. S. HUSSAR *by John Wetherell*—The Recollections of an Ordinary Seaman of the Royal Navy During the Napoleonic Wars.

THE NAVAL BRIGADE IN NATAL *by C. R. N. Burne*—With the Guns of H. M. S. Terrible & H. M. S. Tartar during the Boer War 1899-1900.

THE VOYAGE OF H. M. S. BOUNTY *by William Bligh*—The True Story of an 18th Century Voyage of Exploration and Mutiny.

SHIPWRECK! *by William Gilly*—The Royal Navy's Disasters at Sea 1793-1849.

KING'S CUTTERS AND SMUGGLERS: 1700-1855 *by E. Keble Chatterton*—A unique period of maritime history-from the beginning of the eighteenth to the middle of the nineteenth century when British seamen risked all to smuggle valuable goods from wool to tea and spirits from and to the Continent.

CONFEDERATE BLOCKADE RUNNER *by John Wilkinson*—The Personal Recollections of an Officer of the Confederate Navy.

NAVAL BATTLES OF THE NAPOLEONIC WARS *by W. H. Fitchett*—Cape St. Vincent, the Nile, Cadiz, Copenhagen, Trafalgar & Others.

PRISONERS OF THE RED DESERT *by R. S. Gwatkin-Williams*—The Adventures of the Crew of the Tara During the First World War.

U-BOAT WAR 1914-1918 *by James B. Connolly/Karl von Schenk*—Two Contrasting Accounts from Both Sides of the Conflict at Sea During the Great War.

Lightning Source UK Ltd.
Milton Keynes UK
UKHW040636301221
396391UK00001B/136

9 781782 825623